...re and

...unity

Creative Writing

Education, culture and community

Rebecca O'Rourke

niace
promoting adult learning

©2005 National Institute of Adult Continuing Education (England and Wales)

21 De Montfort Street
Leicester
LE1 7GE

Company registration no. 2603322
Charity registration no. 1002775

NIACE has a broad remit to promote lifelong learning opportunities for adults. NIACE works to develop increased participation in education and training, particularly for those who do not have easy access because of class, gender, age, race, language and culture, learning difficulties or disabilities, or insufficient financial resources.

You can find NIACE online at www.niace.org.uk

Cataloguing in Publication Data
A CIP record of this title is available from the British Library

Designed and typeset by Avon DataSet Ltd, Bidford on Avon, B50 4JH
Print and bound in the UK by Latimer Trend, Plymouth

ISBN: 1 86201 161 3

Contents

Acknowledgements

There are many people to thank as a book like *Creative Writing: Education, culture and community* moves out into the public sphere. This is true of any book, of course, but especially when, like this one, it is a book that has been many years in the living and making.

It is over 30 years since I sat at the back of a Worker's Educational Association poetry workshop in a pub in the centre of Hull. As a student at the university I was out of place among the dockers, secretaries, butchers and shop assistants, all of whom brought along better poems than I did. In my day job, doing English at the university, I was in the company of feminist, socialist, anarchist and marxist political activists and theorists who changed forever how I saw my subject.

It is over 25 years since I found my way to the Federation of Worker Writers and Community Publishers and through them to my own writing and work in community writing and publishing. At the time, I was a post-graduate student at Birmingham University's Centre for Contemporary Cultural Studies. The Federation, and the adult education teaching I did for Balsall Heath WEA and Birmingham Extra-Mural Department, grounded the theoretical work of CCCS in tangible work of social change.

It is 15 years since I went back to Birmingham, as a part-time doctoral student, to explore the changes I had seen in cultural policy and practice during my time in the field. That decision triggered other changes, two university research posts (one in London, one in Cleveland) led eventually to a job at the University of Leeds where I organised and taught part-time creative writing courses for adults. It was during my time in Cleveland that much of the substantive research for this book was carried out.

CREATIVE WRITING

Along the way, many people inspired, cajoled, provoked and befriended me. Too many people to name one by one; too complex a web of ideas and influences to pull single threads from. But I am glad to have known them and continue to be grateful for their encouragement – the giving of courage – to me and to others.

Work on completing this book has gone on alongside the restructuring of continuing education at the University of Leeds. Such events have become a feature of university continuing education and whatever else they are good for it is rarely adult education. Whatever the outcome, at the University of Leeds and elsewhere, *Creative Writing: Education, culture and community* is a testament to the influential role played by university departments of continuing education both in developing creative writing as an academic discipline and facilitating its contribution to social and cultural change. I hope my account of the strengths and limitations attending both projects will be a valuable guide and inspiration for creative writing's participants and practitioners as they move into the new spaces and new arguments of adult education and cultural politics.

Rebecca O'Rourke

Chapter one

Introduction

How much it takes to become a writer. Bent (far more common than we assume), circumstances, time, development of craft – but beyond that: how much conviction as to the importance of what one has to say, one's right to say it. And the will, the measureless store of belief in oneself to be able to come to, cleave to, find the form for one's own life comprehensions. Difficult for any male not born into a class that breeds such confidence. Almost impossible for a girl, a woman. (Olsen 1980: 27)

The last 30 years have been interesting times for creative writing. Creative writing is now one of the most popular cultural activities and educational subjects in Britain. Every regional arts board makes regular provision for a range of activities that include writers – in – residence, festivals, projects and support for small publishers. Writing contributes to major projects in arts for health and social regeneration across the country. Every school has access to schemes that bring professional writers into classrooms to work with pupils of all ages. In adult, community, further and higher education creative writing courses are no longer an aberration or curiosity but staples of provision, with courses offering formal and informal learning opportunities ranging from bite-sized taster sessions through to post-graduate and doctoral programmes. Outside education and the subsidised arts sector there are extensive national and regional networks of independent writers' groups, small presses, festivals and residential course providers, including the acclaimed Arvon Foundation and its Welsh sister organisation, Ty Newyd. These flourish alongside a buoyant commercial sector that supports magazine and book publishing, correspondence and residential courses.

CREATIVE WRITING

The word itself is moving into the mainstream, as the activity becomes both familiar and popular. Most people now know what it means; at least to them. Although creative writing does not warrant its own entry in the Oxford English Dictionary (OED) it is cited in the 1989 definition of creative. This usage dates from 1816, when Wordsworth referred to writing as a creative art, and it entered the language as a means of distinguishing creative from critical, journalistic, academic or technical writing. The first references to creative writing courses occur in the early-twentieth century and are generally negative. The OED entry also states that creative writing frequently refers to a course of study in the United States (OED 2000).

Creative writing's current popularity has been hard won and results from campaigns within cultural policy and literary theory that challenged a model of literary value organised around the scarcity principle. In cultural policy the argument engaged the Arts Council's Literature Department, who were influential both in shaping national literary culture and controlling access to it through patronage of individual writers. Within literary theory dominant ideas about canonical texts were challenged, which not only opened spaces for the alternative and oppositional traditions of writing by women, working class and black writers but also transformed the concept of literary practice and value. The result was a provisional, historically specific way of engaging with a more widely defined social practice of writing that valued making, as well as interpreting, literary texts.

Achieving these changes was not straightforward, and opponents often viewed creative writing with suspicion. At times, creative writing had a totemic status and was perceived as symptom and cause of falling standards in language and behaviour within compulsory schooling, deemed diversionary in the radical tradition of adult education and to lack academic rigour in higher education. Questions of quality and standards were also a preoccupation in cultural policy. The belief that writing was a matter of innate talent and writers and writing of any worth could and should take care of themselves dominated its work for many years.

INTRODUCTION

Cultural attitudes and practices change slowly and unevenly and the campaigns which changed the standing of creative writing also span several decades. During the process several arguments recur. These concern the degree of support and intervention creative writing needs to sustain participation along the amateur/ professional continuum, whether and in what form writing constitutes a professional cultural practice, and the appropriate relationship between education and the cultural practice of creative writing.

As they played out, these arguments became more specific. Educational providers, writers and tutors argued first about whether creative writing could or should be taught at all. Then about how best to teach it and whether what was learnt was what had been taught. Finally, they debate whether such learning can be adequately captured and rewarded by current assessment methods. Cultural policy makers argued first about whether their responsibility was to increase the number of new writers or new readers; and whether widened participation in writing activities led to falling standards. They questioned whether writers and writing needed public subsidy and, in agreeing that they did, debated new values and purposes for writing. As they abandoned elite values and purposes they transposed the literary to the social, ensuring the centrality of cultural activity to social regeneration and inclusion. Creative writing therefore came to hold two quite different, but sometimes overlapping, meanings and sites of practice. It could be understood as a means of training for writers but also as the use of writing for purposes which were not primarily literary. Both tendencies put education, with its capacity to transform individuals and social groups, at the heart of the cultural experience and this educational inflection became a defining feature of contemporary British creative writing.

Creative Writing: Education, culture and community examines the changed status of creative writing through a study of the relationship between those who make and implement educational and cultural policy and those on whose behalf that policy is made. It charts how changes in cultural policy made education central to the reformulation of a more inclusive and participative cultural policy and set in train a number of contradictions. In exploring the consequences of this for creative writing I argue that the current dominance of educational values and processes in cultural policy is problematic for those who advocate cultural action as a catalyst for radical social change.

Section one begins with the charting, in chapter two, of the peculiarities of literature within cultural policy and the way writing is conceptualised within literature policy. I argue that education became central to the reformulation of cultural policy as an agent of social inclusion and regeneration and in this context look at the relationship between the arts and adult education. This sets up one of the central arguments of the study as a whole, that the new managerialism and market reasoning (McGuigan 1996: 62) operating within the discourse of cultural policy is tempered by its turn towards educational values and purposes.

Chapter three develops a critical account of the rise of creative writing and its formation as an academic activity. I show that contemporary creative writing activities in Britain have a longer history than some contemporary commentators credit them with; and that this is a complex and differentiated history. I outline the different sites of creative writing activity in compulsory and post-compulsory education, the arts and arts education, and the commercial and voluntary sector. I argue that while the activity remains fundamentally the same, its different locations and contexts give rise to very different ideas about its value and purpose, and to different pedagogies.

Section two provides an ethnographic study of social writing. This approach begins to close the gap between those who make and implement educational and cultural policy and those on whose behalf policy is made. The research on which it is based was the first of its kind and took place over a period of five years. It included participative observation and a comprehensive range of qualitative investigation. It theorises the policy shift from conceptualising writing as a singular to a socialised activity through the development of a concept of a local culture of writing. My development of the concept of a local culture of writing takes account of the dangers of an uncritical embrace of the terms community and local (Bornat 1992; McGuigan 1992; Smith 1994; Barton and Hamilton 1998). I use the term 'local' in its geographical sense, to specify place, but also in its political sense, where it is allied with a critical understanding of community and a refusal of the concerns and values of the dominant national culture.

This section comprises four chapters. Chapter four discusses the theoretical nature and origins of local cultures of writing with reference to the work of Paul Willis (1990), Mark Smith (1994), Ruth Finnegan (1989) and David Barton and Mary Hamilton (1998). It provides a practical application and illustration of the complexity of forms or organisation and support for writers. This is followed, in chapter five, by an exploration of access to local knowledge of creative writing activities in relation to participation studies (cultural and education) through an account of the catalysts and barriers to participation in the local culture of writing, including popular perceptions of writers and writing activities. It was striking how little people knew about what actually went on, at both the surface and structural level, in creative writing activities. I argue that this represents a major barrier to participation, and discuss this further in the light of a survey of local knowledge of creative writing activities.

In chapter six, I detail the contradictions embedded in pedagogic practices, in formal and informal sites of creative writing activity, through accounts of the organised writing activities, in the form of courses and free-standing groups, with which people become involved. I have anonymised students, tutors and the names of their courses and groups. Individuals have been given a pseudonym, groups were named after rivers I have lived near (Goyt, Mersey, Thames etc) and, because he died while I was writing up this research, I named the courses after my brother's favourite rock climbing areas (Cuillin, Kinder, Llanberis etc). The account I give of the activities, rituals and social meaning of creative writing is organised by an understanding of them as sites of contradiction. The nature of these contradictions includes their relation to structure, the creative writing curriculum, group and tutor dependence, the ambivalence of the tutor-facilitator and the tension between personal development, artistic considerations and commercial or marketised imperatives. A detailed account of a group (Goyt) and a course (Crowden) are used to develop an account of creative writing's pedagogic practices which both illuminates the rituals and behaviours of organised writing activities and provides contextual knowledge for the more issue-based discussions which follow.

Chapter seven is concerned with the experience of creative writing tutors. It looks back to chapter three, where key issues about the nature and purposes of teaching creative writing were identified. These turn on whether writers or teachers are best placed to become creative writing tutors, and debates about where creative writing belongs institutionally. I show how they are underpinned by, and to some extent reflect, different under-standings of the purposes of teaching creative writing and how these in turn relate to different models of the writing process. The chapter charts the relevance of these debates to tutors working in Cleveland through an account of becoming and being a creative writing tutor. It concludes with a detailed exploration of two practitioner-based issues and problems. These are the role of feedback and criticism and the diversity of the student group.

In the final section of the book I stand back from the experi-ence of local cultures of writing to engage with the tensions and differences that mark the wider contemporary discourse of creative writing, especially its engagement with educational access and inclusion. Taking myths of the common writer as a starting point, I challenge much of the common sense (both celebratory and condemnatory) about writers and writing who are neither seeking nor achieving literary or commercial success. The change in policy associated with the move to widen and democratise access to the arts puts greater emphasis on educational values in cultural policy and produces a practice in which the lines between educational and arts apprenticeship activity are increasingly blurred.

One consequence of the greater emphasis on educational values is uncertainty about the degree of independence required or encouraged in participants by creative writing tutors and facilitators. This produces a contradictory situation in which rhetoric of empowerment coexists alongside practices that encourage dependence, both within particular activities and across the culture of writing as a whole. In this way we see how the attack on dependency, which new managerialism in the discourse of education and cultural policy represents, is deflected by the elevation of educational values and practices. However, I argue that unless this educational turn is rooted in a critical and transformative engagement it will not fulfil its potential to empower participants in creative writing, wherever their purpose and motivation lie.

Chapter two

Literature in cultural policy

'We hope you will not find the word "literature" off-putting' (Arts Council 1992). This modest, almost apologetic comment, which accompanied information about how to apply for grants from the Literature Department of the Arts Council, condenses major changes in how British cultural policy conceptualises its mission and purposes in relation to literature and writing. Today, creative writing activities are provided, valued, funded and participated in throughout Britain on a scale that was unimaginable even a decade ago. The changes in cultural policy that underpin this contemporary popularity arise from cultural and educational campaigns with long histories. They chart a movement from away from appreciation towards participation, away from organisation on the basis of scarcity to plenty and from elitism to inclusion. These changes in cultural policy provide the context, material and ideological, within which local cultures of writing develop and thrive.

My initial research interests were in writing as an organised activity for individuals and the communities in which they lived. However, the way in which creative writing activities were organised and engaged in at a local level was bound up with the regulation of literature and literary activities in post-war British cultural policy. Very little attention has been paid to the impact of policy changes on the way individuals and their communities engage with and make sense of organised writing activities. Often, as my study demonstrates, the relationship generates more friction than fit, characterised as it is by mutual distance and disdain, but policy frames the context within which practice takes place and is therefore critical to our understanding of it. This chapter outlines the history and campaigns that led to the de-centring of literature within cultural policy, and discusses its significance for creative writing in education.

Jim McGuigan's *The State and Serious Writing* provides a detailed critical account of twentieth-century literature policy up until the early-1980s (McGuigan 1985) that contextualised my study. Of especial value is the clarity with which he develops his argument concerning the Arts Council's fundamentally contradictory founding imperative. McGuigan makes an important point about that the consequences of the Arts Council's founding vision of raising standards in art forms while spreading access to them as widely as possible. He argues that the tension this produces will result in a basic and recurrent, rather than single, contradiction for Arts Council policy (McGuigan 1985: 29). Conceptualising cultural policy as a series of resolved and re-emerging contradictions enables the development of a more complex model of cultural change which gives due weight to the balance of power between the campaigns, visions and strategies of cultural activists across the political spectrum.

I extend and develop his ideas by continuing the story beyond the early-1980s, albeit necessarily in less detail than his account. As this story unfolds it becomes clear that the 'terminal confusion of Literature policy' he identifies developed in ways he could not have predicted in 1985 (McGuigan 1985: 237). Reports of literature's death were exaggerated. Less than a decade after McGuigan had so carefully delineated the nature and effects of 'serious writing' as a universal, socially detached category which defined and organised literature policy, it had been, as the quotation above indicates, de-centred. The move from literature to creative writing, which drove this displacement, added a new dimension to the recurrent, and irreconcilable, contradictions of literature policy by introducing education as a key component of arts experience. I elaborate this through an account of the changing purpose of literature in cultural policy.

McGuigan's later work on cultural policy has been concerned with the impact of the global reach of market reasoning and new managerialism, features which have become characteristic of late-twentieth and early-twenty-first century public life (McGuigan

1996; 1999). In elucidating the distinctiveness of literature within cultural policy I advance two arguments that engage with McGuigan's ideas on cultural policy. First, that local cultures of writing can act as forms of resistance to the totalising discourse of the market, but do so only if resistance is consciously and actively pursued. Second I argue that literature policy is differently shaped by the discourse of market regulation and new managerialism because of the historical peculiarities with which literature was incorporated into cultural policy. This enables a competing discourse, which emphasises educational values and purposes for the arts, to temper the deregulation of the state's role in general cultural policy where literature is concerned.

Literature and the Arts Council of Great Britain

There was no separate Literature Department when the Arts Council was founded in 1946 although the British Council, which was largely concerned with the overseas promotion of British culture and the English language, did offer considerable support for writers in the form of lecture tours, performances and book promotion. Several possible explanations for this have been advanced, both at the time and by later commentators. They include the absence of an institutional base for writing and literature (Pick 1986: 47) and a confidence in the market's ability to regulate both professional excellence and public access (Sinclair 1995: 165). While these pragmatic explanations have some force, it is possible that the absence of literature from the moral-political project of the early Arts Council (McGuigan 1996: 53–7) is linked to the ideological force with which English as a subject discipline underpinned the moral-political project of compulsory state schooling (Mulhern 1979; Doyle 1981; Hunter 1988; Street 1995).

A Poetry Panel was established in 1963, which allocated bursaries to individual writers and supported the sector through tours, a festival and the purchase of nationally significant manuscripts which would otherwise have gone overseas. Two years later a Literature Panel was established. Although its focus was clearly on the individual writer – all of its 34 awards and four prizes went to individuals – its brief did include consultation with the Publishers' Association about subsidy, especially for translation, and the possibility of publishers co-funding awards to authors as well as the whole area of authors' rights, looking at possible changes in the tax position, and at libraries (Arts Council 1966: 17). However, literature was marginalised by the policy emphasis in the mid-1960s on Housing the Arts. A 1985 survey of British Arts Centres, largely established as a result of that initiative, shows literary events – whether professional or amateur – in a definite minority. Literature also found itself out of step with the Arts Council when the latter repositioned itself more centrally within debates about the social purpose of art. Literature held fast to an out-moded aesthetic that was out of step with the Arts Council's founding Arnoldian mission of civilising society and continued to move towards elitism as the Council more generally took a more pragmatic direction. Nicholas Pearson explored this at length, taking visual art as its focus. He argues convincingly that the moral argument Lord Goodman used to put the case for the new Arts Council Charter in the House of Lords masks a profoundly political agenda (Pearson 1982: 80-2). The focus of Goodman's interest was young people in the context of newly formed distinct youth cultures and the moral panic this had created.

> Young people lack certainties, lack guidance; (...) they need something to turn to; and need it more desperately than they have needed it at any time in our history. (...) I believe that once young people are captured for the Arts they are redeemed from many of the dangers which confront them at the moment. (Arts Council 1967: 11)

Ian Gasse, in his study of arts funding since 1945, identifies six themes in the Arts Council's purpose of which three draw on the civilising mission. These are the transmission and re-enforcement of traditional values and the use of the arts to create quality of life, which often serves to create or maintain social differences between those who do and do not have access to the arts. This, he argues, is related to but distinct from seeing the arts as a form of education and enlightenment. This is still 'culture from above' but it seeks to obliterate rather than maintain social differentiation. He distinguishes cultural democracy from these top-down purposes because of its emphasis on creative self-expression and participation. His sixth theme is culture's dual role in the economics and ideology of national prestige (Gasse 1998: 72–4).

From the outset, the Literature Department refused to define its work in relation to social purpose. In contrast to Lord Goodman's concern about winning young people to the arts, the Literature Panel's chairman balked at supporting even talented young writers:

> I myself do not believe that the young writer, however talented, should have things made easy for him. A period of struggle, adversity, discouragement is a good test of his vocation, his integrity and his stamina (early success is a stern test of integrity, too). It is when he has passed this test that any help we can give him may well be most timely (...) encouraging the older writer when he most needs encouragement. (Arts Council 1966: 16)

This divergence, in purpose between the Literature Department and the Council as a whole shaped literature policy well into the 1980s.

The Department was out of step with everyone: the regions, as we will see later, but also the Scottish and Welsh Arts Council Literature Departments. While these Departments supported individual writers, they also developed pro-active policies designed to shape the broader literary culture well before such ideas were taken seriously in London. For example, the panels in both Wales and Scotland prioritised commissioning surveys of provision and need which they then used to inform strategic policy decisions. Throughout the late-1960s and early-1970s they worked with book publishers, editors of little magazines and the broadcast media as well as individual writers. In 1967, Literature became a policy priority for the Arts Council of Scotland as a whole:

LITERATURE IN CULTURAL POLICY

Literature is (...) of all the arts, the most solitary and the least
organised. (Arts Council 1968: 37)

Several schemes, for example Writers-in-Residence, were prefigured in Scotland several years before their adoption in England
(Arts Council 1968: 38). In 1973 Scotland had Writers-in-
Residence in community settings in Skye and Aberdeen; and
one at Edinburgh Teachers' Centre to facilitate 'integrating the
writer in the educative process' (Arts Council 1974: 42). In 1973
England's first writing residency was established at Hull
University; it would be a further four years before one was located
outside a higher education institution. If England lagged behind
Scotland and Wales, then the Literature Department lagged
behind the Council as a whole. Education became the Council's key
organising concept in the mid-1970s but it was a decade before
the education imperative was fully integrated into the Literature
Department.

During the late-1970s the Literature Department in England
commissioned a piece of research into its grants to writers. That
the findings were not destined to play an immediate role in policy
formation can be deduced from the Council's initial reluctance to
publish the work and their reference to it in the 1980 Annual
Report:

> The report was useful as a history of how the grants system had
> evolved and was administered: it did not, however, provide a clear
> answer to the question whether any of the books whose authors had
> been helped would have been written without grants from the
> Council. (Arts Council 1980: 31)

The Department's work at this time was largely concerned with
grants to writers and a feature of the Grants to Writers scheme
was the interchangeability of sponsor, recipient and panel
member. In some quarters McGuigan's report confirmed a suspicion of the scheme as a self-serving clique or, as McGuigan was
quoted by Morley and Worpole, 'the regularised interconnections
between grant-giver and receiver' (Morley and Worpole 1982:
140). Although panel members were ineligible for awards during

the actual time they served on the Panel, three of the 20 grant recipients interviewed had sponsored other writers, four were former panel members and after his retirement the Literature Director both sponsored writers and received a grant himself. Between 1966 and 1978, 16 panel members received grants before or after their service (McGuigan 1985: 196).

In *The State and Serious Writing* McGuigan explores further a set of issues about grant giving and their recipients. Using Bourdieu's work on education and cultural capital he analyses recipients of writing grants in socio-economic terms. Doing so reveals evidence that supports and demonstrates the operation of Bourdieu's concept of habitus and its role in the accumulation and exchange of cultural capital (McGuigan 1985: 174–88). From the outset, the basis of awards had been stated as need plus quality with the target group identified as full-time professional writers in need of 'a period of time in which to study and practise his art, undistracted by other commitments' (Arts Council 1966: 15). This is a contradictory statement. C. Day-Lewis compares the writer to other professionals – doctors, architects, and engineers. But the comparison is weak. If writers really were a 'hard-core of whole-time professional[s]' (Arts Council 1966: 15) then by definition they would not need to buy out time to concentrate on their writing.

Although the Arts Council often subsidises writers who, for various reasons, do not need subsidy, grant-aid carries a complex significance for the writers receiving it. For several, the grant genuinely enables new work either through funding research, sabbaticals from other occupations or underwriting the move into a full-time writing career. A grant also does important work of legitimisation, both at the symbolic level and in the material uses to which that status and reputation are put (McGuigan 1985: 177). 'Buying time' is, by the 1990s, the key phrase defining the purpose of all grant-aid to writers in supporting documentation from the Arts Council of England and the Regional Arts Boards. The contradiction being managed here is that very few literary, as opposed to popular, writers live by their writing alone (Findalter 1966; Holgate and Wilson-Fletcher 1998).

The term 'serious writing', which McGuigan identified as crucial to the Literature Panel's decision-making is a way of determining seriousness of approach and context as well as classifying the formal and stylistic features of the text. The other key terms in the repertoire are 'merit' and 'quality'. Absence or sufficiency of literary merit determined funding decisions. McGuigan's report provided detailed evidence to support the conclusion reached by Raymond Williams after his term as a Panel member. Williams argued that despite the Arts Council's appearance as an accountable body, in which people with direct and current knowledge of the art form and its field dispose of public money in a responsible fashion, the reality is one of co-optive consensus (Williams 1979a: 160).

McGuigan notes the consensus operating and attempts to unpack the criteria in a series of interviews with panel members and grant recipients. His findings demonstrate how securely, and how uncritically, the concept of serious writing informed Literature policy. As he comments, 'the circularity of the discourse of "serious writing" is quite dizzying' (McGuigan 1985: 220). His lengthy quotation from an interview with Melvyn Bragg, the then Chairman of the Literature Panel, from which I quote more briefly illustrates well the self-satisfied complacency which oiled the Literature Policy machine:

> I think serious writing is represented by those people who think that they represent it at the time. (...) The Arts Council Literature Panel is full of people who could be said to either be writing or representing serious literature in various ways. (McGuigan 1985: 220)

Only one person, the writer Ian McEwan, brought any kind of critical edge to his reflections upon this definition of serious writing. He noted the closure that happens for readers, writers and, by extension, literature policy as a whole when 'serious writing tends to become a kind of self-fulfilling, self-defining category. [...] All there is is good or bad writing' (McGuigan 1985: 221).

At the same time that McGuigan was conducting this study a completely new type of literary formation, the Federation of

Worker Writers and Community Publishers (FWWCP), engaged the Literature Department in a series of well-publicised debates. The explicit focus was funding for their organisation, but this condensed a whole series of shifts in the understanding of, and attitudes towards, literature and the role to be played in its development and promotion by the Arts Council. The FWWCP's experience with the Arts Council underlines the way in which policy debates can use financial arguments to obscure their concerns with making, reproducing and legitimating ideological meanings.

During the late-1970s and early-1980s the Council as a whole continued to move further away from the arts as an issue of national prestige towards questions of extended social access. The internal, as well as external, debates were fierce, as many saw the extension of access as a threat to standards of excellence. Much of the running and many of the arguments were made by the emergent Community Arts movement (Braden 1978; Kelly 1984) but the impetus to change came most strongly from the financial crisis confronting the Arts Council. *Value for Money* (1977) was followed by *The Arts in Hard Times* (1978) as Annual Report titles. The move to increase audiences and define a specific educational role for the Arts Council was at one level simply an astute political judgement about the surest means to secure and retain funding. This was especially pertinent after 1976 when formal routes for business sponsorship through the Association of Business Sponsorship for the Arts were established (Arts Council 1977 and 1985; Shaw 1993). But literature, then under the directorship of Charles Osborne, was marching – sauntering would perhaps be a more apt description – to a different tune.

Literature has always had the smallest slice of the Arts Council cake. Since its inception, the Literature Department's budget never exceeded one per cent of the Arts Council's total spend. Charles Osborne took a perverse delight in this state of affairs, seeing it as evidence both of the market's ability to sustain literature and the scarcity of any talent worthy of grant-aid. The ability of literature to survive without public subsidy had been a common theme since the Arts Council's founding. In the Twenty-Fifth Annual Report, five years after the Literature Department was set up, it was asserted that 'books of importance would continue to be published without subsidy' (Arts Council 1970: 9). Osborne, however, took it to the extreme in 1984 when he voluntarily liquidated his Department following the 1983 general review of the Arts Council, which culminated in *The Glory of the Garden*. The Council found it 'difficult to satisfy itself about the value of much of its present support for literature' (Arts Council 1984: 28) and the sector's strength was deemed to lie in profitable commercial publishing, the teaching of literature in schools and the public library system.

Those aspects of British literary life that Osborne found provided positive evidence of the strength and vibrancy of market regulation were in disarray. Independent bookshops were closing; British publishing houses disappearing in global mergers and the budget for stock purchase, opening hours and public esteem of public libraries were plummeting. This crisis, with its roots in the global restructuring of capital and communications (Murdock and Golding 1974; 1987), had been building for some time. Teaching, especially the teaching of English, was starting to come under the sustained attack from the government and the press, which culminated in the National Curriculum. During this period organised writing activities received little if nothing in the way of state-subsidy directly from the Literature Department. Small grants were made to the FWWCP, which enabled it to support a full-time paid worker and national network. Although these were significant victories for the organisation it was essentially conscience money shamed out of the Department to match funding from the Gulbenkian Foundation. There was no significant national funding of participatory writing activities until the early-1990s, when Alistair Niven's leadership began to effect change, but even then Literature commanded only half a per cent of the total Arts Council budget.

Literature in cultural policy: the view from the regions

At this stage, literature rather than creative writing is still the significant activity under dispute within cultural policy. The relationship between what the Arts Council describes as the centre and periphery has been a source of friction within cultural policy ever since the founding of the Arts Council. Its wartime forerunner, the temporary and privately-funded Council for the Encouragement of Music and the Arts, operated across the whole nation because its primary activity was touring. During its early years the Arts Council worked closely with 12 Art Clubs based around the country, including the Middlesbrough-based Tees-side Arts Guild, but as it developed it prioritised building-based projects in London and side-stepped issues of regional provision. Visual Arts Director, Philip James, expressed what was no doubt a common view in the late-1950s when he made the following observation:

> England is a small country, and the whole area south of the Wash regards London as its Art Centre. (The North is admittedly more independent, but this has been recognised by the fact that one of the Regional Arts Officers lives in Manchester, spending a few days in London each month.) (Quoted in Sinclair 1995: 112)

This attitude continued to inform strategic thinking until the mid-1960s when greater attention to the social purpose of art highlighted questions of access and brought to prominence questions of the regions and their development.

The history of the Regional Arts Associations [RAAs] is one of contestation with and divergence from the centre. The RAAs rejected an identity defined by London and saw themselves instead as centres in their own right. Ian Gasse argues that whereas alternatives and oppositions to central government cultural policy had come from intellectuals, activists and the organised working-class in the 1960s and 1970s, during the 1980s this opposition came from alliances between metropolitan local government and community arts organisations (Gasse 1998:

57–71). Steve Dearden, former Literature Officer for Yorkshire and Humberside Arts, has stressed the way RAAs define themselves less as marginal in relation to London and more centred within other geographies:

> We were part of, or our own centre in, a network that included Ukraine, the Asian sub-continent, the West Indies and the USA. (Dearden 1998)

The cultural framework represented by the various ethnic communities in Britain also actively de-centres notions of a centre and its peripherary. The RAAs, later Regional Arts Boards (RABs), arrived at these expanded, more inclusive and diverse, definitions of, and audiences for, literature activities much earlier than did the Arts Council. For example, from the outset, individual member groups of the FWWCP were regularly funded by their RAAs for a range of activities including one-off publications, readings, attendance at the Annual General Meeting and salaries and running costs for local publishing, writing development and book-selling projects. Unlike the Arts Council, where supporting the FWWCP absolved the Department from any further responsibility towards participatory writing, in many RAAs support for the FWWCP was part of a wider strategic approach to literature. This consciously distinguished cultural policy in the regions from that which prevailed in Piccadilly and Great Peter Street. Whereas the Arts Council prioritised the professional writer, the RAAs emphasised widened access to the arts. They reconfigured the vertical hierarchy (of amateur and professional, high and low, paid and unpaid) which underpinned 'serious writing' into a horizontal continuum along which people could move in both directions. As early as 1981 Yorkshire Arts Association was debating the value of creative writing fellowships on the grounds that they produce 'only marginal benefits to the region as a whole'. The decision to retain them was based on changing their emphasis to 'personal involvement with readers and aspiring writers rather than the author's own creative development' (Dawson 1982: iii). Several RAAs adopted a reformulated mantra of quality along the lines suggested by

CREATIVE WRITING

Steve Dearden, Literature Officer for Yorkshire and Humberside Arts:

> The progress or development between A & B rather than the attainment of the mysterious Z. (Dearden 1998)

In keeping with this, RAAs tended to support activities with an inclusive, often educational, reach such as festivals, courses and workshops. These activities were strategic, intended to develop support networks for new and emerging writers. This often brought them into conflict with the Arts Council who controlled their budgets. The relationship was particularly fraught between the mid-1970s and early-1980s, when Roy Shaw was Secretary-General. Shaw's background in adult education ensured that he sought to place the Council's educative responsibility at the forefront of its policy. He used his final Secretary-General's Preface to the Annual Report for a personal credo:

> In the 1950s the Council's tasks were crystallised in the words 'raise and spread'. Then, my distinguished predecessor as Secretary-General, Sir William Emrys Williams, argued forcibly the need to concentrate on raising standards, believing that too great an emphasis on spreading would lead to the diffusion of mediocrity. When I became Secretary-General in 1975, the climate of opinion had changed, and Williams' views seemed like 'elitism'. (Arts Council 1983: 7)

However, Shaw's commitment to education, as a result of which the first Arts Council Education Officers were appointed (funded, ironically, by the Gulbenkian Foundation in the first instance), saw the purpose of education as a process of induction into the codes and values of high culture. In this he came into direct conflict with the emergent Community Arts movement, which had several advocates in the RAAs.

Shaw's 1983 Preface contained a scathing attack on Su Braden, one of the movement's leading activists, and her book *Artists and the People* (Braden 1978):

> The arts the Arts Council funds do not appeal to a majority (...) Miss Braden's claim that Shakespeare, Constable, Beethoven are not

'relevant' to working people is nonsense. I have seen all three – and many more examples of so-called bourgeois art – interpreted to working people so that they saw and felt the relevance that was not immediately perceived but was made plain through the mediation of a good teacher. (...)

The difference between many middle-class people who enjoy the serious arts and many working-class people who don't, is not that the arts are bourgeois but that they are difficult and that most middle-class people have had more opportunity to study them and become familiar with them, not only through formal education, but most importantly through the almost subliminal educational influence of a cultivated home background. (Arts Council 1983: 8)

Although Shaw might not disagree with the existence of cultural capital and the concept of habitus as elucidated by Bourdieu as material facts, he reaches a very different strategic position in relation to them from Bourdieu and the cultural activists of the time who were influenced by his thinking. The RAAs developed and supported the regional literary infrastructure through grants to small magazines, festivals, residencies and writing development projects and work in partnership with the local authority and other local agencies. This produced a number of effects; notably an increased number of people participated in organised writing activities, which, in some regions, created a critical mass strong enough to challenge London's stranglehold on the literary profession. The Glasgow school, Huddersfield's claim to be the nation's poetry capital, the innovative literary festivals held (amongst others) at Ilkley, Lancaster and Birmingham, Liverpool's commitment to developing theatre writers through The Everyman and the work in Manchester of the North-West Playwrights' Trust, the pre-eminence throughout the 1980s and early-1990s of the North East's little magazines and small presses all contributed towards the subtle shift in defining and valuing who writers were, and what they wrote about. They began to make a tangible and significant challenge to the idea that London connections were a pre-requisite of literary ambition and achievement.

CREATIVE WRITING

The regional activities also challenged a narrowly defined and selective literary culture in other ways. It was there that participation in writing activities that emphasised the creative process and the socially purposeful nature of arts activity was more likely to be positively encouraged. There were also further, far-reaching changes. Although the economic and ideological significance of the arts in national and international terms had been acknowledged for many years it was the arts partnerships with local authorities, most notably but not exclusively in the Greater London Council, that enabled a view of the arts as cultural industries to gain credibility throughout the late-1980s. In 1984 *The Glory of the Garden* devolved increased responsibility for direct arts provision to the regions but without commensurate financial arrangements. The RAAs had to seek match funding – variously called challenge and incentive funding – to unlock the centralised budgets which were, in real terms, falling throughout this period and continued to do so for the next decade. Abolition of the Metropolitan County Councils and the Greater London Council removed a valuable strand of arts funding. During this period, perhaps under this stringency, a new theme, the economics of culture, entered cultural policy. Debates about the social value of the arts were now recast in terms of the arts as an economically productive sector:

> The issue is now not so much whether the arts have an economic dimension. Rather, what is the specific and distinctive economic contribution the arts can make? (Myerscough 1988: 2)

In his report, produced for the Policy Studies Institute, John Myerscough argued that art was a productive activity providing employment and spending by the arts organisations and their customers as well as contributing to less tangible aspects such as the quality of life and urban renewal.

Contributors to the European Journal of Cultural Policy (Bennett 1994; Hansen 1994; Puffelen 1995) later called Myerscough's findings into question. But they were influential at the time in encouraging both local governments and businesses to pick up the gauntlet of 'investing in the arts' thrown down to them by Sir William Rees-Mogg (Rees-Mogg 1985, Arts Council 1985). It was an interesting way of looking at the arts. Instead of asking what the arts cost, Myerscough and the local government officers and arts administrators talked about the ability of the arts to generate income. The arts' contribution to economic growth and regeneration was seen to lie either in direct income generation (for example, the money theatre audiences spent in the local economy on meals, drinks and travel) or indirect savings (for example, the costs of vandalism averted by a Community Theatre or Public Arts project). Figures supplied by the Office for National Statistics show that the arts contributed 25 billion pounds to the UK's Gross Domestic Product in 1998. This compares with 11.8 billion from agriculture, 18 from mining and 33.7 from construction (RAB 1998). At the same time, cultural activists associated with the Greater London Council borrowed the idea of 'cultural industries' from European commentators on civic culture (Mulgan and Worpole 1986; Landry et al 1996). Again, this saw the arts as productive – sites of employment and income generation – but what often remained a crude economic determinism in Myerscough was, in the work of the Greater London Council's Cultural Industries Unit, the basis of policies which articulated the arts with leisure to look at the culture which 'matters to most people most of the time' (McGuigan 1993: 7).

The emphasis on cultural industries gave local authorities a more central role in arts funding and policy. Not only did the Arts Council devolve responsibility to its RAAs, but also in several regions, including Cleveland, provision was further devolved to Local Arts Development Agencies. As diversity, social access and social purpose became key objectives within arts policy, the role of the local authorities in managing social life became central to its success. The growth, for example, of the arts equality and arts and health movements, which had often begun as single-issue self-help or campaign groups, developed synergy with local authorities whose community development units, social services and health care departments provided the context and clients for much of this work. Similarly, arts and arts-related activities were included in social and urban regeneration projects funded by various

European schemes and later by UK lottery funding each of which were managed by the local authorities. This created a local infrastructure for arts activities with the potential to resolve the old polarisation of cultural policy – amateur versus professionals, producers versus consumers, raising or spreading excellence.

McGuigan, quoting the Arts Council's first Secretary-General, Mary Glasgow, reminds us that this solution was not as new as it liked to think it was when he talks about ' "the claims of art" in a narrow sense winning out over "those of social service" ' (McGuigan 1985: 38). The National Inquiry into Arts and the Community proposed that the distinction between arts and community arts had become redundant in the 1990s as the specialised concerns of Community Arts now characterised the arts more generally (Community Development Foundation 1992: 1). In terms of literature, this shift was marked by the creation of a new professional 'the Literature Development Worker', and the development of a project-based practice, concerned with institutions, infrastructures and tangible outcomes. Both changes were ushered in as a result of the 1991 National Arts and Media Strategy (NAMS). Although the framework of political and cultural policy has continued to change, NAMS represents a significant point in the story of creative writing in cultural policy. It is here that the turn away from literature, as an elite and restricted practice to writing is secured; and it is also here that educational values are most clearly invoked to manage and guarantee that turn.

The national arts and media strategy

In 1990 the Arts Minister, Richard Luce, sought to develop a national strategy for arts and the media. Financial considerations were inevitably to the fore but they stood alongside imaginative and wide-ranging questions of purpose. The strategy was to be developed through extensive national consultations and documents were produced for the various art forms and for specific sectoral interest groups. Literature was paper number 29 of 45 and the overall exercise sought the views of 90 local authorities, 197 organisations and 93 individuals. Sixty strategy seminars were organised directly from the NAMS Unit and many RAAs and some local authorities organised additional seminars (Arts Council 1993). The consultation document contained questions, organised under various headings such as: developments in the art form, public funding, literature in society and management, training and resources. It also contained a document to prompt discussion, which distanced itself from an official view. This formed the basis of a series of public meetings with what would now be termed 'stakeholders', a broad cross-section of writers, educators, booksellers, publishers, librarians and arts administrators. These various responses were compiled as a second consultative document, *Towards a National Arts and Media Strategy*, responses to which formed the final document submitted to the Secretary of State for National Heritage in the Autumn of 1992 and published as *A Creative Future* (Arts Council 1993). The consultation seminars were exciting events, with participants aware of the actual and potential break with past traditions and ideologies they were enacting. Although it often felt like a victory for activists and campaigners who had promoted a cultural-democratic or radical opposition there was also a sense of unease. Delegates to the Yorkshire and Humberside Arts NAMS broadly supported its intentions but were concerned that ministerial change might derail its intentions. They were also concerned about the extent to which the introduction of a National Curriculum would undermine its attempts to relocate cultural activity at heart of social life and inclusion at the heart of cultural activity. Several people also took the initiative to task for its failure to embrace the full implications of the cultural democracy argument it advanced.

Keynote speakers and delegates challenged its silence about the writing process and references to literature rather than writing. They saw this as evidence of 'a monolithic definition of literature to which new ideas and influences must and will adapt, rather than perceiving the changes in the definition of literature itself which have resulted from their emergence' (Yorkshire and Humberside Arts 1991: 5). There were criticisms of the assumption that access to writing and reading could only happen within narrow, formally defined educational contexts such as school, college or university.

The seminar also highlighted what have continued to be key issues in literature policy. First, there was unanimous opposition to the proposed National Centre for Literature. In Yorkshire, just as at the national seminar held in London, it was felt that a national centre, particularly one sited in London, would be a backward step. A number of centres, serving regional audiences, were to be preferred. Second, many people felt that the public library system and community publishing projects either already provided this function or could do so given adequate funding and a policy steer.

The second issue concerned training for writers working in education. Gillie Bolton, a keynote speaker from the National Association of Writers in Education (NAWE), put a forceful case for a national training strategy and expressed support for the development of a National Vocational Qualification (NVQ) for writers in education (Yorkshire and Humberside Arts 1991: 3). NVQs were introduced in 1987 and quickly established their centrality in further and vocational education. Several creative industries developed NVQ but writing proved intractable and in 1993 it was agreed to abandon work on the writing NVQ. NAWE went on to play a significant role in the informal, and unaccredited, development of professional practice amongst writers-in-education as part of its vital networking and co-ordination role. In 2001, it formed part of a consortium (with the National Association of Literature Development Workers and the Federation of Worker Writers and Community Publishers) to manage and deliver an Arts Council sponsored training programme for writers working in education.

Jim McGuigan's analysis in *Culture and the Public Sphere* (McGuigan 1996: 51–73) and his more recent *Rethinking Cultural Policy* (McGuigan 2004) helps to clarify the contradictory reactions cultural activists had to NAMS. Using the work of Bourdieu and Habermas to support a materialist analysis of cultural policy in relation to wider economic and political changes, he argues that the last 20 years have seen a rhetorical and organisational shift from state regulation to market regulation of social and cultural life. This represents a discursive shift from a social-democratic discourse of social access to the market reasoning and managerialist rhetoric of the New Right:

> The most profound accomplishment of the New Right government in Britain may not be that it literally rolled back the state in order to release the full blast of market forces but, rather, that it inserted the new managerialism and market reasoning into the state and state-related agencies of the public sector, in effect calling upon organisations that are not themselves private businesses to think and function as though they were. (McGuigan 1996: 62)

The argument is elegant, well documented and persuasive at a general level. But in relation to literature, something else is going on. Because the Literature department had, unlike the rest of the Arts Council, refused to ally itself with the social-democratic discourse, that discourse was not secure enough to be replaced by that of market reasoning. The new organisation and purpose for literature envisaged by the NAMS consultation actually represents the legitimisation of the social-democratic discourse. The conflict between this and the ethos of market reasoning is resolved, where it is resolved, through recourse to educational values and attitudes. It is for this reason that I consider the impact of education upon the literature discourse to be as important as the effects of the new managerialism and market reasoning, which McGuigan analyses so incisively.

McGuigan states at the outset of *Culture and the Public Sphere* that one of its catalysts was the desire to engage practically with the politics of culture, as opposed to the critical abstractions of cultural politics that had hitherto characterised cultural studies, by linking theorists and analysts of culture with its agents. My study tries to go one stage further in suggesting that it is not only the agents of cultural policy but also its subjects, those with and for whom cultural policy is enacted, with whom cultural studies must engage. It is here, at the experiential level, that resistance to totalising discourses will be found:

> I do not mean to suggest that a total ideological closure has occurred. This, specifically in Britain, is related to the incompleteness of the Thatcherite project and the resilience of expectations cultivated under social democracy, perhaps best exemplified by the inviolable principle of public health care, if not necessarily its practice in straitened circumstances, that is still represented by the National Health Service, in popular consciousness. (McGuigan 1996: 72)

The power of resistance signified by the NAMS Literature consultation was only partly the result of its content and ideological position, radical though they were. It gained greater power through its demonstration of the range and standing of practitioners, policy makers and arts administrators who shared, or could debate, a vision of literature organised by inclusion, diversity and participation. The discussion document proposed that four key elements should inform a future literature strategy:

> It must seek to facilitate enjoyment of reading by the largest number of people; to support new writing; to promote literature in education; and to encourage an international and multi-cultural view of literature. (...) The voices of our writers and storytellers are our literature and without them there would be no publishing industry. Our libraries would be empty and above all our minds and spirits would be poverty-stricken.

> Language is the mainstay of our means of communication and so in the widest sense everyone is an author in that they use and manipulate words. (...) Everyone should have the opportunity to express themselves in imaginative language, and continually to improve their skills of doing so. (Niven 1991: 3–9)

This envisaged a radically different understanding of both literature and the role of the Literature Department. There were no references to literary merit or maintaining standards, rather the emphasis was on an inclusive definition of literature. In emphasising the role of literature in education there was the potential for the arts to cease being a place at which the educated arrive and to become instead part and parcel of the journey.

(Education, for the purpose of this document, was primarily but not exclusively understood as taking place in schools.)

Although these attitudes and values were new to literature policy at the level of national cultural policy they were familiar to the RAAs and to those who had, since the 1970s onwards, sought to develop close working partnerships between the arts and adult education. In thinking about the impact of policy change upon those who participate in the arts it may seem, therefore, that there is little change. But the differences which NAMS created and represented, and its influence upon subsequent policy and funding for literature, notably through the Lottery and the Cultural Diversity initiative, have been of great significance and continue to feed through and influence the cultural sector (Arts Council 1998a; 1998b, 2003).

The differences are of three kinds. First, there is now equal importance attached to reading and writing, readers and writers, whereas previously the focus had oscillated between them. Second, the emphasis on widening participation in literary activities of all kinds recognised that the seemingly natural profile of both the arts audience and the artist practitioner was a cultural construct, open to change and redefinition. Third, there was a decisive break with previous definitions of literary value, quality and standards.

From the 1970s onwards there had been sustained challenges to an absolute notion of literary value and to the idea of a fixed and stable literary tradition. This challenge came from a number of sites within artistic and educational practice. It was initiated partly by the interaction between popular adult education, through the work of academics such as Edward Thompson (1968), Richard Hoggart (1957), Roy Shaw (1978, 1987) and Raymond Williams (1958, 1979b), who also became actively involved in developing cultural policy. This constituted both a critique and a challenge to the values and knowledge base of mainstream education, which also helped to produce British cultural studies as an area of intellectual-political work in adult and higher education. This in turn led to more sustained critiques of the relationship between mass and high culture which fed back into and changed the disciplines of English, History, Politics and Sociology.

Within these debates, it was rare for questions of value to be engaged with directly. Indeed, value was often treated as if it was an irrelevant or tainted concept. McGuigan offers a critique of this cultural relativism arguing for a critical and politically informed engagement with popular culture (McGuigan 1992; 2004). He discusses the link between the campaign for cultural democracy, especially in relation to community arts, and argues that a crude cultural populism dealt the deathblow to the crude elitism, which had previously organised cultural policy and practice in Britain. However, this leaves unresolved the issue of what a more refined practice and policy might look like.

Throughout the 1990s, as they grappled with these issues, value became a key area of enquiry for cultural theorists (Frow 1995; McGuigan 1995; 1999; 2004). The issue also exercised practitioners. For many, as we will see in later chapters, the response is an awkward silence about value. But such silence, as Terry Eagleton noted in a discussion with the poet Simon Armitage, is difficult to maintain:

> Value is a transitive term but talked about intransitively. It is not arbitrary and subjective – it is present: conventional and situationalised. We can't help thinking things are good and bad. (Eagleton 1993)

Where questions of value, quality and standards were opened for debate they were almost always linked to questions of exclusion and purpose. If literature could be seen as an arbitrary category, just one possible development from writing, then literary merit might equally be seen as a relative, socially constructed category rather than an absolute truth. The implications of this, in respect of a move from narrowly competitive views of writing and writers to a more inclusive and expanding definition, has come to define organised writing activities since the early-1990s. Within these activities, the idea that everyone had creative potential and was therefore entitled to resources and opportunities, which would enable it to develop and flourish gained ground.

This change was not without critics. In addition to those, notably the *National Inquiry Into the Arts and the Community* (Community Development Foundation 1992), who felt it had not gone far enough, there were those, including P.D. James, then Chair of the Arts Council Literature Panel, who felt it had gone far too far. Sinclair quotes her as damning 'a silly age of little enthusiasms. I don't understand why we concern ourselves about women in the arts, a development for this or that, disablement or ethnic minorities. Our concerns should be literature' (Sinclair 1995: 298). Unease about literature's changing purpose continued as the diversity agenda took hold, and was aligned with anxiety about the shift from arts to heritage. William Scammell, in a letter to the *London Review of Books*, expressed it as 'the foolish notion that poets and novelists are or should become (cheap) social workers' (Scammell 1997: 4).

As Eagleton indicates, value judgements are constitutive of literature and so the work of recasting literature policy into a differently valued frame of reference, which NAMS began, was an enormous undertaking. Various strategies were adopted, including the populism signalled by the title of Violet Hughes's report *Literature Belongs to Everyone* (Hughes 1991) and Alastair Niven's attempt to specify how different purposes for literature operate with their own different value systems. But, to the extent that this shift in thinking about value has taken place, it has done so by incorporating educational values into mainstream cultural policy and practice.

Education became both agent and guarantor of these changes. We can see this in the way that from the late-1980s onwards the extent and quality of education work became an important funding criterion. In 1998, the minister for Culture, Media and Sport prioritised educational values and targets in his report on the spending review. He talked about policy drivers in terms of promoting access, pursuing excellence and nurturing educational opportunity before setting targets of 300,000 new experiences in the arts and 200,000 new educational sessions (DCMS 1998).

Education and the arts

The arts and adult education are not frills, but basic to the business of living; not the icing on the cake, but the yeast in the dough. (Adkins 1981: iii)

Education has often been invoked as the means of providing passage from elite to inclusive cultural policies in relation to literature. Indeed, during the mid-1980s interregnum, when the direct funding of literature activities ceased, it was the collaboration between RAA Literature Officers and remaining staff in the Literature Department to develop a policy for Literature and Education which ensured its continuity and survival (Arts Council 1987: 20). This also laid the groundwork for NAMS and partly explains why education underpins its strategic thinking and later implementation.

There is a strong affinity between the teaching of English (at all levels and in adult education) and both the socialist and liberal-humanist commitment to personal growth and development, which became allied with the social democratic discourse about the arts in the 1980s. Although several commentators have drawn attention to the contradictions implicit in this position (Hoyles 1977; Batsleer et al 1985; Doyle 1989; Dixon 1991; Street 1995) the connection is clearly established and, as we shall see as this study unfolds, continues to inform individual and institutional involvement in the writing culture. It is therefore not surprising that education came to play a significant role in the democratisation of cultural activity. However, it is important to note that educational discourses are not monolithic and are always managing competing tendencies towards liberation and repression. Bill Forster is one of the few commentators on the relationship between the arts and adult education to draw attention to, and make a case for, the distinctive appeal of each:

They (arts activities) are enjoyable precisely because they are not educational. (Forster 1983: 20)

But other major commentators in this area (Adkins 1981;

Hutchison 1982; Hutchison and Feist 1991 and Community Development Foundation 1992) both identify and urge synergy between the arts and education. This has been a distinct trend in arts provision as the emphasis on participation has tended to recast the artistic experience as an educational one, and funding has certainly followed educational rather than aesthetic priorities.

Robert Hutchison argues that the Arts Council's devolution of responsibility for amateur arts to the voluntary sector through the Carnegie UK Trust and the local authorities indicated the low value set on these activities:

> Amateur activities are seen not as having intrinsic merit and strength
> as arts activities but as part of some wider general social service.
> (Hutchison 1982: 50)

He saw the increased professionalisation of the community arts movement as significant both in extending its range and countering this attitude. However, he noted also that the demystification of culture represented by the community arts movement was often couched in anti-culture arguments. As a counter to this trend, later identified as 'uncritical cultural populism' (McGuigan1992: 244), he sees a role for adult education. Adult education's tradition of simultaneously providing access to and a critical perspective on education could be used in the arts context too (Hutchison 1982: 54).

These themes are revisited and expanded upon in the report into the role of amateurs in the cultural life of the UK, which he and Andrew Feist prepared for the steering committee of the Voluntary Arts Network (Hutchison and Feist 1991). In this report, Hutchison and Feist attempt to bring greater sophistication to the task of distinguishing between amateur and professional arts involvement. They begin by stating that there is no necessary opposition between standards of excellence and amateur practice, although they note that the assumption that there is underpins cultural policy, particularly the various arts-initiated educational schemes in which professionals work with amateurs.

They argue against the standard definition of amateurs doing voluntarily what professionals earn their living from. In particular they note that within many ethnic minority communities cultural activities are not hived off as the preserve of a few but are passed on through the generations as an expression of the whole way of life. With reference to the dominant, class-stratified white culture they develop a useful schema which positions practitioners along an amateur/professional continuum in terms of their age, motivation and opportunity. This is probably a more accurate reflection of the way professionals build arts-based and craft-based careers, especially in literature where there is no formal education or training route of the kind available to fine artists or musicians. Its suggestion that the transition to professional practice is as much about developing an attitude of seriousness and purpose towards the art form as it is about receiving payment is supported by Ruth Finnegan's study of music-making and Cherry Anne Knott's account of crafts (Finnegan 1989; Knott 1987).

In this context, the importance of formal and informal adult education is noted. It shows students how a professional or semi-professional career can be developed and provides tutors with an economic base that supports their activities. The interdependence of adult education with amateur arts and crafts creates an amateur/professional interface across which skills, methods and motivation are transferred, audiences are created and developed and practitioners – whether students or tutors – can create opportunities for the practice and validation of their art or craft. Important as this is, it is also important to note that many of those who participate in arts and crafts activities, often with a high degree of seriousness, skill and commitment, do not wish to develop this side of their life in professional or commercial ways.

At the same time as cultural policy was redefining its practice to make education central to the experience, informal and formal adult education was finding it harder and harder to retain space for arts education. Although often informal and oppositional in its rationale, delivery and pedagogy, adult education became increasingly tied to formal educational practices and values as assessment and credentialism, in the guise of mainstreaming came to define the sector. Throughout the 1990s funding and credit frameworks that elevated individual use and purpose over those of groups and communities regulated educational activity. Where adult education had once been able to provide forms of social and cultural association that enabled individuals and groups to access and develop forms of cultural activity on the basis of need, interest and use they now had to work within a framework driven by individual progress. One consequence of this was that adult education could no longer provide an infrastructure for collective cultural activity. It becomes, following the distinction made by Danish philosopher Jurgen Habermas (1984), system rather than lifeworld. Habermas's work is complex and often difficult but there is a resonant simplicity in his central idea that we live between what he calls 'lifeworld' – the areas of renewal, creativity and critical insight; and 'system'-regulation, imposition and conformity.

We have travelled a long way from our starting point in this chapter, which was to track how literature in cultural policy became a site of inclusive and participative activity. Cultural change is often a process rather than an event, and the move towards a more inclusive understanding of ideas about the social practice of literature and writing is no exception. We now move on to consider, in the next chapter, how attitudes towards creative writing in education change throughout the same period. Together, these two contextual chapters provide insight and background knowledge of the forces that shapes opportunities for writers and writing available locally.

Chapter three

The rise of creative writing in education

This chapter explores how creative writing became a subject discipline within British education. My account challenges the tendency to locate creative writing's origins exclusively within higher education (Harper & Kerridge 2004). The teaching of creative writing has deeper and more divergent roots than the founding of undergraduate or postgraduate degree programmes and the rehabilitation, via rhetoric and arts education, of their respectable ancestors. My account reaches outside the carefully planted and tended gardens of the academy into the wild woods of cultural practice. These practices, and the cultural policies they are linked with, include the participative and community arts movements, adult and community education, compulsory education, commercial and state providers. Together, they combine to produce and maintain the local cultures of writing which exist alongside and interact with the experience of teaching and learning creative writing as an academic subject discipline in higher education.

The chapter has two purposes. First, to counter the somewhat insular account creative writing in higher education gives of itself by providing a history of creative writing provision in other sites of formal and informal education, most of which considerably pre-date higher education provision. Second, to show how ideas about the role and purpose of creative writing in relation to artistic practice and to education have changed over time; and to argue that one consequence of this has been to replace artistic values and practices with those of education. In turn, this situates those who teach, just as much as those who learn, creative writing (whether they do so in its formal or informal sites) in a highly contradictory position which I describe as being in and against education.

Creation myths

The stories we tell about how we arrive at any given point provide clues to our current preoccupations. The story of the discipline formation of creative writing as an academic subject within British education is no exception. Its story of origins is generally told from the standpoint that creative writing belongs only to higher education, although commentators may disagree about their precise nature and about with whom and where the story starts. For many years it has been an accepted wisdom that creative writing is an import from North America. Creative writing courses certainly featured in the USA higher education system a good 30 years before they appeared in British universities. But, in Britain, summer schools, correspondence courses and adult education provision in creative writing were established long before David Craig launched the undergraduate programme at Lancaster University in 1969 and Malcolm Bradbury the postgraduate programme at the University of East Anglia (UEA) in 1970.

Nevertheless, North American experience acts as an important reference point for the introduction of creative writing to Britain. Teaching writing in North America has both a more extensive history and organisational base than it has in Britain. When this phenomenon crossed the Atlantic it brought two distinctive elements with it. First, teaching writing along a continuum from composition (what Britain calls the critical essay, expository or academic writing) to creative writing challenged ideas of writing as natural and untutored. Second, the writers' workshop provided a pedagogic model for such teaching and learning. There was, however, a third aspect of American creative writing, which was often lost in the passage to Britain. This was the way the educational activity sat alongside wider cultural interventions designed to develop a wider writer's community. This partly reflected the different organisation of higher education in Britain and America, with the latter's flexibility regarding matriculation, age of entry and full- or part-time forms of study, and partly the more democratic and participative approach to cultural life and activity characteristic of North America.

It is, therefore, interesting to see that now, as Britain moves towards mass higher education, the recognition that universities hold cultural capital that could – and some would argue should – be available to its wider region has brought creative writing into dialogue with initiatives that support cross-curriculum writing activities, academic literacies, outreach and capacity building. Many of these changes reflect the emphasis on partnership and regional development which follow from reconfiguring higher education as lifelong learning, including the different needs and capabilities of the undergraduate population in the wake of successfully starting to widen participation to Britain's universities. It is commendable that universities now take seriously their responsibilities to the city and region in which they are located. But these initiatives are not new. They continue the traditional extension role of university extra-mural departments and of adult and community education provision as varied as community colleges, the Workers' Educational Association and local community education services.

The view of creative writing as an America invention gained ground partly because of publicity surrounding the first British MA programme at UEA, which foregrounds the connection with North America even as it attempted to distance itself from the association:

> Angus Wilson and I – fellow professors of literature at the then new University of East Anglia – came up with a shared literary inspiration (...) to start up a postgraduate programme in something we decided to call 'creative writing'. We disliked the term, and certainly the idea then had a very negative aspect to it. In Europe, 'creative writing' was generally thought of as a suspect American import like the hula-hoop. (Bradbury 1994: 20)

UEA always attracted a good deal of publicity. This was partly because its director was an established writer and critic who regularly featured in the media, partly because it was innovative and partly because UEA launched several of its graduates, from Ian McEwen onwards, into spectacular literary careers. This has overshadowed other sites for teaching creative writing in higher education, including some which predate it. Most notable amongst these are David Craig, who established undergraduate and postgraduate teaching in creative writing at Lancaster University and Peter Abbs, who reconceptualised the teaching of English, and the training of teachers of English, as an arts, rather than humanities, subject at the University of Sussex. Philip Hobsbawm is important here, too. As a student and then tutor at the universities of Cambridge, London, Glasgow and Belfast he set up informal writing groups that nurtured the talents and careers of writers such as Seamus Heaney, Michael Longley, Derek Mahon and Jeff Torrington.

The conflict surrounding writing in education stems from the antipathy between English and creative writing. This is a conflict with several dimensions, initially framed as whether you can, and whether you should, teach creative writing it has now become more an issue of what you teach, and how. There is also the question of where creative writing teaching is located. Writing is unique amongst the creative industries in having no formal routes into and through employment. As a profession, writing is sustained by a web of public and private patronage and writers are trained in 'invisible colleges' (Miller 1993: 20-32) – largely informal networks of affinity, example and opportunity that are nevertheless also sites of significant social power. The late-twentieth century saw the opening out of a range of professions that had once also operated in these informal, grace and favour ways, but writing has proved more intractable than most. There are advocates of creative writing as a craft and profession, as well as an expressive art and intellectual activity, who seek to establish educational courses that will provide this vocational grounding. They are more frequently found in the areas of script and screen writing, where there are more direct links between industry and education, but this approach is beginning to inform provision more generally, especially when it is located outside English departments.

CREATIVE WRITING

For many years the prospect of even very modestly conceived creative writing options within English undergraduate programmes were strongly contested, especially in the pre-1992 universities, and only in the past decade has creative writing become relatively common as a postgraduate or single or joint honours undergraduate subject. As creative writing finds a place within British higher education, the conflict between English and creative writing is recast. One position, outlined by Philip Hobsbawm in the influential critical collection *Teaching Creative Writing* (Monteith and Miles 1992) and consolidated in the work of practitioners such as Paul Mills (1996), Rob Pope (1995) and Linden Peach (1995), situates creative writing as a contemporary outcropping from rhetoric.

Another position, exemplified in Graeme Harper's research project *Creative Writing in Academe* (2001), puts a different spin on the affinity based account of origins when he argues that it is universities, rather than departments of English, that provide (and continue to provide) for the making of writers. He makes this argument to challenge the defensiveness of creative writing in the academy but his position conflicts with affinity based accounts because, unlike them, he does not argue strongly for links between English and creative writing. Rather, he seems to propose that the skills associated with creative writing are 'caught' rather than 'taught'.

In contrast to debates about whether or not creative writing is part of the English subject discipline, there have recently been strong cases argued for creative writing as a wholly innovative body of knowledge, with a consequently different approach to learning and teaching. These can differ radically in their focus. So, for example, Celia Hunt and Fiona Sampson (1998) of Sussex University see creative writing as a powerful therapeutic tool, aligning its creative possibilities not only with the arts but also with art therapy. Jeremy Hooker (1997) values creative writing for the contribution it makes to educating the imagination, arguing that it is only possible to enable, not to teach, writing. David Ball, of Anglia University, extends the personal development model of creative exploration to argue for a more socially purposeful engagement with the content and meaning of writing, which he terms social literacy (Ball 1998).

An area that could be of greater interest to creative writing practitioners in higher education is making the connection to applied linguistics through academic literacy. Writing is central to academic practice and it is slowly being realised that all students benefit from explicit development of their writing skills. Applied linguistics adds theoretical underpinning to the learning support services provided for home and international students and blends with recent interest in integrating student skills across the whole curriculum. It has the potential, too of underpinning creative and professional writing courses with theoretical frameworks distinct from literary critical theories that continue to prove resistant to the notion of agency. There is, though, rarely synergy between these various engagements with writing in higher education, despite the rich opportunities for collaboration and shared experience in teaching and research.

All the accounts of origins, whether they concern under-graduate or post-graduate teaching or creative writing as a single or combined subject, share a tendency to put creative writing in higher education at the centre of debates about the practice and pedagogy of creative writing. This is in spite of its formation, and significantly longer history, in other contexts of formal and informal educational sites, and sites outside education. It is to this other story of origins that we now turn.

De-centring higher education

Complex, vibrant and important as the teaching of creative writing in higher education is, it is not, as sometimes represented, unique or self-contained. An alternative story of origins for the teaching of creative writing brings into focus the native, non-higher education based traditions of teaching and learning creative writing that sit alongside and are articulated in higher education.

This alternative story has two aspects. First, it includes a critical history of the other institutional sites where creative writing is, or has been, taught. In this way higher education becomes simply one of many sites where creative writing is taught and learnt. This acknowledges the multiple flow of influence, often conveyed directly by practitioners moving between these sites horizontally or vertically as they develop their careers. Such sites include schools, prisons, adult and community education, adult literacy, further education and teacher training. Second, it looks at teaching and learning creative writing in a completely new way, not as a discrete activity but as a material and socially located practice within a culture, or cultures, of writing.

Cultures of writing

A culture of writing is the aggregation of sites, agencies, projects, outlets and networks of a specific time and place in which creative writing activities take place. These include sites of formal and informal education across the whole sector, commercial enterprise, state-subsidised arts activities, including arts regeneration and capacity building projects, self-directed activities across the amateur and professional matrix, and writing apprentices and patronage across mainstream, avant-garde, small press and community publishing. Its concern with process and agency, meaning and value creates a social practice of writing. By this I mean that creative writing activities are not just about things – whether these are pieces of writing, published and unpublished, writing groups, publications or performances – but about the making of meaning through, and alongside the lived relationship of making or engaging with, those things. All these activities are, theoretically, accessible to anyone. In practice, they are always restricted. Participation is determined by real or perceived educational disadvantage – what Bourdieu terms cultural and symbolic capital (Bourdieu 1990). The concept of a culture of writing bridges the gap between individual lived experience and the broader social relations of educational and cultural policy and practice.

Within cultures of writing, even in educational sites, the activity of writing – doing writing – takes priority over teaching and learning writing – doing education. This is finely balanced and tutors and learners often perceive themselves in opposition to educational practices and values even when this is clearly where they are located. The relationship of these practices to education is complex. Education determines them – most powerfully by organising literacy, social and cultural capital – and can influence activities at several removes. The area of self-determined leisure activity, for example, relates to education but is often defined precisely by the ways in which it is not-education: freely chosen, negotiable, outside a framework of control organised by assessment and so forth. Much writing activity across the amateur/professional matrix takes place here. Such activities build, as well as interpret, local, common and national cultures of writing. Adult and community education is ambiguously and therefore powerfully, located in relation to these cultures of writing. Until very recently, its marginal status gave adult education scope to develop socially transformative qualities that allowed it to become a resource for local cultures and communities. During the last decade, this scope has been curtailed by the close regulation and scrutiny that adult education has experienced. Changes in cultural and educational policy over the last ten years have restricted this scope in the now formalised adult education sector. At the same time, cultural practices incorporated into social regeneration and health care initiatives adapt many of the values and practices associated with radical adult education. This suggests that informal education is a powerful precondition for socially transformative adult education.

De-centring education

The first social practice that defines a culture of writing is so rooted in our common sense of writers and writing that it receives very little critical attention in discussions of teaching creative writing. It is patronage and writing apprenticeships. Experienced, and perceived, as individual and personal, patronage is profoundly social and material. It is conducted through invisible colleges, as informal learning and teaching, and it also forms part an important hidden curriculum of some higher education, especially Oxbridge. Patronage also flourishes as a form of work-based learning in the literary institutions of publishing and journalism and it shapes the work of individual writers who gate-keep, broker and mentor entry into and progress within their profession. Writing apprenticeships are the powerful and often overlooked structural element underpinning all cultures of writing.

A second, equally powerful, equally overlooked, underpinning structural element is the commercial sector. This is even less researched and considered than patronage or apprenticeships. It exists in two forms: as markets for writers, and as a service industry. Commercial or popular writing is often excluded from teaching creative writing, especially in higher education, but students and participants engage with it, often alongside the formal teaching and learning they do – as extra-curricular rather than hidden curriculum. The commercial aspect is important in the ideological struggles over writing within cultural policy and education. At the policy level, the market has been invoked to withdraw or refuse subsidy to literature and writing. Within education, the emphasis on an open-ended educational process that invokes either literary values or personal development has often been seen as incompatible with market-led writing. Market-led writers are often found in Writer's Circles or Clubs where the experience of learning and teaching creative writing is framed by an anti-expressive, anti-romantic pragmatism. However, those who participate in the range of creative writing activities available do not make the same distinctions between commercial, artistic and educational activities, as do those who provide them.

Next, I want to outline the elements of creative writing's service industry:

> There are firms of which I would warn you, which want so much down to cover incidental expenses, and which later tell you that they have found a man 'who loves your poems and would like to print them in

book form'. But when you go into the question the amiable man is not rich and would want you to help a little (a small matter of about twenty pounds), and you, who are aching to see your words printed, are sorely tempted. Please don't be! (Bloom 1938: 120–1)

Warnings about vanity publishing in the 1930s indicate how long a history writing's service industry can claim but it would be dishonest to present this aspect as the whole story. Some of its activities do take pecuniary advantage of a writer's desire to see their work in print but others, while run for profit, provide valuable information or services to writers and would-be writers. Magazine and book publishing is both a service to writers and a successful market niche in its own right. The proliferation of distance learning courses, editorial agencies, holidays and conferences likewise provide opportunities for writers, but also create an income for those providing the service. These activities cross the borderline between writing as education and as leisure. This reminds us that writing, like other art forms, has its hobbyist dimension but it also reflects changes in the organisation and funding of adult education and community arts that have forced many tutors and providers to become entrepreneurs in order to survive at all.

Some services for writers are clearly part of, and provide for, the writer as enthusiast, especially those linked to small societies and associations that must be run entrepreneurially if they are to survive. Nevertheless, the pages of *Writing, Mslexia and Writers News* are thick with adverts offering self-publishing, reading services, plot generators, IT packages, courses, holidays and writing spins on all kinds of sales. The expanding lists of books for writers indicate the market's buoyancy, as does Barry Turner's *The Writer's Handbook*, which has been published annually since 1987 and complements *The Writers' and Artists' Yearbook*.

Self-help manuals on imaginative writing, writing good English and literary style have been produced for a self-improving adult audience throughout the twentieth century. Martin Secker's series *The Art and Craft of Letters*, with contributions from Frank Sidgwick and Lascelles Abercrombie, addresses itself primarily to readers but there is an implicit address to writers too. The 1970s and 1980s saw a steady interest in books about writing, ranging from the reprinting of Dorothea Brande's 1934 classic *Becoming A Writer* with a foreword by John Braine (Brande 1983) to John Fairfax and John Moat's *The Way To Write* (Fairfax and Moat 1981). The three major publishing companies in this field, A & C Black, Allison and Busby and Elm Tree Books, consolidated their lists by publishing manuals for a wide range of genres and forms, a trend that continues to the present day. There are also regular promotions in *Writers News* of a Writers Book Society, which offers a chance to buy USA imprints as well as UK publications, including those produced by small presses and Writers' News Ltd, that are rarely seen on sale in bookshops. 'How to Books' has recently launched a successful writing list of 30 titles with the emphasis clearly on the market-led writer.

In all these creative writing manuals the reader-writer is constructed as an individual, working in isolation and focused on publication and the editorial relationship. During the 1980s this changed. Books emphasised creative expression and the writing process and constructed the reader-writer as part of a group, engaging in socialised writing activities. This reflects the collective forms of organisation ushered in by feminism and community writing which was taken up by creative writing in adult education. Its expansion generated the need to develop and share a repertoire of activities and ideas on practice. Julia Casterton's *Creative Writing* illustrates the rationale of her teaching for the City Lit (Casterton 1986) and Julian Birkett's *Word Power* (1998) first accompanied a TV series, shown on Channel 3 in 1982, which stressed the value of writers' groups.

From the mid 1990s, another shift occurred, with manuals and guides now aimed less at the self-improving adult and more at the undergraduate student and creative writing tutor. These include *Teaching Creative Writing* (Monteith and Miles 1992), *Writing in Action* (Mills 1996), *The Creative Writing Handbook* (Singleton and Luckhurst 1996), *The Creative Writing Course Book* (Bell and Magrs 2000) and *Running Good Writing Groups* (O'Rourke and Robinson 1995). They illustrate the professionalisation of creative writing activity and its subsequent incorporation into a pedagogic framework. The commercial dimensions of writing and writing development shaped, and continued to interact with, the infrastructure which cultural and educational policy began to build for creative writing from the 1970s onwards.

De-centring higher education: adult and community education

Creative writing has been taught in adult and community education for far longer than it has been taught in higher education. However, although adult education can be broadly characterised and differentiated from compulsory and higher education, it is important to recognise that it is not a monolith. The differences between forms of adult education provision and participation can be as great, or greater, than those between these sites and other educational sectors. This is particularly pertinent in the context of accreditation. Credit frameworks paradoxically soften the distinction between higher and adult education at the same time as they sharpen it between formal and informal education.

Geoffrey Adkins argued that one legacy of the 1973 Russell Report into adult education was the separation of arts education from work with disadvantaged and community groups (Adkins 1981). Although he argued against the inevitability of that separation, socially purposeful adult education throughout the 1980s showed an increasingly sociological bias. There were exceptions. David Evans's included creative writing workshops in the community education programmes set up by Liverpool University. This led to the establishment of two independent groups, Scottie Road Writers and Liverpool 8, who became founding members of the FWWCP and later part of the ambitious REPLAN/NIACE project, Working Through Words, 1984–86, which in turn led to the setting up of the Community Resource Unit (REPLAN/NIACE 1988). However, the account of community education in Liverpool that became a founding text for training adult educators does not discuss this cultural work (Brookfield 1984). With women's education there was greater crossover between sociological and cultural work, including writing, most notably in the work done by Jane Thompson in Southampton that culminated in the writing and publishing of *Learning the Hard Way* (Taking Liberties Collective 1989). In general, though, arts activities were marginal to social regeneration until well into the 1990s (Thompson 2002; Fegan 2003).

London's City Literary Institute ran one of the largest and most ambitious writing programmes within liberal adult education in the British Isles. They encouraged students to adopt a professional approach to their work and supported them in this by employing published writers as tutors. The Writing School was recognised as an exceptional provider of creative writing activities for adults and, in the late-1970s, became the first English institution outside a University Department to host a writer-in-residence. City Lit not only offered a wide choice of general and specialised courses but also a structured educational experience. The Writing School's success was bound up with its tutors, yet the definition of a good tutor and good tutoring was implicit:

> A good teacher of creative writing knows what to do. (…) If you have real writers and real writers who are also committed to education, and to City Lit, and possess certain personal qualities then it works. (Mercer 1991)

This model of teaching creative writing in adult education is reminiscent of the founding principles of the Arvon Foundation. It privileges the writer's status as writer, not teacher, and relies on a tacit pedagogy in which knowledge is caught without formal instruction.

> Teaching involves two complementary concerns – one is training and practice in the craft; the other is, in the classical sense, education ('leading out from'), which amounts to a facilitating of that self-discovery implicit in all self-expression. The two cannot realistically be separated. And the matching of these two in a way that is individually appropriate can be undertaken only by someone whose authority is,

and is felt by the student to be, unquestionable. (...) Authority, originally, is the quality of being an author, in other words the unquestionable knowledge that comes with having 'lived' the making of something. (Moat 1985: 65)

Such practical pedagogic issues continue to be debated by higher education practitioners. The City Lit's prestige and central London location ensured it had the pick of tutors and permanent waiting lists for many of its writing courses. Elsewhere in the country, smaller, less mobile populations and a more limited pool of tutors to draw on, meant the provision of writing courses had to be organised differently, as we see with The Adult College, Leicester and South Western District WEA. Each example raises curriculum issues that continue to inform creative writing practice.

Creative writing courses were first offered at The Adult College, Leicester in 1953. In 1958, former students established Leicester Writers' Club and in 1964 The Writers' Club began to organise a programme of creative writing courses for The Adult College, which continue to the present day. The founding circumstances of the original creative writing classes illustrate both the historical reach of creative writing provision and its changing ideological formation. The college principal appointed a former elementary school teacher to provide remedial classes in all but name. From this instrumental beginning, the activity quickly developed a more specialised concern with commercial creative writing and for 30 years The Writers' Club monopolised creative writing teaching in Leicestershire. It organised a range of activities: guest speakers and manuscript meetings at The Club, an annual programme of structured classes, Beginners, Intermediate and Seniors, offered day and evening, plus two or three specialist courses each year and an annual residential summer school. In addition, its former students and tutors taught creative writing courses and workshops throughout the county for the WEA and Community Colleges. The ethos of this work was that product was more important than process, and that value was realised in commercial terms. The tutor was present in the classroom not as a writer, but as an editor, and the authoritarianism of this position was reproduced in the teaching style.

The development of creative writing courses by the WEA in the West Country provides another example of how adult education helped to initiate and sustain creative writing teaching. Writing courses were first requested by students taking literary courses in the early-1950s and initially met with suspicion from the organising body. Short follow-on courses were provided in 1953 and 1954 but the students still wanted a full creative writing course. This posed a problem for the WEA who were bound by the terms of their grant aid to provide arts appreciation rather than practical classes. But, struck by the students' willingness to write critically and creatively and the quality of insight their creative writing added to their critical work, they offered 'The Pleasure of Writing' in 1955. It fostered networks and initiatives for writers that continue to the present day.

The principles on which this programme was established differ from those of both the City Lit – to make writers – and Leicester Adult College – to make money. Its premise was that only a few students would have the combination of talent and application needed to succeed as professional writers. The course might act as a springboard for them, but they were not its prime focus:

> No claim is made that students can be taken in from the streets and taught *en masse* to write creatively and well. But most would-be writers can be helped to develop the craft of their art, and their imagination and creativity can be stimulated whether or not they go on to pursue writing as a vocation: this process, it is felt, is worthwhile in itself. (Hough 1983: 35)

The value of creative writing for personal development sits within the distinctive social purpose framework of the WEA, although the hesitation with which South Western District WEA agreed to run creative writing courses was repeated over several decades by adult education providers throughout the country. Nevertheless, its standpoint came to inform creative writing provision by local authorities, adult education departments in the universities and, increasingly, mainstream undergraduate teaching:

Although many Creative Writing courses are able to recruit selectively, they do not exist solely for those students who are already gifted writers. The discipline also has responsibility to students without great imagination or facility with words. It can help all students to improve their writing skills and experiment with rhetoric. Creative Writing is a practice-based discipline but it is not vocational in any simple sense, and programmes cannot claim that all of their students will be able to make careers as professional writers, or teachers of Creative Writing. (Holland et al 2003: 5)

De-centring higher education: schools

Creative writing in schools also has historical reach. The first positive references to teaching creative writing occur in 1917. References to a backlash against creative writing in schools can be traced back to at least the 1930s in North America and the debate about whether writers or teachers should teach creative writing to 1947. Schools made several critical contributions to teaching creative writing and the development of cultures of writing.

The attention to writing process in the work of Britton et al (1975) and Holbrook (1964a, 1964b, 1967a, 1967b) provided a point of contact and exchange between Britain and America. It established a forum for debate about the nature and purpose of creative writing teaching and learning which acted as a conduit for North American experience and was quickly elaborated beyond schooling and children by writing tutors who crossed backwards and forwards between schools and adult education. When these arguments appear ten or 15 years later in community, adult and higher education contexts their elaboration in relation to compulsory schooling provided a point of reference from which commonality and divergence was explored.

Creative writing options and strands were included in B. Ed. programmes from the 1960s onwards which provided models and rationales for teaching creative writing in higher education as it moved into the undergraduate curriculum more generally. It may also account for the number of English teachers who became activists around creative writing: setting up an Association for Writers in Education in 1987, teaching in adult education, becoming involved in the Regional Arts Association and contributing to community-based creative writing activities. Schools also channelled the principles and practices of Arvon back into other sites for teaching creative writing. Arvon began as a project aimed at school children, running closed courses and training sessions for teachers, and only later developed work with adults. It emphasised the authority of the writer, as opposed to the teacher, eschewed coercion and stressed doing the writing above formal instruction and tuition. Many contemporary creative writing tutors were first exposed to this approach to writing while accompanying their school students to Arvon and it provided them with a model for teaching and learning creative writing better adapted to adult, community and higher education (Moat 1985: 66).

Schools played an important part in founding community publishing. Teacher Chris Searle, who was sacked for publishing *Stepney Words* in 1971, and Ken Worpole, who founded Centerprise Publishing Project in 1973, both enabled their pupils to write books that more fully represented their lives and identities. Schools also acted as links to community arts projects in East London, Brighton and Bristol, which in turn were linked with radical adult literacy campaigns influenced by Paulo Freire's *Education for Freedom* (1972) and, later, in Liverpool and elsewhere, the Second Chance or access movement in further and higher education. Out of this political and cultural mix several community-based writing, oral history and publishing projects were founded which, in 1976, formed the Federation of Worker Writers and Community Publishers [FWWCP].

Today schools are central to Creative partnerships, a scheme that brings significant financial and cultural resource into local communities. This work can be traced back to the Writers in Schools scheme (founded 1969 and devolved to the regions in 1980) which acted as a nodal point from which many community writing and writing development projects grew. They laid down a pattern of partnership working between local authorities and regional arts associations (later boards) that enabled the successful implementation of the current arts and regeneration agenda.

De-centring education: enthusiasts and social movements

Commercial creative writing activities draw on a loose aggregation of writing enthusiasts, just as the educational and arts based initiatives do. Sometimes these are the same people and sometimes they are quite distinct but there is a sense in which all writers are enthusiasts, or amateurs. Although there clearly is an employment sector called writing there is no clear-cut route into writing as a career choice and arts and educational initiatives are usually explicitly non-vocational. It is customary, too, for even established writers to combine writing with another career.

Keith Jafrate, commissioned in 1994 to research literature and writing activities in Leeds in preparation for a writing development project, was surprised to find strong separatist tendencies amongst Leeds writers and writing organisations (Jafrate 1994: 1). Writing enthusiasts, like other self-help groups, are finely differentiated, opinionated and volatile. All cultures of writing have groups, which despite a broadly shared vision and practice of writing, argue and split. Where groups do not share a frame of reference, they maintain significant distance from each other, often expressing their differences robustly.

It is important to highlight the diversity within the field of non-professional voluntary writing as a check to the inclusive, and generally socially progressive, claims made about the voluntary sector (Elsdon et al 1992). There are several instances of people organising together to achieve their ends – and showing self-actualisation and realisation – but doing so without the values and social purpose foregrounded in more explicitly political arts activities, such as the FWWCP.

The FWWCP is the leading umbrella organisation for socially purposeful cultural political work in literacy, writing and publishing. The writing workshop, and the publication and performance of writing, is central to its work. Much was taught and learnt in the FWWCP, but it is significant that originally membership excluded groups that had been set up by or met in educational contexts. FWWCP writers groups valued autonomy and self-determination. They had affinity and solidarity with the radical and socially progressive traditions of adult education but were wary of the dependency such classes could create. The groups ran as workshops, a collective organisation in which all have an equal right to participate and be heard. The debate in these workshops – about content and meaning, as much as style and form – was often in direct reaction to the political and literary blandness of the writing enthusiast and hobbyist. 'Serious writing' was a significant term in discussions of cultural policy throughout the 1970s and 80s but in the FWWCP it had as much to do with social purpose as literary ambition.

The significance of the FWWCP's distance from traditional educational values and practices – the espousal of a critical, self-determined education – became greater throughout the 1980s and 1990s. The cultural democratic campaigns of the 1970s led to changes in cultural policy in the 1980s and 1990s. Cultural policy was now characterised by an emphasis on participation, social inclusiveness, an entitlement agenda and cultural diversity. But there was a catch. A campaign about the arts, cultural capital and social relevance was resolved with recourse to education. People wanted a different kind of artistic or aesthetic experience and were offered, in many cases compelled to have, an educational experience. Education thus became the guarantor of widened participation and a keystone of cultural democracy and diversity in the arts. Uncritical education is concerned with regulation rather than transformation or transgression. It is, largely, what we get, and stands very little chance of delivering its promise.

This chapter set out to demonstrate the complexity of creative writing's origins and contemporary location in education, community development and arts activities. It alerts us to the possibility that within any given creative writing activity a number of traditions, definitions and purposes, some in competition with each other, will be in play. It argues that whatever the actual site of this activity, it will be over-determined by educational practices and values. It points towards the key issues which practitioners and policy makers alike, in education and the arts, have to engage with as they implement, or resist, moves to widen participation in creative writing. These hinge on three central questions. The first is whether writing is conceptualised as an artistic or an artisanal process. Second, whether being a writer is conceptualised as a singular preoccupation, and by implication restricted to fewer people, or seen as something which sits alongside a range of other identities and activities in ways which allow different degrees of involvement from a wider range of people. Finally, whether writing can be taught in ways that enable its mysteries to be learnt, and if so, how this teaching and learning should best take place. We take these questions with us into the exploration of Cleveland's local culture of writing.

Chapter four

Local cultures of writing

Although ideas about writing and its audience changed as elitist cultural policies gave way to those emphasising inclusiveness and widened participation, a gap still remained between those who made and implemented policy and those on whose behalf it was being made. Policy makers assume a practice of writing but do so on the basis of a limited dialogue between policy and practice. The understandings of writing practice that do exist are largely drawn from the metropolitan experience of literary elites. Consequently, creative writing policy makers and practitioners have had at best only a partial understanding of how writing fits into the everyday lives of the people with and for whom they work. This chapter attempts to close the gap between policy and practice through an exploration of writing as a social practice. Using the concept of a local culture of writing I describe the complex ways in which forms of organisation and support for writers develop, in specific times and places, the ways in which writers participate in these activities, and the meaning they attach to them.

What is a culture of writing?

This concern with process and agency rather than cultural products draws on Paul Willis's concepts of symbolic creativity and the grounded aesthetic (Willis 1990). This means seeing creative writing as a social practice: not just about things – whether these are pieces of writing, published and unpublished, writing groups, publications or performances – but also about the making of meaning through, and alongside, the lived relationships of engaging with those things. Willis sees symbolic creativity as 'roughly equivalent to what an all-embracing and inclusive notion of the living arts might include' (Willis 1990: 11) and argues that its vital role is in producing human identity and capacity. *Common Culture*, as a commissioned study of young people and the arts, reflects Willis's expertise as a leading commentator on youth culture. The rationale he outlines for his focus on young people – that they are crucially and self-consciously concerned with issues of who they will become (Willis 1990: 7) – also resonates with adults, who make up the majority of the participants in cultures of writing, and who are often catalysed into writing as a result of specific experiences which disrupt their everyday lives and identities.

I also drew on the work of Ruth Finnegan to formulate the concept of a culture of writing. Finnegan studied music making in Milton Keynes. Her starting point was the musical family and she explored the nature and extent of their involvement in music-making activities and the ways in which they and others valued their activity. Her discussion of the value of music making is extremely useful as she considers the question in anthropological rather than aesthetic terms. Her argument about the role of music in public ritual, observations about performance as gift-exchange and her interest in music-making as a pathway through urban life were all suggestive routes into understanding the complex negotiations individuals make when they become involved in organised writing activities (Finnegan 1989: 303–7, 331–6).

This helped me to formulate creative writing as a social, rather than individual, activity, by providing a reference point from which to plot the ways writing conformed to or diverged. Amateur and professional are key categories in cultural policy and they take on a complexity in their lived reality that challenges the binary opposition into which public policy and perception puts them. Finnegan described this as a complex continuum, showing that people moved along it depending not only on their skill, ability and interest in the practice but also on where they were in their life span and personal circumstances. This had great resonance with how I observed writers moving in and out of engagement with writing, publishing and associated organised writing activities.

There was, however, a fundamental difference. Initial participation in music making arises through and is sustained by a process of acculturation, people are drawn into the activity gradually because others do it and this familiarity sustains their continued involvement. By contrast, involvement in writing activity was often precipitated suddenly, with writing activities providing a refuge for individuals from friends and family. Like Willis's young unemployed people, these writers were often 'painfully grounded in "normality" rather than in radicalism or the transcendental' (Willis 1990: 120) and, like his young people, exploring questions of identity as life changes destabilised their identities and situation.

Willis dealt with a broad and inclusive canvas – a common culture. My interest was the relationship between a specific, local organisation of the writing culture, often characterised by opposition and diversity within itself, and its points of contact with metropolitan and national literary culture. This may seem a very laborious way to talk about something most people would recognise as community writing. But, although I do use the term, I have reservations about it.

Throughout the campaigns against elite cultural policies during the 1970s and 1980s the term 'community' – as in community writing, writers in the community, community publishing – was in common usage. I prefer to use this term only in that historical sense. Although Raymond Williams (Williams 1976: 76) found that, unlike other terms of social organisation, community was never used unfavourably, throughout the 1970s its widespread and often imprecise use rendered it problematic in cultural and political analysis. By the 1990s, the Conservative Government's co-option of 'community' for their repressive and socially destructive policies – community charge, care in the community, community policing – emptied the term of what residual radical content it retained.

McGuigan's critique in *Cultural Populism* (McGuigan 1992) echoes a tension that emerged in the mid-1970s between the FWWCP and the emergent community arts movement. Although in practice there was often co-operation between the FWWCP and various community arts projects, the FWWCP took a different ideological and organisational stance from the community arts movement. In the context of the Arts Council, this was about keeping the argument within, and about, literature, despite well meaning efforts from supporters on the Literature Panel to move it to Community Arts. But it also reflected a wider concern (which I still share) about the way 'community' muffles conflict by setting up a two-tier system that deflects attention from the inequalities inherent in the values and practices of the mainstream. The emphasis on community also makes it harder to articulate the differences within specific communities which preoccupied radical theory and practice throughout the following decade. At the same time, as Barton and Hamilton make clear in their discussion of the concept of community, it is an enduring term which can be useful in delineating the local social relations which mediate between the private sphere of family and household and the public sphere of impersonal, formal organisations (Barton and Hamilton 1998: 15–16). Nevertheless, my preference is still to use the term 'local', although I am aware that the concept carries many of the same reservations and limitations as 'community'.

Kevin Robins argues that the 'struggle for place' is at the heart of much contemporary concern with urban regeneration. He counsels a wider view of the local: one that recognises its relation to the economies and cultures of globalisation as well as its relation to the national and metropolitan (Robins 1991: 34–5). Making a useful distinction between locality and local, seeing the latter as relational and relative, and accepting 'the perceived and felt vitality of local cultures and identities', he argues that globalisation positions cultural localism 'in ways that are equivocal and ambiguous' (Robins 1991: 36) before warning against nostalgia, introversion and a parochial sense of local attachment and identity.

These are fair points, well worth bearing in mind as we move into the local writing culture of Cleveland. But I would add a rider: it is as necessary to understand this 'parochial sense of local attachment and identity' as it is to judge it.

Writing is ordinary

Cleveland is not an auspicious site for cultural or literary activity. This makes it ideal to demonstrate how pervasive and how ordinary the impulse to write creatively is, and to chart the social practices which collect around it.

Writing activities are too finely specified a category to be picked up in any useful detail by national surveys of leisure and learning and social trends (Mass Observation 1990, Sargant 1991, 1997, 1998; Sargant et al 2000; DfES 2001 Central Statistical Office 1992). The Arts Council of Great Britain did commission Research Surveys of Great Britain (RSGB 1991) to include questions on arts participation in their regular surveys. They showed that writing, like the majority of other arts activities, is a minority preference. Photography, participated in by 19 per cent of the adult population surveyed, was the most popular. Writing stories, in the medium range of popularity, had 4 per cent participation, and writing poetry, at 2 per cent, was not quite the lowest return: 11 of the 52 options presented to respondents recorded participation rates of 1 per cent. However, the sampling methodology they employed is not well suited to untangling the complexity of participation in writing. Having noted over many years the hesitancy with which people attending (and sometimes leading) writing groups and courses claim identity as a writer unless they are widely published leads me to suspect under-reporting in large-scale surveys such as this.

In their 1990 survey of amateur arts, Hutchison and Feist tried to flesh out the bald statistics uncovered by the RSGB Report. They tracked competition entries and unsolicited manuscript submissions as an indicator of amateur writing activity. They counted 400 small poetry presses that received between a few hundred and five thousand submissions annually. Major competitions, such as those organised by the Poetry Society, Arvon Foundation and Bridport attracted between 4,000 and 32,000 entries. The Royal Shakespeare Company, which in the 13 years prior to 1990 had only ever staged two unsolicited plays, received 400–500 unsolicited manuscripts per year. The British Broadcasting Company, which broadcast 217 plays in 1990, received between 10,000 and

13,000 submissions annually, with a further 5,000 going to light entertainment (Hutchison and Feist 1991: 128–30). Although not entirely reliable, (these outlets are also used by professional and semi-professional writers), they give some indication of the overall level of writing activity, and the blurring of the divide between amateur and professional practitioners supports their argument about the unhelpfulness of that distinction (Hutchison and Feist 1991: 10). The Internet has created new opportunities to channel and develop this interest. Flagship sites, such as Trace On-line Writing Community or the BBC Get Writing board, have active communities of membership and receive thousand of hits each month.

Elements of local cultures of writing

I referred earlier to the culture of writing as the aggregation of sites, agencies, projects, outlets and networks of a specific place and time in which creative writing activities take place. It is now time to specify what this means in practice. This is a two-stage process. It involves identifying at a general level the elements of the culture of writing. Then, using this as a template, mapping particular occurrences in a local form.

All local cultures of writing exist in relation to regional, national and international forms of organisation and association for writers. The most obvious connection between them is the market, but they also offer a variety of networks and support. These include the Society of Authors and the Writers' Guild of Great Britain, the Arts Council, with funding and strategic overviews, and specialist organisations, either for specific art forms, such as the Screen Writers' Guild and Romantic Novelists Association, or campaign and interest groups, such as the Disability Arts Movement (DAM) or the Association for the Literary Arts in Personal Development (LAPIDUS).

Residential courses for writers, positioned along the education/recreation spectrum, draw on a national catchment area. These include the Arvon Foundation and many smaller

61

charitable or private enterprises. Similarly, a range of distance learning opportunities are provided by traditional – National Extension College or Open University – or specialist – Open College of the Arts or Writer's Bureau – providers.

The culture of writing develops from the interaction between these institutions of writing – the forms of organisation and activities – and their providers and participants. Each form carries and reproduces a range of meanings in its practice, a meaning concerned both with the particular form and its wider significance. Within any culture of writing, then, it is important to ascertain and understand several levels of meaning and legitimisation, including who is and is not recognised as a writer, what the purpose and value of writing is understood to be, what the craft secrets are understood to be and how they are transmitted to new writers. Such meanings are never totalising, although distinct writing cultures have organising, or ascendant, ideas. Barton and Hamilton's concept of 'the ruling passion' (Barton and Hamilton 1998: 18), developed in literacy studies, helps us understand this. It counters the prevailing functionalism of literacy theory by exploring its emotional dimension: the ruling passion in people's lives and literacies. This idea transfers easily to creative writing where it helps to explain what it is that catalyses and sustains writing and writing activism. In this way, we can see the ruling passion not only of individuals but also of groups and agencies. Within local cultures of writing, finding out about, and making use of, national resources for writing requires a high level of motivation. In my study, such connections were rarely made and when they were, they were more likely to be with the market-led and commercial sector.

The regional infrastructure can link local and national cultures of writing but it often functions as an alternative to both. Statutory arts associations provide a strategic overview which they underpin by granting or withdrawing funding directly or by brokering partnership arrangements. These support publishing initiatives, individual writers, writing residencies, festivals and special projects. There are also non-statutory regional associations, which operate with varying degrees of formality in terms of membership, for example, Northern Playwrights or Northern Shape. However, these are very much single-issue groups with tightly defined agendas that do not often extend to playing an advocacy or campaigning role. Networking and information exchanges is vital for writers to negotiate their way around the writing field, whether nationally or regionally, but the amount of information to be processed, and the cost of doing so, makes it a difficult undertaking for a voluntary organisation. It is a role better performed by the RAB. With the advent of the Internet, these functions become easier to manage and regional initiatives more easily claim national status. A good example is the Save Our Short Story campaign, which was initiated by Northern Arts but has stimulated national publicity and intervention. Similarly, the Internet enables national initiatives to more easily accommodate regional specificity, as is the case with the BBC's Get Writing Community.

All these national and regional elements are, theoretically, accessible to anyone from a local base. In practice, there are always restrictions. These may be practical, such as the time and means to travel being adversely affected by age, unemployment, gender or disability, or based in a lack of knowledge about opportunities and how to access them. This shades over into the way participation is determined by real or perceived educational disadvantage – what Bourdieu terms cultural and symbolic capital (Bourdieu 1993). This will be returned to later in the chapter. Here, it alerts us to the way local provision can support and encourage writing activity. While still subject to the same processes of exclusion and intimidation it is, nevertheless, by virtue of its spatial and temporal closeness, able either to break down some of the barriers or simply to create unpredictable, slightly risky gaps for individuals to slip through.

Locally, loose groupings of enthusiasts are commoner than formal organisations. The ruling passion, rather than strategic policy, is in command and leads to an emphasis on specific local sites of activity, projects and networks, supporting and supported by courses, groups and workshops and any publishing initiatives, local competitions and performances they organise.

These general ideas about cultures of writing, developed in response to the multitude of events and positions encountered during the early stages of my fieldwork studies, provided a grid against which to map the specific writing culture of Cleveland. It is to this I now turn.

'A hole like that'

In '"A hole like that": The literary representation of Cleveland', Andy Croft (1990) uses this comment, made by a character in a Kingsley Amis novel, to introduce his account of the way Cleveland has been by-passed by both mainstream literary culture and its heritage reprise. It is against this background that the indigenous writing culture develops, and the contempt for Teesside goes a good way to explain the defensive local chauvinism, which Robins (1991: 36) would identify as parochial local attachment. This is, though, only one feature of Cleveland's culture of writing. In the 1990s, when I carried out the research, it was also characterised by a commitment to broadly based and inclusive understandings of creative writing. This, with its related commitment to demystifying the practice and process of creative writing, put community-based writing and writers at the heart of its activities, and in doing so saw them simply as writing and writers. It had taken time and effort to reach this place. It seemed like the calm after the storm at the time. With the benefit of hindsight it is easier to see it as the deceptively still eye of a storm that still rages.

The storm has several sources of energy. First, change is constant, something apparent in the account of the formation of Cleveland's culture of writing which follows. Second, the 1990s saw two major policy changes that bear directly on the infrastructure supporting Cleveland's culture of writing. In education, the central government review of university-based continuing education in 1994 imposed mainstreaming and accreditation, which removed funding from community-based work. At the local level, this meant that the responsibility for funding and organising creative writing courses, which had devolved to the University of Leeds' Adult Education Centre, came to an end. Changes also took place within cultural policy as more pro-active, participative policies were implemented. Finally, the very interventions that produced and sustained Cleveland's culture of writing created its own developmental dynamic, for individuals and groups, which continued to generate areas of growth and change.

The first interventions: 1960–1972

There are no blank canvases for policy makers and activists to work on. An historical analysis of writing in Cleveland shows early formations and trends pre-figuring later developments, such as the University of Leeds' Adult Education Centre (AEC)'s role in co-ordinating and supporting cultural initiatives, the provision of meeting space by the libraries and the promotional role of the local media. In the 1960s, the AEC functioned to all intents and purposes as an Arts Centre. Its core educational activities were overshadowed by its work with affiliated societies, film club, exhibitions, annual trip to the Edinburgh Festival and general contributions to Teesside's social and cultural life (Saunders 1983; Chase 1996). There are, then, important continuities, as well as differences, between the culture of writing in Cleveland in 1990 and 1960. What distinguishes one period from another is often the combination of critical mass, attitudinal shifts and cultural policy that either encourages or blocks change.

I found no record of writers' groups existing before the early-1960s when a number of writing groups were established. The first of these was a writers' circle, Middlesbrough Writers' Group (MWG), which supported writing across all genres with the emphasis on a professional, market-led approach. Various activities, including guest lectures, were organised but the focus was firmly on members' individual commitment to writing and publishing, with the provision of market information a high priority. Writers' Circles locate themselves outside the educational sector and, due to the high number of genre fiction and non-fiction writers who make up their membership, are often excluded by the subsidised arts sector. They see their role as providing a service for professional, but non-literary, writers and ambitious amateurs. MWG closed in 1994. It had not retained sufficient new people to step in as death and illness undermined its ageing organisers, nor had it become a key provider of creative writing in adult education as several writers' circles in other parts of the country had done. During its final years friction developed between some members of MWG and those involved in promoting new ways of organising local writing activities. Sometimes expressed in terms of organisational style or openness to new members, it reflected a fundamental difference in the way writing and the writer was conceptualised:

> We do a terrible disservice saying anyone can do it, come and join us, because there are fewer and fewer outlets for writers. I sometimes feel very anti 'creative writing'. The only analogy I can find is somebody who has spent years learning to make beautiful hand-made furniture and some dickhead from MFI comes along saying: 'I know how to do that.' (Beatrice)

Poets were not well served by MWG. In 1962 Poetry 20+, which alternated discussion of member's work with reading from the poetry tradition, was formed. It met at the AEC then moved to a nearby Library. As with MWG, founding members were the core membership, which made the group unsustainable beyond one generation, and it closed in 1993.

There were several poetry initiatives. During the late-1960s and early-1970s these were often connected with the radical politics of the time, were informally structured and short-lived. A late-60s poetry group that met in Guisborough library and members' homes and a writing group based at a neighbourhood centre in central Middlesbrough had left no documentary records but were still part of popular memory. An early-70s initiative at Thornaby Pavilion, a local authority leisure centre, also left no records but was remembered by a local poet. It prefigured community arts principles.

About four of us, including John Longden, arranged Sunday afternoon poetry readings. We invited members of the public to bring either their own work or any poetry that they were interested in. (...) They attracted an enormous audience from widely differing backgrounds. It attracted elderly people reading Tennyson's poetry and it also attracted very young people reading experimental verse. (...) We got children peering round the door and in an unguarded moment I remarked that we should have a separate group for them. The manager of the Pavilion, striking while the iron was hot, said: 'Are you volunteering?' so I more or less had to, and I used to go in on Saturday afternoons and run a kind of glorified crèche loosely connected to creative writing. (Nell)

Equally of its time was Housecall, a local radio programme that featured creative work alongside music and supported a listeners' writing group and held regular competitions. Housecall continues to broadcast but the writing group and its local publishing ceased during the 1980s.

Mersey Writers was formed in 1972 by people with shared left-wing political values. A key founder member came to the area as an LEA English advisor. He exemplifies a recurrent feature of Cleveland's culture of writing, that of incomers introducing experiences and ideas originated elsewhere. He introduced the writer's workshop to Cleveland. Its emphasis on peer evaluation and expressive imagination challenged the more authoritarian, market-led approach of the writer's circle. Exposure to debates and movements surrounding progressive English teaching had influenced his professional life but he had also spent time in Lancaster as a member of a writing group run by Gordon Ayles, which David Craig (who pioneered undergraduate creative writing in Britain) also attended, and in Leeds, where he had attended a university extension poetry class run by Jon Silkin in 1963.

Similar groups were forming elsewhere in the country at this time but Mersey Writers differed from them because it remained a closed group and did not include outreach as part of its activities. It met in people's homes, membership was by invitation and it rarely participated as a group in local writing activities, such as the later Writearound festival or local publishing, even though individual members were prominently involved in these initiatives. The group provided a conscious alternative to the ethos of Writers' Circles:

> This isn't the sort of group that has a prize for the person who earned most in the preceding month. And we don't clap if anyone does get published. (Mersey)

Until the late-1970s, then, both dominant and alternative writing cultures in Cleveland were shaped by the perception of writing as a singular and largely solitary activity realised in and validated by publication, and the forms of association that developed sustained this perception. This began to change in the mid-to-late-1970s as trends and movements in the political and social sphere began to democratise previously individualised cultural experience. The changes were uneven in their impact. Some organisations, such as MWG and Poetry 20+, continued much as before and many individual writers continued to write the same things in the same way. But for others, especially a younger generation who had not been attracted by or welcome in MWG and Poetry 20+, these ideas were influential. This generation became activists in the late-1970s and early-1980s and transformed the values and infrastructure of creative writing in Cleveland.

Student activism and community development: 1980–1984

This period saw the underlying ethos of creative writing activities change radically. Previously, they had been self-selecting, self-managed and largely self-financed by people who identified themselves as writers. Throughout this period, evangelising activities designed to stimulate interest in writing amongst a broad cross-section of people who would not necessarily see themselves as writers, and the financial underwriting of these activities by education, arts or local authority agencies, became the norm. The impact of incomers was at its strongest here, and the link between radical politics and writing was asserted, first through feminism, then the youth unemployment campaign, the peace movement and finally the Communist Party. The community arts movement, with its focus on celebrating shared experience and common identities – as women, young people, members of a particular race, class or region – was a powerful national force at this time and several incomers brought experience of this with them. Some influences owed more to happenstance than design. During this period, for example, the development worker for the FWWCP lived in Newcastle, barely 45 miles away, and there were several active groups in nearby County Durham and Tyneside, but the link between Cleveland and Federation activities came later, through a friendship that developed between one of the founding members of Writearound and a London-based member who holidayed in his village.

The local women's liberation movement, which received some funding from community development sources, organised a Women's Festival in 1981 that included two writing workshops. In 1982 several women who had attended these went on to take part in the region's initiatives around the national promotion of women in arts and entertainment, Women Live. This coincided with setting up the Village Arts Project in East Cleveland. It developed a writing group that campaigned strongly about the region's unemployment. It produced a successful anthology, *The Cleveland Way*, and provided a focus for writing activity in East Cleveland. It also modelled the pattern of group involvement in writing and publishing that came to characterise the Cleveland writing scene in the mid-1980s. This early lead by feminists is submerged both in later developments and accounts of their origins. There are a number of explanations for this, including the general decline in feminism as a social movement, but it has particular resonance in Cleveland, where one consequence of the 1987 child sexual abuse cases was a profoundly damaging split amongst local feminists and virulent hostility from the media and general public towards feminist activism of any kind.

In the early-1980s several mature students with prior experience of community arts came to Teesside Polytechnic. They set up societies, publications and performance spaces, which helped to channel and maintain energy and support for the other initiatives. There were two little magazines: *Poetic Licence* (1982), a local open access magazine with a broad local appeal; and *Station Identification* (1983), a more avant-garde magazine. *Poetic Licence* had a link to Housecall, through the latter's monthly competition, and acted as an informal focus for networking in the area until 1984 when its editor left Teesside.

The Multi-Media Society was formed in 1981 by Trevor Teasdel, a mature student with prior experience of community arts, who was to play a significant role in Cleveland's culture of writing. The society promoted events and organised workshops on and off the polytechnic's premises and made links with the town's Youth Unemployment Campaign. This led to a permanent performance group, The Castalians, which was launched in June 1982 at Cleveland's art centre in Stockton. Monthly meetings provided networking and performance space for local writers, musicians and songwriters and, with National Poetry Secretariat support, several visiting poets and performance groups came to the area.

The Castalians brought together several people who developed further initiatives, such as the Writearound festival and *Outlet* magazine throughout the late-1980s. By autumn 1983, following low attendance, The Castalians was relaunched but the focus of writing activity had moved to Middlesbrough and in autumn 1984 it was wound up.

In Middlesbrough, community arts initiatives laid the basis of wider cultural activity. The first project was based at a youth and community centre in North Ormesby in 1983, where several feminists who had been involved in the Cleveland Women's Festivals worked. In 1984, community arts projects were extended to the whole of Middlesbrough and included plans for a writing workshop. Trevor Teasdel, who had now graduated, stayed on in Teesside. As a volunteer with Community Arts Middlesbrough, then employed on a Manpower Services Commission project he remained involved with writing activities.

During this time related but unconnected initiatives were

happening elsewhere in the region. Stokesley WEA launched an evening creative writing class in 1983. This quickly established itself as a writing group, producing an anthology, *Leven Lines*, in 1986 and meeting outside term-time in members' homes. In 1984, the WEA and University of Leeds Adult Education Centre jointly launched a creative writing course on a newly built council estate. This group produced an anthology, *Lazy Tees*, in the early-1980s. In Hartlepool, a creative writing group was started at the Unemployed People's Centre. There was no development agency to initiate or co-ordinate these projects. Cleveland Arts was established in 1982 but had no specific brief for or expertise in Literature. It was only in 1991, when Cleveland Arts set up an Arts Equality Unit, that writing became a significant part of its work and even that reflected the skills and interests of the first post holder. She had previously been involved with writing groups and brought that dimension into her work, initially by including writers in the teams of artists running projects in elderly people's homes and day centres.

In 1983 Northern Arts established a writer-in-residence, Bob Pegg, at the Dovecot Arts Centre, in Stockton. This was a parachute initiative, planned and implemented with a minimum of local consultation, even though Cleveland Arts were largely funded by Northern Arts in part 'to advise and assist arts organisations in their dealings with Northern Arts' (Cleveland Arts 1984: 4).

The writers' workshop Bob Pegg set up at Teesside maintained the momentum of student involvement in Cleveland's writing culture as a new intake of students became involved in existing initiatives and later developed their own – Entertaining Hope (1987) and Teesside Poly Arts Festival (1989). As Teesside has always had a high number of mature home-based students there was greater integration between student and town culture than is usual with higher education arts initiatives. By the mid-1980s, the scene was set for consolidation of the local culture of writing. Several key agencies – education, arts, and community development – were in place, individuals had begun to establish informal networks and the volume of organised creative writing activity had increased.

Laying down the foundations: 1984–1986

This period saw considerable integration of community arts and adult education initiatives but it was not strategically planned. Rather, it relied on individuals who crossed between these sectors, saw opportunities for synergy and made it happen. The high level of public political activity linked to the miners' strike, ecology and peace campaigns and the greater flexibility that adult education had to organise work that explored these issues, facilitated this. The political campaigns used cultural, as well as traditional political, forms of protest such as banners, festivals, newsletters, songs and poetry. These acted as both rationale and outlet for the community art activities that had been developing in Cleveland.

In 1984 Community Arts Middlesbrough launched Teesside Writers Workshop (TWW) and invited Tyneside Writers Workshop, a FWWCP group, to the opening. The event was well attended by people involved with the range of the writing activities Cleveland offered and the intention was that TWW would become a worker-writers' group on the Tyneside model. This expectation, combined with the instrumentality of TWW's formation, created difficulties for the group. Its membership fluctuated as volatile meetings drove many people away. Trevor Teasdel, who persevered with the early meetings, described them as a battleground. The conflict was about who the group was for. TWW had attracted several confident and established writers who wanted a group that would challenge its members but it had been envisaged as a community arts project that would meet the needs of its least confident members. These aims proved incompatible.

A split developed, which came to a head during the production of an anthology in 1985. One side wanted to include work from all members and the other wanted to select work. The situation was resolved by setting up a WEA short course that several people left TWW to attend. When the course ended, it formed a new group, Write Now. Three people attended both groups and relations became more amicable. They travelled together to attend events in Durham and Newcastle with FWWCP groups and took part in local performances together. TWW was active in publishing and performing during this time but it did not admit any new members. The number of writing groups in Cleveland expanded during this period. Older groups, such as the writers' workshop for women in East Cleveland, thrived and new groups started, including one linked to a second Northern Arts residency. The WEA responded positively to requests for creative writing classes and started several in the area.

During this period writing activists in Cleveland began to interact more with the FWWCP that, towards the end of this period, took a much more pro-active role nationally. In addition to co-ordinating the work of its member groups, the FWWCP was also promoting its participative, community-based approach to writing and publishing to sympathetic individuals and agencies around the country. It secured funding for a series of regional training events open to non-FWWCP members that combined discussion and performance. Several activists and writers from Cleveland attended these events, which provided a stimulus to local and regional networking. Cleveland, however, was not a key-player in these larger networks. Its culture of writing was marked by 'the discourse of beleaguerment' (Bennett 1995: 215). Although coined in an entirely different context, to describe the unease in the cultural sector about the new funding arrangements of the early-1990s, it captures not only the defensive chauvinism of writers and writing activists in Cleveland but also the attitude of outsiders which fuels it:

The Write Together events got going and I remember we held one in Darlington as a sop to the Teessiders. I have a sense of Newcastle as the centre of the region. I don't like Middlesbrough much as a place, a bleakness comes over my soul when I think about it. (Armstrong 1993)

Cleveland desperately wants a regional identity because it hasn't got a very positive one. The tension created between the national and the local, in terms of what the regional identity would be and who it looks to, can be stimulating and positive. But it can be negative. For instance, people really limit themselves by shunning some of the events that bring in national writers. (Atalla 1993)

CREATIVE WRITING

These comments, from a founding member of a FWWCP group and Literature Officer of the Regional Arts Board respectively, partly explain why local forms of organisation and provision have such priority within Cleveland. Although Cleveland turned inward, it did so with a strong commitment to networking across its own region. Initially, this focused on producing a magazine to publish local writers' work and provide information about various activities going on locally. Attempts to raise external funds for the project were unsuccessful and the Write Now group self-funded the first issue of *Outlet* in November 1986.

Outlet was edited by a collective of eight people, seven of whom were or had been involved with TWW and was primarily, as the name suggests, a place for people to send creative work. It also acted as a discussion forum and information exchange. Its focus on new writers, and 'those who may not see themselves as writers with a capital W' (Tutor, Llanberis), brought conflict with Northern Arts. They questioned the low-key production style and the emphasis on encouraging and recognising effort:

> One Northern Arts adviser suggested we 'were doing these people no good by publishing them'. Our experience was that it often did 'do them good' in that the writers concerned, instead of giving up, became enthusiastic, joined classes, responded positively to feedback, learnt from the variety of styles in the magazine, joined writers' groups and often over a period of time we would see vast improvement in style and confidence. (...) Some pieces that were considered to be 'rough diamonds' would be published and feedback given by one of the editors to help the writer develop their work. Positive discrimination might be given to very young writers with potential, or elderly writers who'd written their first piece aged eighty-seven – a very brave step. This was part of the community and developmental nature of the magazine. (Tutor, Llanberis)

Despite its reservations, Northern Arts funded *Outlet* for several issues. The first print run of 500 rose to 1000 for the next six issues and 2000 thereafter. The magazine was free and distributed through libraries, bookshops, writing groups and an individual mailing list. As well as helping to unify and co-ordinate creative writing activities, *Outlet* was also a means of identifying need. The collective's links to the WEA and Community Arts Middlesbrough enabled several mutually supportive and developmental connections. Members of one group, for example, who complained of having to travel, were guided through the procedures of setting up a local group through the WEA, and its founding meeting was advertised to local contacts. In this and other ways the importance of *Outlet* as a prototype of literature development cannot be underestimated. However, it is important to remember that this activity was entirely voluntary. Grants were given strictly for production, distribution and promotion.

The success of *Outlet* helped to strengthen the case for a writing festival. There was no doubt about local interest in writing, *Outlet* provided a skeletal publicity and promotion network and there were a number of committed individuals with experience of working productively together. Realising this objective took Cleveland's writing culture into a new phase.

Consolidating the culture of writing: 1987–1993

Writearound was established in 1989 and quickly came to dominate external perceptions of the writing culture in Cleveland. That these were largely favourable is an indicator of the extent to which the social-democratic discourse by then shaped cultural policy nationally. But there were reservations and Northern Arts, the main backer, was always more comfortable with a rationale for the festival that privileged ideas of selectivity and merit over participation:

> Cleveland is homogeneous enough to be genuinely inclusive. The Writearound competition is just the right thing to discover talent amongst the grass roots. There will be loads and loads of really awful stuff but good writers too. (Attala 1993)

Symbolically and practically, Writearound was the most important event to take place in the writing culture at that time, but there were other related activities that form an important part of the Writearound story.

This period saw a rapid expansion in the number of creative writing courses in the region. Several were organised through the WEA but the local Further Education Colleges also began to run courses, usually with an inflection towards the commercial end of the spectrum, and the AEC ran a Writing for Pleasure and Profit course, taught by a member of MWG.

It was WEA policy to fund courses for one or two terms with the expectation they would then continue as free-standing groups. Some did, but rarely as successfully as when they were tutored courses. In the late-1980s, due to changes in policy and funding, the WEA was unable to continue even this minimal level of support for creative writing classes. At the same time, funding at the AEC became available for community education work for the first time and was used to organise creative writing classes in Cleveland. Unlike the WEA, a full-time staff member who was able to devote considerable time and attention to it managed this programme. AEC also offered repeat funding to courses. They set up some new courses but also took over courses and groups that the WEA had established. The number of courses continued to grow and by 1995, when the withdrawal of funding ended the programme, it employed sixteen tutors to provide one hundred classes, with a minimum of ten students in each, each year. This programme played an important role in consolidating Cleveland's culture of writing.

The Writearound Festival

The idea of a local festival of writing was first mooted in 1985, during a car journey to Newcastle for a Write Together event. The idea didn't go away, but it was 1987 before it was taken forward by the tutors of Llanberis and Cuillin. Llanberis's tutor had stayed on after studying in Teesside. Cuillin's tutor ran a newsagents in a coastal village between Middlesbrough and Whitby that supported a small fishing fleet and settled community alongside tourism. He describes himself as an ordinary working bloke who had started writing poetry in his late 30s in response to a personal crisis a good decade before Cleveland's culture of writing began to form. He picked up news of various writing groups through the local press, contact with the Arvon Foundation and his friendship with a regular holiday visitor who worked for a FWWCP Project in London and eventually he joined TWW where he met Llanberis's tutor. The workshop became the forge in which the various writing interventions were shaped.

Just as there had been arguments about where to pitch TWW and *Outlet*, there was conflict over the festival. Here the argument was about incorporating writers from outside Cleveland. Cuillin's tutor, as a result of his positive Arvon experiences, favoured doing so whereas Llanberis's tutor argued for a wholly local orientation. The outcome settled towards a grassroots emphasis. They approached Cleveland Arts, who took the idea forward with heads of the library service and education, Jenny Atalla of Northern Arts, representatives from the local authorities' leisure services and representatives from local writing groups. It took two years to plan and launch the first Writearound:

> They were impossible meetings for a long time. People who weren't used to meetings, people who wanted to say something about everything. They didn't follow procedures, some personality clashes. (...) It was such an amateur operation people couldn't possibly have expected it to be anything other. (Tutor, Bleaklow)

The steering group polarised into two camps, professionals and non-professionals. It is interesting the Northern Arts representative credited one of the few professionals in the 'non-professional' camp with Writearound's successful realisation, although he would be the first to make clear he was very much on the fringe of writing activities in Cleveland when Writearound was first mooted:

> Cleveland is Writearound: writing groups vociferously demanding a festival. Its grassroots with (Bleaklow's tutor) standing there like a colossus. Those early meetings were total chaos – he held it together

CREATIVE WRITING

and moved it on because he had the ability to organise and to organise others. It wouldn't have happened without someone who could do that. (Attala 1993)

Although his work did not include organising creative writing courses at this time, Bleaklow's tutor utilised cultural capital gained from previous experience of managing meetings, organising and planning adult education programmes and political activism. It would have been difficult, given the grassroots nature of the project, for the meetings to continue to be chaired by Cleveland Arts or one of the other agencies, but devolving chairing to Bleaklow's tutor enabled the professionals to relinquish control to the non-professionals while ensuring it was exercised in ways they recognised.

The Festival had several elements. It ran a competition, restricted to people living in Cleveland and its immediate environs (Darlington and Whitby), for poetry, short stories and non-fiction articles or local tales, each year until 1994. Prize-winning entries, together with several from the short-list were published in an anthology. A competition for children was introduced in 1993. The awards ceremonies proved the most popular festival events. In 1993, 165 people attended the launch of the children's anthology and 80 the adult anthology. That same year, an audience of 80 people came to hear Roger McGough and 60, Jane Gardam. Festival events were varied. They included library-based events for children and adults, readings and discussions from visiting writers, readings and performances by local writers, writing workshops and open readings. In addition to events organised by the committee several other events, such as theatre productions and exhibitions, were promoted under Writearound's umbrella.

The grassroots character of the festival was achieved through the mix of events and the decision to hold them throughout the region at a variety of venues. The events were directly linked to the various writing groups, with each hosting an event. In most cases, visiting writers shared the stage with members of the host group, an arrangement that worked well in most cases.

The process of deciding on events and venues offers further

examples of the grassroots orientation of the festival. The planning process began with each group being circulated with a questionnaire about the previous festival and asked for suggestions about the forthcoming one. The groups were consulted about whether they wished to put on their own event or host a visiting speaker, and then further negotiation took place to match speaker to group. Wherever possible, events took place at the group's usual meeting time to ensure a core audience. The festival grew and developed. The first lasted a week, which expanded to two and finally three by 1993. In 1992 a part-time administrator was appointed.

The success of Writearound generated a new wave of activity in 1990 and 1991, with the launch of a new small press, Paranoia, and several new publications, *Tees Valley Writer, Exile.* Middlesbrough's local newspaper, *The Evening Gazette*, launched 'Noticeboard', a monthly column for writers edited by Bleaklow's tutor. By now, he had become a central figure in Cleveland's writing culture. This was partly due to his role in Writearound but also reflected the way in which the community-based writing courses he co-ordinated for the AEC were a central focus for creative writing activity. He also initiated a monthly poetry event, Poetry Live! that brought established poets to Middlesbrough.

Although some new people had begun to help organise the various writing activities this did not happen in sufficient numbers for the original activists to take a back seat. There was a tension for them between writing activism, their own writing and their domestic and working lives:

> Unfortunately, the more I've got involved in publishing other people – and let's be honest, Writearound is publishing other people – the less energy and intuition you have left for your own writing. That's one of the sad things of it. Your own writing doesn't do very well. (Tutor, Cuillin)

Under these circumstances, it became easier to let responsibilities fall on those who could pick them up as part of their paid work and this increasingly happened. At the same time, though, there was a strong sense of popular ownership of Writearound. For example, when Cleveland Arts appointed a Literature Development Worker in 1993 the Writearound committee discussed whether or not he could join them. It was inevitable, and proper, that he should, but indicative of the tension surrounding professional and amateur engagements in Cleveland's culture of writing that the question arose and was taken seriously.

The 1993 festival staged 50 events attended by well over 2,000 people. This made it one of the best-attended literary festivals in the country yet this did not guarantee financial security from ticket receipts (many events were free or offered at a charge which did not cover costs), sponsorship or grant aid. Although 1993 saw what was in many respects the most ambitious and successful Writearound, it also signalled the beginning of major changes. These were led in part by funding pressures, and the impact of the newly appointed Literature Development Worker but they also arose from the working through of an internal dynamic. Writearound had been developmental, setting up and engaging in a process of change. Five years on, it had to reassess where to go next, and how to take into account the changed expectations and needs of the local culture of writing it had succeeded in developing. The Chairman's report on the 1993 festival is largely a series of questions and an appeal to local people to join the debate about its future:

> Should Writearound continue to grow ? (...) Should Writearound try to appeal to (...) both writers and readers? Can it be both a 'literary festival' and a 'writer's festival? (Writearound 1993)

At this point, though, Writearound's future lay less with the people it served and more with the funding agencies. The festival had always been financially insecure and relied heavily on donations in kind and of time from its management committee. Northern Arts and Cleveland County Council provided the major funding and both were soon in jeopardy. The abolition of Cleveland County in 1995 not only threatened the funding of countywide activities but also made planning and administration difficult. Liaison and negotiation now had to take place with four separate library, arts, leisure and education officers. Where a Borough Council was generous in its support, as Middlesbrough continued to be, the absence of matching funding from other Boroughs made it hard to justify programming events there. At the same time, the emphasis on financial stringency from Northern Arts put pressure on the committee only to organise events that would be well attended and show a profit.

Northern Arts had never offered Writearound revenue funding and by 1994 its grant aid took the form of a guarantee against loss. It failed to mention the festival in its 1994 review, *Promoting the Arts in the North* (Northern Arts Board 1994) and began to compare Writearound unfavourably with the recently launched, and distinctly non-grassroots, Durham LitFest. This may have been no more than the tyranny of innovation, which is a characteristic weakness of all arts funding, or a misguided concept of fairness in response to inadequate resources. But the knives were out for Writearound, which was criticised for its lack of business sponsorship, the low production values of its publicity material and its administrator's lack of literary standing. In 1995, under pressure from Northern Arts, her contract was not renewed and joint literary directors were appointed to organise and run the festival.

Writearound continued but its community base soon took the form of closed workshops in schools and prisons, reflecting the focus of funding for the Literature Development Worker's post, rather than the network of local writing groups and activists it had once served. Writearound was unable to secure independence from the vagaries of the current arrangements for funding the arts. Under those constraints it became a leaner festival, retaining workshops and guest writers but winding up its competition and publications (except those for children, which the local newspaper sponsored), open readings and shared local and guest per-formances. It was sustained as part of a wider package of lottery-funded writing activities managed by Buzzwords, a Teesside-based literature development project within Cleveland Arts, which drew together the whole gamut of activities – creative writing courses, newsletter, work in schools, local publishing and residencies – that fed into, and created, the culture of writing. Finally, these targeted activities, increasingly limited to work with children and young people, predominated and eventually Writearound ceased to exist at all.

Writearound's fortunes demonstrate the inability of the statutory funding bodies to respond adequately and appropriately to cultural innovation. It aptly illustrates Robert Hewison's proposition about English cultural policy:

> To have a cultural policy means having a vision that encompasses ideas, images, values, that encompasses both artists and audience and which has a long term goal of improving opportunities for creativity, and of giving as much access as possible to the productions of that creativity. But no policy is possible without the structures to deliver it, and the money to make things happen. (Hewison 1997: 2)

The trajectory of the Writearound Festival describes a complete shift in focus from amateur activists to the professionals. It was not a conspiracy, although inevitably some activists saw it that way. It illustrates the truth of what John Pick, in an article anticipating the effects of lottery funding, called the 'final victory of the state planners over artistic freedom' (Pick 1994: 5). Ken Worpole, in a discussion of the voluntary sector in leisure, speculated about how to resource such traditions without killing them. He worried about flooding the voluntary sector with money and consequently professionalising it (Worpole 1991: 148).

In Cleveland, the flood was a trickle but it was just as effective in breaking apart the elements of mutual aid in Cleveland's culture of writing. Cleveland was unusual in that its activists were well established before they asked for professionals to help them legitimate their activities and gain access to resources. Yet gradually activists lost the balance of power. It is easy to romanticise these conflicts and to idealise the past but from the outset Writearound, just like *Outlet* and all the societies and groups that preceded it, was meshed into forms of institutional provision and their structures of power that made the outcome fairly inevitable. There was no free space to be usurped by paid administrators and development workers but when these positions were held by incomers they made wonderful scapegoats for tensions and conflicts that may always have been present.

After Writearound

Throughout the late 1990s Cleveland's local culture of writing was characterised by professional initiatives both in the provision of educational and arts activities. The Literature Development Worker appointed by Cleveland Arts worked with the National Association of Literature Development Workers to ensure Cleveland was well networked into regional and national initiatives for training, project funding and authors visits and exchanges. Buzzwords, an arts agency that combined publishing, workshops activities, public events and targeted project, was established and secured funding from several sources that enabled a wide range of work to take place. Increasingly, though, this work was defined by social purposes as much as it was by cultural or artistic consideration as funding increasingly emphasised first contact with arts activities rather than recurrent funding and prioritised bringing arts experience into regeneration and health promotion projects. This meant that people involved in existing writing activities were no longer directly supported in their activities.

Some writers who had come up through these routes were able to gain work experience facilitating these projects but the majority experienced this period as one of retrenchment and sometimes resentment as writing activities increasingly focused on schools and young people, healing arts and closed institutions and public art. At the same time as the local arts activities became more specialised, the community-based writing courses were cut back as funding was withdrawn. Adult and continuing education was increasingly tied into accreditation frameworks, which represented a significant change in their organisation and delivery. Whereas the AEC had previously been able to respond to student demand and interest, the imposition of mainstreaming and the consequent compulsory assessment and drive towards a programme-led curriculum meant there was less flexibility for both students and tutors, some of who severed connections with the AEC. Elsewhere in the adult and community education sector, accreditation frameworks codified progression and curriculum for students, which, in the case of creative writing, emphasised its connection to formal language studies rather than its expressive and creative aspects.

The AEC took as positive a view of mainstreaming as it could, using the need to develop a programme of courses as an opportunity to address issues about curriculum and pedagogy in ways that tried both to foreground the radical and transformative aspects of the community-based programmes and address some of the shortcomings that had emerged. Issues of progression were addressed, as was the need to develop independent learning and student control of the process, within a framework that encouraged a critical engagement with creativity and self-expression. While never achieving the same volume of students that the community-based programme had, the programme flourished for nearly ten years until a further round of review and reorganisation ended all of the AEC's provision. The local culture of writing continue to thrive, with students, tutors and activists connecting to regional initiatives from the subsidised arts sector, running self-determined performance and publishing projects and lobbying for adult and community education providers to run creative writing courses. No longer as visible or buoyant as it was a decade ago, the local culture of writing continues to provide new, emerging and established writers with activities and events to sustain them. Currently, the University of Teesside is developing work for its undergraduate and lifelong learning students in partnership with the local arts agencies under the regional development agency banner. Teesside has developed international standing for its work in animation and digital media which it is finding ways to make available to the whole community, and a whole new phase of development for Cleveland's culture of writing is poised to develop.

A note on cultural diversity

I have analysed Cleveland's culture of writing in terms of its institutional framework and its ruling passion and in doing so I am conscious that it tells a story only about white writing. Racism has had a powerful impact on national, regional and local cultures of writing. In general terms, initiatives around race have been less frequent, less visible and less successful than comparable work on issues of class, gender and disability. Nationally, a very small proportion of creative writing teachers or literature development workers comes from the black and ethnic minority community. Cleveland, unlike coastal areas with Atlantic seaports, has never had a large Black and Asian population. This reflects its trading patterns which have tended to be with Scandinavia and Northern Europe. Nor has Cleveland attracted post-war immigration on the scale of other industrial areas of Britain. Until very recently it was a predominantly white town. A small Kashmiri population ran shops, restaurants and taxi firms, a small number of Chinese and Pakistani people ran shops and restaurants and there were a small number of Indian and African professionals (usually doctors and dentists) and a very small Somali refugee population.

Cultural diversity has increased since the turn of the twentieth century, due in part to increased numbers of refugees from a greater variety of countries and to the expansion of higher education and national health provision in the area which has attracted culturally diverse migration both from abroad and from within Britain. A consideration of the local culture of writing needs therefore to engage with issues of race.

There has been one writing project specifically for the Asian community. In 1988 Cleveland Writers' Project was established. This was a one-year residency that originated with a head teacher at the only Middlesbrough junior school with a high intake of Asian pupils. It was supported by the English Adviser, funded by Middlesbrough Borough Council, Northern Arts and Marks and Spencer, and co-ordinated by the Artists' Agency and Cleveland Arts.

There was an extensive and wide ranging job description, covering work in schools, oral history with older men, youth theatre, writing workshops for men and women and a final publication (Ahmad 1990: 2). The writer appointed did not relocate to Middlesbrough but co-ordinated the project from London with the help of a job-share with a BBC Radio Cleveland presenter who had an interest in writing and a local support group. The project highlights some of the difficult issues concerning cross-cultural initiatives in writing.

The Cleveland Writers' Project was not intended to be integrationist, rather it sought to make available to the area's Asian population some of the empowering and pleasurable activities associated with writing. Although well-intentioned in this respect, it spread its resource thinly trying to be all things to all people, and failed to take into account the implications of running a writing project with a cultural group who had no tradition of written culture. A much more successful initiative came through the Writearound festival, when it made links with the Mush'ara, a poetry festival rooted in the oral tradition. As a result of advertising the Mush'ara as part of Writearound several white writers attended and a small number of Asian writers began to attend courses and events. Despite this, very few people crossed over into each other's culture, even as visitors. Consequently, the detailed account that follows is, in its mono-culturalism, an accurate reflection of the absence of cultural diversity in Cleveland's culture of writing.

In the next chapter I look at how people find their way into and around the culture of writing. I base my analysis on the interviews and observations I carried out in Cleveland, including a survey of local knowledge, which explored barriers to participation. I then explore why people get, and stay, involved, with writing in terms of their expectations and the meaning and value they find in their activities. This involves specifying the range of purpose – personal growth and development, recreational, artistic apprenticeship, socially purposeful, and commercial – which informs creative writing activity.

Chapter five

Peopling local cultures of writing

Introduction

The previous chapter outlined in broad terms how Cleveland's culture of writing developed. Here, the focus is on those who got involved in Cleveland's culture of writing, and their reasons for doing so. These people successfully negotiated the barriers to participation that can exist in local cultures of writing. This chapter also considers the issue of participation – and non-participation – in writing activities more generally. I begin by considering participation from the standpoint of those who do not get involved.

Audience development became an issue for cultural policy from the mid-1990s onwards. Prior to this, the *laissez-faire* approach that had characterised cultural policy meant participation did not receive a great deal of attention. Where it had been studied, as in the mass observation surveys (Mass Observation UK 1968, 1974, 1976 and 1990), the Policy Studies Institute survey of amateur arts (Hutchison and Feist 1991) and the National Institute for Adult and Continuing Education Reports on leisure and learning (Sargant 1991, 1998) it was so broadly focused that the specificity of particular art forms was lost. Nevertheless, the Mass Observation Surveys are a useful reminder of the way that class, age and gender differentiate whether or not adults go outside the home for leisure in the evenings at all and, when they do so, where they go (Mass Observation 1974: 54).

The surveys also point to the complexity surrounding studies of participation. They note that knowledge of opportunities is significantly higher than the use made of them, for example 94 per cent of those surveyed in Sheffield had heard of The Crucible Theatre, but only 24 per cent had ever visited it (Mass Observation 1974: 59). Similarly, their survey of non-participants found that although material factors, for example, price and transport, played their part, the commonest response, at 41 per cent of the sample, 'not a theatre goer/prefer cinema/TV etc' (Mass Observation 1974: 69) suggests attitudinal or cultural factors were strong determinants. These were not explored in the surveys, which concluded that audience expansion lay in persuading those who went occasionally to go more often. The 1990 survey of Londoners' attitudes towards the arts also concluded that the most effective barriers were psychological, rather than practical, (Mass Observation 1990: 3) but again, this was not explored at length.

The policy shifts that gave greater weight to participation and inclusion highlighted the need to change attitudes towards the arts in order to both increase and widen participation across the full social spectrum. Information was hard to come by, as major surveys were only rarely commissioned. The 2001-survey commissioned by the Arts Council surveyed attitudes, attendance and participation in the arts. This was the first survey of its kind since 1986. It provided data to monitor changes in eight categories, which did not include literature. This is evidence of how marginal literature was to cultural policy generally (traditionally claiming less than 1 per cent of the Arts Council budget) and how issues of housing the arts and major capital investment associated with opera, music and theatre preoccupied cultural policy for the last two decades of the twentieth century. When the 2001-survey was repeated, in 2003, its focus was on cultural diversity, signalling a further shift from elite and minority attitudes towards the arts. Both the 2001- and 2003-surveys were conducted jointly with the Council for Museums, Archives and Libraries and the inclusion of films, carnival, festivals and clubbing and breaking music down to include live and recorded listening, indicated a radical break with the old categories of cultural activity. Books and writing had high participation rates, 73 per cent read for pleasure, but figures for writing increased only slightly, with three per cent respectively for writing poetry and stories. All the 'doing' activities (with the exception of clubbing under dance) were significantly lower than participation as consumption or attendance. However, it is interesting that participation was less differentiated than was attendance by socio-economic status and there were 'no noticeable class differences in participation in many activities, including writing stories and plays or poetry' (Arts Council 2002: 38). This adds substance to the assertion made by many writing activists that writing is a more democratic and open art form than many others. It was partly a response to such limited information about cultural participation that led me to look closely at who came to the courses, groups and events.

Local knowledge of events and opportunities

I surveyed awareness of creative writing opportunities amongst Cleveland library users for two reasons. First, to ascertain how effectively information about creative writing activities circulated through its main publicity outlet. Second, to understand the factors that influenced participation in creative writing activities from the standpoint of people who were not necessarily part of Cleveland's creative writing networks.

I targeted library users because the library service played an important role in Cleveland's writing culture. Classes and groups met in branch libraries throughout the region, libraries displayed newsletters and publicity leaflets, and they jointly funded the Writearound festival. I surveyed six libraries, which both spanned the county's socio-economic range and were within the catchment area for AEC courses.

I visited each library twice, when the regular writing activity was going on and when it was not, and stopped everyone who came into the library during my visits, which lasted between three and five hours. I wanted to see if there was evidence, other than attendance at writing groups or courses, of engagement with creative writing from the general public. If there was, I wanted to explore the factors that influenced participation in creative writing activities.

CREATIVE WRITING

Although libraries were key sites for hosting and publicising information about creative writing groups, classes and other related activities, the library users I spoke to were significantly unaware of the range of events taking place. Of the library users, 71 per cent did not know that a writing group or class met in the library and 91 per cent had never heard of the local Writearound Festival. Such lack of awareness must influence whether these events attracted their optimum audience, as a third of the people who had not known about Writearound expressed interest in attending it. However, raising awareness does not automatically lead to participation.

The majority of people who wrote and knew that a writing group met in their library reported that they chose not to go along. In some cases this was an informed choice, a reminder of the number of writers within any locality who do not want to participate in any socialised writing activities. But the majority gave reasons for not attending that indicated a profound lack of confidence in their ability. Despite never having visited the group or knowing anyone who had, people decided they were not good enough:

> I don't feel I do enough writing. (Man, Acklam)
> I'm not up to that standard. (Woman, Acklam)

In relation to writing groups and courses, the reasons people gave for not participating envisaged an aptitude range which included them, albeit humiliatingly at its lowest point. With Writearound, something different was going on. Although several people mentioned an unwillingness to travel to festival venues, especially at night, people talked about not attending the festival in ways that suggested they felt completely outside its frame of reference. Their talk about feeling out of place or being unsure what was expected of them conveyed a belief that such events were not intended for people like them. Ironically, they articulated precisely the exclusions to cultural participation that Writearound set out to challenge:

> I know I shouldn't really, but I'd feel inferior. That it wasn't for me. That

PEOPLING LOCAL CULTURES OF WRITING

I wasn't clever enough. It's a bit above me. I'd feel out of place amongst all those professional people. (Woman, North Ormesby)

When I asked people whether or not they wrote, and if they had considered joining a writers' group or course, I was testing two assumptions that inform local arts and educational provision. First, that significant numbers of people want to write; and second, that without intervention, in the form of courses, groups and networks, only a minority of them would continue beyond the required writing of school or work. My findings confirmed an interest in writing amongst people who would not define themselves, or are defined by others, as writers. There is very little research into any aspect of writing, creative or not, amongst adults. Two valuable exceptions are David Barton and Mary Hamilton (1998) and an earlier study by Morwenna Griffiths and Gordon Wells (1983). This latter considers the school-based writing development model of Britton et al (1975) from the perspective of its end-point: the different types of writing adults actually do, their writing habits and their feelings and attitudes towards writing. Their research findings are directed largely towards the teaching of English in schools and take the form of a critique of the rigid distinctions between transactional and expressive writing. For our purposes, it is valuable to note their finding that 25 per cent of their sample had attempted to write stories or poems at least once and their conclusion that 'the frustration that is felt there is less one of capability than of opportunity' (Griffiths and Wells 1983: 151).

Of the Cleveland library sample, 12 per cent would, or had, joined a writers' group, with a further nine per cent saying they would seriously consider it and 22 per cent of the sample described themselves as currently writing but not in, or intending to join, a writers' group. As people talked to me certain experiences and themes recurred. These can be summarised as the way writing had slipped from the possible to the impossible, suggesting that factors experienced as individual and personal were, in fact, social and cultural. As people talked about their practical relation to creative writing, they revealed their beliefs and assumptions about it. The most frequent was that writing had universal appeal:

> I've thought about writing. I think everyone does. (Man, North Ormesby)

> In every person there's one good book, if only about their past experiences. (Woman, Ormesby)

The second most common assumption about writing was that it was a gift or talent rather than a skill. With few exceptions, people believed writing could not be learnt or developed. This was often expressed through comparison. A principle of community arts practice is that example will act as an incentive. Here it seemed at least as likely to discourage, although the familial context may be significant:

> I can't make up stories.
> How do you know that?
> Because my sister does. She's brilliant, she's got an amazing imagination. She sends poems and stories off all over. I couldn't match her. (Woman, Ormesby)

People talked about imagination a lot. They saw the gift of writing, and the decisive difference between writers and non-writers, as the ability to translate imagination into words on paper. This is interesting because within the broad spectrum of activities provided by community-based arts and education there has been a definite bias towards realism, which has sometimes blurred the distinctions between creative writing, autobiography and local history. While this can be a good way into writing, it risks hardening into an orthodoxy, and one that cuts across popular conceptions of writing's nature and purpose.

The relationship to writing that was most frequently reported confirmed little has changed in the decades since Griffiths and Wells conducted their study. A youthful interest in writing was gradually eroded by lack of opportunity or the pressure of working lives and domesticity:

I used to be good at school. Composition as we called it was my favourite subject.

What happened?

I just went into my dad's business, and then I had six children. I had no time and no encouragement. (Woman, Guisborough)

There was considerable testimony to the ordeal of learning to write, and being required to write, at school. A legacy of this struggle into literacy was the destruction of any pleasure in writing. For many, this was also the consequence of enforced letter and report writing required by work:

I had too much difficulty learning to read and write for it ever to be a pleasure or passion to me. (Man, Guisborough)

There were also several people whose potential interest in writing was blocked by lack of confidence in their writing skills:

I've got a fairly good imagination but I couldn't put it down. I can think of a storyline for days but the minute I try and put it down it's gone. (Man, Berwick Hills)

It's all up there in my brain. Most people want to write a book.

What do you think stops you?

Lack of confidence. Scared of not having enough English. (Man, Ormesby)

Because people who do join writing groups and courses are often just as unconfident about writing, it raises the question of what prompts some people to own that fear and join a group or course and write whereas for others the wanting-to-but-not-feeling-able keeps them away. Griffiths and Wells (1983: 150) note 'it was disturbing how many people said that they were uncomfortable about their basic capabilities, and that they wished they could write better.' Ray Brown, a writer with many years experience of writing residencies and placements in closed and semi- closed institutions and a long standing WEA tutor, defines his approach to creative writing in relation to literacy:

I've seen people who've suffered from the fears and prejudices
people bring about writing. For example, a 79-year-old man had
written an autobiography of his life in the first 16 years of the century
in Ireland and had sat on it for 20 years, out of a fear of not knowing
how to write English. I spent a year saying: 'You're doing all right'.
(Brown 1993: 1).

Getting into writing: profile of participants

The University of Leeds Adult Education Centre [AEC] provided
most part-time creative writing courses in Cleveland by the 1990s.
Provided by the Community and Industrial Studies [CIS] section,
they were free and ran on an open door, rolling programme basis.
Most were held in libraries; only those organised in partnership
with the Equal Arts Unit of Cleveland Arts were not open to the
general public. They ran in settings with closed or restricted
access: a prison, day centres, residential homes, mental health
users drop-in centre and an international family centre. Most
courses attracted between eight and fifteen students.

When students enrolled they completed a form, which asked
about their socio-economic status and previous educational
background, and registers were kept, enabling a participation
survey to be conducted. The socio-economic profile of students
attending these courses conformed to national profiles for
participation in adult education (Sargant 1997). They were
predominantly female, over 50 and white. The CIS programme
was designed to provide educational opportunities to people and
communities experiencing social and educational disadvantage.
Evaluating the extent to which the creative writing programme
achieved this was not straightforward. The North East performs
so badly against a whole raft of national socio-economic indicators
that it could be argued that any provision in the region contributes
to countering an overall profile of limited opportunity and
disadvantage. Similarly, women are, in broad terms, socially
disadvantaged in comparison with men and with 64 per cent of the
students being female, the courses were serving people

experiencing social disadvantage. At the same time, though, social determinants, especially social class, interacted to displace, override or secure disadvantage in ways which maintained rather than challenged patterns of social inequality and the tensions that resulted did inform the AEC programme.

Students came from the older range of the population: 43 per cent were aged between 45 and 64, with 16 per cent 65 or over, and they were predominantly white (98 per cent). Nearly half (44 per cent) had a disability of some kind, a relatively high figure perhaps explained by the proportion of retired students and the provision of courses specifically for people with disabilities.

Educational disadvantage was a complex issue for this group who were, in many ways, a testimony to post-war social mobility and the significant role adult education itself had played in this mobility. More than half (56 per cent) had left school at 16 or under, but only eight and a half per cent had no qualifications and just over half of the 46 per cent with a higher education diploma or degree had gained their qualification as mature students. In occupational terms, just over a third of the sample (36.5 per cent) identified themselves as professional: non-managerial, of whom 20 per cent worked in education. A further 20 per cent held skilled manual jobs, 12 per cent had full-time domestic responsibilities, eight and a half per cent worked part-time and 17 per cent were unemployed. The highest and lowest occupational categories – professional: managerial and semi-skilled and unskilled respectively, made up the smallest groups with two per cent in each.

Less than ten per cent of students had addresses on the council estates or other working-class areas where courses were often held. The majority of students travelled in to attend courses, often doing so from affluent suburban areas. Not only were local students less likely to attend classes, they were also the students most likely to leave the course within its first few weeks.

It was more difficult to gather this sort of socio-economic data in the free-standing groups. Observation was a reliable means of ascertaining age, gender, disability and race but an unreliable guide to occupation and educational attainment, which was pieced together from indirect references during discussion. The groups appeared much more clearly socially demarcated than the courses. People attended their local group and its social composition reflected its area. So Thames and Humber, situated on council estates, were exclusively working class whereas Goyt and Annan, in market towns several miles from the Teesside conurbation, had a more mixed membership in which middle-class professionals predominated.

The issues of opportunity and disadvantage are further complicated when asked in direct relation to the subject or activity provided, in this case creative writing. Bourdieu's work on cultural capital theorises the experiential knowledge of cultural activists and adult educators, that access to cultural activity is determined not only by education and broad socio-economic factors but also, and especially in Britain with its strong metropolitan bias, geography (Bourdieu 1993). In this context, providing educational resources to support the development of local writing and publishing was a radical intervention that resources individuals and communities with cultural capital.

People attending the courses had different experiences of writing. The courses were advertised as suitable for beginners and experienced writers and were remarkably similar in their composition. This was also the case with free-standing groups. Only the groups that selected their members were homogenous. A typical group would be eight to twelve people. Of these, never more than one or two were completely new to writing. Slightly more, perhaps three or four, would have been keen writers in the past. The majority would have some current experience, generally gained through adult education, in writing and writing groups and perhaps one or two had considerable experience of writing activities, possibly with modest publishing success.

A minority had a strong interest in writing poetry, drama, autobiography or fiction but the majority had general interests in writing, often including letters for publication, articles and features alongside imaginative writing. Ambitions to be published or to perform, as opposed to writing for personal, often therapeutic, purposes, were frequently found amongst group and course members. These provided the continuum along which individuals positioned themselves and which gave groups their characteristic emphasis or style.

In addition to observing and interviewing writers from groups and courses I also interviewed a selected sample of individual writers. This was not representative in the classic sense but did match the emerging profile of the culture of writing in Cleveland. The sample included a spectrum of new to experienced writers, with a matrix of attitudes towards writing and publishing. I included writers who were and were not anxious to publish, those whose interests were profit-led, those seeking personal development, those keen to develop a professional approach to writing and those for whom writing was a hobby. I interviewed writers who had never belonged to a group or course, writers who belonged to formal and informal groups, and students on taught courses.

Getting into writing: routes and role models

In *The Hidden Musicians* Ruth Finnegan demonstrated the importance of family and peer influences in creating participation in musical activities (Finnegan 1989: 308–11). No such pattern exists for writers, for whom writing is almost always an activity that separates them from family and peers. Although the majority of people I talked to participated in social writing activities, their interest had begun in individual, often isolated, circumstances. Those who talked about having always written were unable to recall other children in their school who had shared their interest in making up stories or rhymes. In all my conversations with people engaged in writing activities there was testament to the relief of meeting and mixing with others who shared an interest in writing:

> I never tell people I write. They think you've got illusions (sic) of grandeur. You can see them thinking: who does she think she is?
> (Woman, Froggat)

CREATIVE WRITING

> You can talk and talk at home and just get glazed eyes, but here people talk back. (Woman, Annan)

Accounts of writers' lives show that whatever their gender, race or class position, aspirations towards a career in writing is rarely encouraged. Although sometimes seen by those at several removes as an easy route to riches, writers usually hedge their bets with a more reliable day job, often in education or the media. For others, especially women, writing comes after work, whether paid or domestic, in middle to old age.

This tangential relation to the labour market sustains the apparent democracy of writing and publishing: Mary Wesley, a successful novelist with several lucrative television adaptations, published her first novel when she was 70; Jeff Torrington, a Scottish working-class man who had attended adult education writing workshops for several years, won a prestigious literary prize with his first novel, *Swing Hammer Swing*, which had been several years in the writing; Willy Russell started out as a hairdresser and ended up as a stage and television playwright; William Ivory's television series, *Common as Muck*, drew heavily on his own work experience as a bin man; the prestigious Arvon/Observer Poetry competition is as likely to be won by poets published in small magazines as by those with established reputations.

But despite a steadily increasing public profile, albeit always defined by their difference, for writers whose backgrounds were neither particularly privileged nor whose routes into writing straightforward, there was no evidence from my sample that these examples had in any way influenced their interest in writing. Indeed, it was striking how little reference was made to contemporary literary culture.

This was highlighted by the enthusiasm with which Dean discussed Jack Kerouac, Charles Bukowski and Norman Mailer. In his early-twenties, Dean came to writing via the music scene, which in the late-1980s had revived interest in the American Beat generation. His admiration for these old men was very apparent:

PEOPLING LOCAL CULTURES OF WRITING

> The Rock journals were always talking about Kerouac, Bukowski, Norman. So I went to Bukowski's reading and he blew me mind, that was it really. (...) It's so like controversial and all. It just winds up the – I don't know, like the bourgeoisie. It winds them up and I like the idea of that. It just goes against the mainstream. That's the whole point of it. (Dean)

Ken Worpole (1983) has argued that American fiction held a particular fascination for working-class British men because of its narrative realism and vernacular language. Arguably, Dean is simply continuing this tradition. But this passion for America indicates not only the poverty of the culture in which he lives, and about which he was scathingly articulate, but also his lack of awareness of alternative cultures closer to home. The work of James Kelman and the Glasgow school, Irvine Welsh, Roddy Doyle or the Liverpool screen writers, such as Jimmy McGovern or Willy Bleasdale offer just as much potential for going against the mainstream. When he spoke about writing 'American-based stuff' I asked if he had ever tried to write about England in an American style. He struggled to conceptualise doing so:

> It would be difficult. I mean, that's a problem. You're living in Hartlepool and you're setting your stories in New York and people are saying: 'Well Christ, this lad's from Hartlepool. What does he know about New York?' But what do you do? I mean, I don't want to be the stereotyped writer from the North East who writes about unemployment and drinking beer. Sometimes you do think: 'Am I wasting my time here?' But then again, what else is there? If I pack in writing I'm just like the rest of them, aren't I? Just a robot walking about. (Dean)

So, if example or role models were not decisive factors in bringing about or reinforcing a commitment to writing and organised writing activities, what was?

The hidden apprenticeship

One of the most striking features to emerge from the interviews with individual writers was that more than half had a long-standing interest in writing, often going back to their time at school. Yet they struggled to see this as writing at all, just as they struggled to see themselves as writers:

> I don't think, as I said to start with, I am a writer in the sense that I want to produce something and dedicate my life to it. (Rachel)

Very few participants were able to articulate a sense of their development as writers which gave due weight to the process of becoming, as well as being, writers. Had they done so, the more private uses and purposes of writing which the majority reported would have been seen to belong on the writing continuum with more public forms of engagement, which they more readily saw as writing. Several reported a domesticated relation to writing in which letter-writing, diary-keeping and storytelling for children predominated. Writing as a resource for others also figured here. Together, they make a foundation of involvement with, and interest in, language and writing which is more heightened than everyday literacy, but is different again from the more conscious and committed commercial engagement with writing and publishing which for the majority defined a writer:

> I always knew I had the ability to write from going back to my school days but I really did nothing at all with it for the best part of thirty years, other than write short pieces for the company magazine and reports – I was always writing reports. (...) All the time I was in the forces I always made a point of writing home once a week (...) The early 60s and 70s there was a lot more letter writing went on. It came easy to me. (...) I turn out a good letter, and people even today will come and say: 'Look, I want to write a letter but I want it to sound right and I want it to be good' and so I'll draft a letter for them. (Greg)

In discussion, people clearly saw these periods of their lives as wasting or marking time when set beside the real business of writing. But I would argue the continued involvement kept writing alive for them in ways that enabled them to develop their creative and imaginative faculties at a later date. It formed an important part of their apprenticeship to writing. We see this clearly in the following extract:

> I've always done it. My earliest memory of actually writing was on my seventh birthday party and I wrote a story – I've got this old great aunt, heading on for 90, and she's always been very flamboyant and a real character, and I remember I wanted – she was coming up for the party and I wanted to produce something 'cos she's a very good storyteller. (...) And that's my earliest memory of writing. I've always done some bits of poetry through my teens and I wrote a female James Bond novel. (...) And then it stopped, although I've always used poetry as a kind of a form of a diary. I didn't ever stop but I was never structured in my approach to writing, and then jobs and boyfriends just kind of came along. But I always did a little bit. I'd always have an exercise book on the go. (...) My first job was in a plumber's office and the manager used to take the Northern Echo, and Sid Chaplin had a column in it and that's when I realised that you didn't have to be middle-class to write. (...) I think I would have carried on writing even if I hadn't, but I would have been going the long way round, writing poems about clouds and green grass and stuff which is not really what I'm interested in. (Tina)

For many the continuity was less explicit, though no less valuable, for being carried through letters and diaries. A legacy of romanticism sees writing as inspired and the influence of this idea was evident in the way people separated out imaginative writing from its more prosaic purposes and uses. Doing so made it harder for them to tap into the positive and productive relationship between writing that is perceived and experienced as ordinary and that which is extraordinary. Some embraced this romantic understanding of creativity explicitly, talking about being driven to write:

> I always knew that there was something way down inside, that I was compelled (...) to write the same as a runner feels compelled to run. (Greg)

Others talked about the way this romantic understanding had been tempered:

> I discovered that whether I was committed, whether it had welled up from inside of me or not, it was still me. That therefore I could see all of a sudden that you can be in conscious control of writing and it can have the validity which I have previously only seen it as having when it welled up from inside. (Al)

The experience of the majority of the people I spoke to demonstrated a pre-disposition to writing which a combination of circumstances, their own willpower and external agents released or developed. There were, however, some for whom involvement in writing would have been difficult to predict from their previous experiences. These experiences challenge a *laissez-faire* approach to cultural policy, demonstrating as they do the complexities of the position that maintains that people know what they do and do not want to do with their lives and leisure.

Kim was running a mother-and-toddler group when it was visited by writer-in- residence, Kathleen McCreery, who was trying to set up a writers' group in the area. The writer was rudely ignored so out of embarrassment Kim agreed to go to the meeting. When no one else turned up, Kathleen invited Kim to another group. Kim took along an autobiographical piece Kathleen had suggested she write:

> Kathleen read it out and made it sound really brilliant, and it wasn't. Looking back on it now, it wasn't. But I thought it sounded really lovely and I just thought: 'I'll keep doing this'. (...) I don't know whether it was 'cos, like, that was the first time that I've really felt I was good at something, 'cos I've never really done well at school and so to have somebody saying to me: 'That's really good, what you've had to say,' it was very important. (...) I always thought I was a bit stupid, you know. (Kim)

This combination of chance and positive encouragement kept Kim involved in something she would never voluntarily have found her way towards. Doug reported a classic, bravura boast, which he then followed through on. Unemployed, with time on his hands, he set out to prove that writing was easy: anybody could churn out the rubbish they put out on the television:

> I got drunk one night (...) sat down and wrote in a book. (...) It was just diving in at the deep end. So me next step was I wrote a novel (...) a person who doesn't know anything about writing, I wrote a novel which never, ever got published and then I wrote a couple of humorous articles which I sent off to the Transport and General Workers' Union paper, which were published straight away. I think if they hadn't have been published I would have just packed in. (...) It was a completely new departure. When I left school, I left school at 15, the only writing I ever did after that was writing letters home from prison and filling in sick notes or official forms, you know, so I never – up to the age of 40 I never even thought of writing. (Doug)

Amy reported being asked to write poetry as part of a New Opportunities for Women course she took after being made redundant from nursing. When another woman from the course told her about a writing class starting up in the area she went along 'to make the numbers up'. Her interest in writing poetry was triggered by the course requirement, but she was receptive to this because she already read modern poetry.

This illustrates how getting into writing can be a matter of chance as much as inclination, but it also underlines the extent to which all writers, whatever their predisposition to writing, are catalysed into the activity by events outside their control. Because there is no formal apprenticeship or recognisable career structure to sign up to, and because writing is always competing with other demands on the would-be writers' time, people rarely drift into writing. There were decisive catalysts that repeatedly came through the accounts. The commonest were motherhood, divorce, bereavement, ill-health, relocation, unemployment, redundancy and retirement, with the last the most frequently cited. Change, usually externally imposed, is common to them all. Writing comes into focus at a time when personal identity, direction and values are in crisis. It becomes a means of coping with life's difficult periods:

We acquired a word processor and shortly afterwards I was injured at work, in the winter months. I had three weeks off work and I was bored silly and the boredom drove me towards the word processor and it just came. It started there. (Greg)

The very early roots stemmed from a form of therapy, difficult teenage years, keeping a diary, university life, all the trials and tribulations of that. (...) It was a way of putting them on paper and confronting and dealing with them. (...) I had a terrible teenage life really. My mother had schizophrenia. It sounds fairly commonplace nowadays but in the early 70s it wasn't, it was dreadful. My father left home. We weren't taken into care because we kept it secret. (...) I don't know, looking back, how we came through it, but we somehow did and I can just remember all this anger pent up inside and it (writing) was just a way of getting that out and dealing with it. I didn't consciously think that's what I was doing, but that's what I did. With hindsight, that's what was happening. (Mona)

Rachel began going to writing classes out of curiosity, not really knowing what they were and with no defined writing project. She ended up writing about the painful and silenced history of her mother's Jewish background. She commented on the way writing groups establish a deeper level of contact and trust between their members than do other social or educational gatherings:

Straight away people would uncover parts of their lives and their attitudes to things. It would all come out in their writing (...) I thought it was absolutely wonderful, in a way it's like – sort of like going into psychotherapy without all the scary things of you are now going to be deemed sane or insane. (Rachel)

Through writing a letter to an aunt in Canada, whose parents had both been killed in concentration camps, Rachel was able to face what she had lived in fear of her whole life. Her parents, wanting to shield her from the war's horrors, had never discussed it with her. Yet, as children do, she had absorbed their terror.

She talked about how when studying sociology at university she had been unable to join in discussions about fascism or the holocaust and how unbearable it was when the tutor, knowing she was Jewish from her name, put her on the spot. Rachel worked on the letter for several years. Its circulation was no wider than the writing group she was attending when the project began and those members of her family she decided to give copies to (her aunt and a cousin). It is no less significant for this intentionally limited circulation, having helped her to confront the profound inner conflict and distress that she still finds difficult to talk about, as the hesitation and increasing grammatical incoherence of this extract reveals:

> I just sort of wanted to, like, say something about although this was only what I thought afterwards, but to say something to them about how I felt as after all, you know, I'm part of them and I'm part of their experiences. Even though I wasn't directly the recipient of all the Nazi terrors, I I absorbed it, like you do with your family and I wanted it to become something that I could say something about, because this is a new generation and we feel it and we interpret it in our own way, and it's valid. You know it's a strange thing, all that business about nationality and what what when people say 'Where – ?' It often comes up. They say: 'Where are you from?' and you automatically dry up, you think: 'Well, where are you from?' you know. (Rachel)

Staying involved

There is an important distinction to be made between getting into writing and staying involved. The writing itself, as Rachel illustrates, can be its own means of sustenance. Within the culture of writing more widely, encouragement was an important means of sustaining involvement, and all the more valuable because family and friends unconnected with writing activities rarely gave encouragement. People distinguished between the general encouragement they received in their group or course and individual encouragement from a writer-in-residence, course tutor, editor or publisher.

CREATIVE WRITING

The majority of those involved in writing rarely talked about it to other people, such as family, friends or workmates. Their reticence stemmed from feelings of vulnerability associated with the very personal nature of their writing and self-consciousness about other perceiving them as failures if they had not succeeded in publishing their work. Writing is different from other craft, leisure or educational activities in these respects and its lack of tolerance for amateur practitioners mirrors the professional arena:

> Writing is unfortunately rather less generous towards mediocrity than other professions. A mediocre solicitor can do useful work, enjoy a comfortable salary and the respect of the community, so may a mediocre hairdresser, radio producer or travel agent. The mediocre writer on the other hand – and few writers can entirely escape the suspicion that they are mediocre – risks both a more self-loathing and a more poverty-stricken fate. (Holgate and Wilson-Fletcher 1998: xiv)

The attitude towards writing from people around the writer can be significant in enabling or blocking their development. Winifred, who stopped writing for 35 years because her husband considered it a waste of time, and Barry, whose wife cited writing in their divorce proceedings, are extreme cases. However, all the writers had to negotiate a place for writing amongst other demands on their time and energy.

The majority of people felt they had received encouragement, but the nature of this encouragement was heavily gendered. Men rarely perceived themselves as receiving encouragement from those around them, choosing instead to focus on encouragement from those connected with creative writing activities – tutors, writers-in-residence, editors. Women, on the other hand, talked about being encouraged in ways that sounded more like accounts of permission. This suggests that while men assume the right to their own leisure, women with domestic responsibilities do not. Consequently they remain dependent upon goodwill from the men and children in their lives.

Encouragement helped people to continue work on specific projects and to continue to write at all. Men sought publication, and cited it as a source of encouragement, far more frequently than did women. It seemed to legitimise writing for them. When women sought publication, they were more likely to do so through local and regional outlets whereas men had ambitions for commercial success and a national audience. When women were published, it seemed to carry a different significance for them:

> I used to compose little poems when I was a kid and then I won this competition at school when I was nine, in 1939. It was a little poem about the war, and then I just went on from there. When my children were growing up I used to write poems about them (...) and I've had quite a success in getting published in different magazines. (...) But on the whole I didn't bother about publishing. I just wanted to write (...) I just liked to do it. (Chrissie)

> I'm entitled to call myself a writer simply because I've had stuff published. I think that gives me entitlement. (Greg)

Sometimes, staying involved with writing meant confronting direct ridicule and disapproval, as Kim had to do:

> This bloke who lived next door, sometimes I would chat with him and I said that I'd joined this, like, women's writers' group and he said: 'Oh, you'll be burning your bra and moving to Greenham Common next. I didn't think you were a feminist.' I didn't even know what the word meant then. (...) I'd been running this mother-and-toddler group, which was all women, and nobody felt that there was anything unusual about that, but the minute I joined women's writers' group everybody thought that was a bit strange. (Kim)

A divorced single parent living on a council estate, Kim had always been active in voluntary youth and community work. She reported that the most positive reaction she had to her writing from friends was 'complete disinterest'. As she got more involved in creative writing activities – taking over as facilitator of a writing group and later joining the Writearound Committee – she developed a network of support for her writing. But whereas men seemed to draw support from local activities in ways which benefited and advanced them as individuals – seeing their work published or performed, receiving prizes or awards – this was much rarer amongst the women, whose tendency to get involved in organising and providing the various activities often conflicted, as happened to Kim, with their own writing needs.

Writers were more often encouraged and sustained in their writing by people they met within the culture of writing but there were rare examples of support from within a family. An aunt took one writer to a Mills and Boon conference:

> She said: Well, Mills and Boon might not be the sort of thing that you want to write, but it will give you an idea of what you're dealing with.
> (Woman, Etherow)

Various people reported fathers, mothers, sisters and aunts who were neighbourhood or work place laureates and, occasionally, published authors. A neighbourhood or work-place laureate is my term for someone who marks shared events with poems, stories or sketches intended for public, as well as private, consumption. The number of people I met who had performed, or knew of someone who had performed, such a role intrigued me. The writing was often, but not always, comic.

Joining the courses and groups

The four most popular reasons given for attending a writing course were the discipline and motivation, to learn craft and techniques, to improve, and hearing other people's opinions on work. This last was sometimes explicitly linked to ambitions regarding publication. These are unremarkable purposes, with much in common with reasons for attending any adult education activity. What was surprising was how diffident people were – or claimed to be – about the actual process of finding and joining a writing course.

Several had joined at someone else's suggestion: perhaps a friend, who took an interest in their writing; or a tutor on a return to learning or GCSE English course. A handful had come by chance, either to support a friend or in the apocryphal circumstances of intending to join another class which was full. It was unusual for anyone to say they had looked for a course to join. Those who did were new to the area, and hoping to meet people, or had been in writing groups elsewhere in the country.

Chance played a considerable part in determining how people got to the courses and groups. Organisationally, it was clear that people paid more attention to word of mouth recommendations and features in the newspapers than they did to publicity leaflets. The publicity leaflet reinforced the decision to attend a writing group or acted as an *aide memoire* for its dates and times of meetings, but was rarely sufficient on its own to encourage first attendance. Building on local networks in this way has positive dimensions and enables adult education to link organically into the local community but is also likely to replicate the patterns of exclusion and dominance which structure that local community. In the Cleveland context, this partly explains the absence from creative writing activities of younger people, and those from ethnic minorities. Both the literature development workers specifically targeted these aspects and several projects were established but they had only a slight trickle down into the existing membership of courses and groups.

Money was often a significant factor in deciding whether or not to join certain classes. FE courses charged a substantial fee but AEC courses were free. Although some students expressed the view that anything free couldn't be very good (always making an exception for the actual class they were attending), quality was not a central issue for the majority of students. The absence of a fee enabled them to take a chance on the course and see what happened. Several people echoed this sentiment:

> I wouldn't have been so quick to come. If you have to pay, you have to commit yourself, you have to really want to do it. (Woman, Froggat)

The local nature of provision was also influential but there were occasions when a course was chosen precisely because it wasn't local. Men especially often sought out a group some distance from where they lived:

CREATIVE WRITING

I come here because no one knows me. It's a little bit off my patch.
(Man, Roaches)

Some more experienced writers attended two or three AEC courses simultaneously and were also likely to have experience of previous creative writing groups and courses. In some cases this appeared to be a displacement of their individual discipline as writers onto a constant search for external stimulus and motivation, but in others it was a search for the right mix of values and attitudes in the group. Several people reported being put off by an excessive emphasis on publication, others reacted to a group's style.

The importance of adult education in creating access to amateur arts activities (Hutchison and Feist 1991) was confirmed in the study. In Cleveland, of the eight free-standing groups who participated in my research, five were either continuations of adult education courses or had been started by people with previous experience of an adult education course. The ways in which new members found their way to the groups, and the expectations they brought with them, highlighted two issues that did not arise as explicitly in the courses. These were the shared purpose of the writing group and tensions around inclusivity. The majority of people who attend writing groups are already writing and join seeking solidarity with other writers, development in their writing style or their writing ambitions and the general stimulus of being with other writers. As with the courses there was often an incentive to join the group, which did not relate directly to writing but to major life changes, which foreground the personal sphere and raised issues of self and social identity, meaning and purpose.

Redundancy was one of these factors, and it is complex in the context of writing. Not only has it become increasingly difficult for unemployed people to follow non-vocational courses and remain eligible for benefit but also joining a course was often experienced as giving up and accepting long term unemployment. Many of the older men in particular linked decisions to come along to a writing activity with accepting that their opportunities

110

for paid work were over. Doug was one of the few unemployed men actively seeking work who attended the writing courses, moving in and out of them as work came and went. Today, the combination of pressure on completion rates and changed regulations about availability for work, would make this much harder to do.

As with the courses, very few people actively looked for a group to join. What tended to happen was that advertising triggered their interest or curiosity about writing in a period when they were available to pursue the interest. Whereas the decision to join a writing course could take place over a period of months or even years, as anxieties were confronted and overcome, joining a writing group happened more decisively. One of the commonest reasons given for joining a writing group was to overcome isolation. People talked about how writing was an isolating activity that others perceived as strange. Writing can seem strange to those around you, but it is also easier to talk about feeling isolated because of your writing than it is to talk about simply feeling lonely, left out of things, unsure who you are now that you are no longer working or no longer actively looking after a family. Perhaps social isolation manifests itself in feeling isolated as a writer?

Similarly, people often offered two reasons for joining a particular group. They answered direct questions with practical concerns. It met at a convenient time or there was no travelling involved. Once people started to talk about their expectations, though, it became clear that many of them had experience of a number of writing groups in the area. Although people had talked about selecting groups on the basis of chance or convenience, it emerged that previous experience of creative writing groups in the area also played its part. Tweed's founder reported her experience with another group:

> I expected a fairly informal idea of what was expected of us and what we got was two old men bickering, the rest of us never got a look in. (Woman, Tweed)

When asked what the bickering had been about, two other

members replied simultaneously: 'About who was in charge'. Clearly, several people had joined and left this group before making their way to Tweed.

Initial expectations: groups and courses

Members of the groups and courses were asked to remember their first meeting as a way of tapping into what those outside, but about to join, creative writing activities make of them. What sort of hopes and anxieties do they bring? What do they think they will encounter? In both the groups and courses this was usually the first time the group had actually sat down and talked to each other about their expectations and ambitions as writers.

Several people had no expectations in the sense that they didn't know what to expect, and genuinely didn't know what they were coming to. The then relative newness of creative writing as a subject for adult and community education and as an activity within community development meant people did not know what to expect. This was compounded by the way writing is both naturalised as an activity – something everyone does – and surrounded by mystique – something only some people have a gift for. So people are genuinely unsure what a writing group does or how they might be taught in a creative writing course in ways that do not apply to, say, learning how to drive a car or paint:

> I expected a magic formula. It was a shock being asked to write.
>
> (Woman, Bleaklow)

This surprise at being asked to write is commonly and widely reported amongst practitioners. In my study, it was humbling to hear the accounts of vulnerability prompted by my question about expectations. In every visit to the courses, at least half the people present reported significant fear and anxiety. In the groups, it was the first thing people talked about. Although affirming how non-threatening and positive the group is through an epic account of origins may form part of a bonding process, fear of the unknown and a sense of inferiority were also powerfully present. This reaction is similar to, but much more extreme than, that felt by any returning adult:

> All professional people, published writers. I didn't expect people like yourselves. (Man, Roaches)

> People who know more than you do and are quick to point it out. To point out what rubbish you were bringing. (Woman, Roaches)

> A group of intellectuals, that I'd stick it out for an hour and then run away. (Woman, Kinder)

This perception that the group would be made up of people who were unlike them, and that their cleverness would be a decisive differentiating factor, was encountered time and again. At the same time, people talked contemptuously about intellectuals and about being made to feel stupid. This points to an ambivalence. Writing is an intellectual activity and it does set those engaged in it apart from the mainstream of life. Were people projecting their own fears and anxieties onto the unknown group, or genuinely asserting a different relation to intellectual life?

Once the group had been joined, and the common ground between them established, these expectations could be viewed humorously, as exemplified by the woman who had expected 'tweedy, earnest types', prompting another member of Froggat to enquire 'hand knitted muesli?' to general laughter.

These preconceptions both stereotype writers and link them to unconventional lifestyles. I asked the group where these images came from. There was no hesitation, or disagreement: the media. Where else would they gain knowledge about writers? They were all too old to have benefited from the Writers-in-Schools scheme and they lived at great geographical and cultural distance from metropolitan literary culture. The only place they encounter the writer, as opposed to the writer's work, is on television and here, as they pointed out, 'you see them all sat round looking very earnest.' This is certainly how a 1998 BBC television series, Writing Masterclass, presented writers when it adopted an excruciatingly earnest format of novelist Nigel Williams reading an essay to an invited audience of members of writing groups.

Perhaps because there is such limited access to writers and cultural representations of writing as work, expectations about writing groups focused less on issues of writing and more on intelligence. The people I spoke to were rarely concerned that the groups and courses would contain better writers than them. Their greatest fear was that people would simply be cleverer than they were. It was as if even before they got to the act of writing itself, they had to overcome a lack of entitlement rooted in intellectual inferiority:

> I think a lot of people think about coming here. They think they wouldn't be able to handle it, think they'd show themselves up. (Woman, Froggat)

Almost everyone had needed courage to attend their first meeting but their vulnerability was gendered. Both men and women were fearful, but only women admitted to feeling stupid. Even in Mersey, which invited membership and attracted people with professional backgrounds, women talked about being 'overawed if you haven't got a literary background' or feeling 'very much the novice'.

On the courses, and perhaps unsurprisingly, the commonest expectation was of formal teaching. This was expressed in comments about the content and organisation of sessions:

> Like a classroom with a teacher to teach you good and bad, I thought there would be homework and he'd mark it. I thought we'd all do the same. (Man, Bleaklow)

> I thought we'd be sitting around with a leader doing all the talking, telling us how to write, giving advice and guidance. (Woman, Bleaklow)

> It's a bit of a disappointment to me. I hoped to learn more. An expert
> would tell me the techniques. I'd expected lectures, someone at a
> board. (Woman, Bleaklow)

Although the expectation of formal teaching was a common response across all the courses and from a significant number of people within them, it was more frequent in people attending classes based at the Adult Education Centre itself. This suggests that moving the community education programme out of the Centre and into community-based premises had reduced the expectation of formal tuition.

The persistence of romantic myths about writing as an inspired activity can be seen from the number of people who feared the group would be detrimental to their writing by imposing its own standards and values. This view was frequently expressed, and more often by men than women:

> I thought I'd be far too impressionable, that I'd alter my writing to suit
> what people said to me. (Man, Mersey)

Finally, it is important to stress that people's expectations were not always fearful and that even amongst those who came with trepidation and anxiety, there was also great anticipation and excitement. They came in spite of the pretentious or arty people that they felt sure were going to be filling up the room. They came prepared to make a go of it. Many people reported expectations of encouragement, which they received:

> I'd been writing for many years. It was hidden, piles of paper in plastic
> bags all round my house. I came for a month and never said a word.
> It helped me release a lot of frustration and it's given me confidence.
> (Woman, Annan)

What is common to all the expectations is the idea of difference. People did not expect to find people like themselves. This must relate to the alienation that they have personally experienced, where to write is to be strange. It is as if they make sense of this by deciding that they – as an ordinary, normal sort of person who just happens to be interested in writing – are the exception.

They too buy into the notion that all writers are odd, so they go along expecting it from the writing group or course. We have travelled with our writers to that first meeting of the course or group. We have seen the anxieties they carried, and their courage. Now we look in more detail at what goes on in the courses and groups.

Chapter six

Inside the groups and courses

You come along and imagine someone will say the magic words: you
will write my dear. But it isn't like that, it's hard work. (Woman, Froggat)

Introduction

This chapter aims both to describe and analyse the social and
pedagogic processes at work in creative writing groups and
courses within adult education. I argue that the egalitarian impulse
behind tacit and non-directive approaches to teaching and learning
creative writing inadvertently creates a fixed template for
organising and participating in creative writing activities; and that
this can undermine creative writing's radical potential.

A sense of belonging

There was a strong sense of local identity in each group or course
I visited. This identity was often established through comparison
with others in the area. There were only ever a minority of
members with experience of other groups or courses to draw on
for these comparisons yet the whole group shared in the sense of
difference, also usually superiority, they sustained. The key factors
differentiating groups from each other was the perceived degree
of objectivity and honesty with which work was commented on,
how seriously they took their writing and how pretentious
members of other groups were alleged to be. The way local

identity was often expressed as rivalry with other writers' groups was in marked contrast with the drive to develop networks and collaborations, which often characterises policy initiatives focusing on community writing. Courses, perhaps because they felt a degree of loyalty to their tutor, were often much more confident about their way of doing things being the best, or only, way to behave whereas some of the free-standing groups did express uncertainty. The most dismissive description of other groups or courses was to refer to them as mutual admiration societies.

Four themes emerged as the key activities of the groups, although their ascendancy varied both from group to group and from meeting to meeting. These were socialising, validating writing as an activity, giving feedback on work-in-progress and encouraging publishing. These were also key activities in the courses but they structured the groups and courses in two importantly different ways. First, the courses because they were tutored, relied to a great extent on the tutor's knowledge, experience and authority to manage, introduce and develop these themes with participants. Groups, on the other hand, although often organised by an informal hierarchy of experience and knowledge, as could be seen in Mersey and Tweed, set out to offer support and stimulus on the basis of mutual aid. Second, groups can be distinguished from courses by the seriousness with which members pursued writing activities and the degree of independence they brought both to the running of their group and to their own writing. People rarely came to writing groups without some prior experience of creative writing experience, however minimal, whereas people often attended the courses with no significant or recent experience of writing.

Directive and non-directive approaches in the groups and courses

Initially I made a distinction between free-standing groups and tutored courses. I anticipated differences of experience and ambition as well as differences in the type of activities. But in Cleveland's local culture of writing was not as sharply differentiated in this way as I had expected. People not only moved both ways between courses and groups but many attended both simultaneously. People talked about courses as if they were groups and there was a tendency to play down the educational dimension of their activities. This was as true of tutors as it was of students. Asked about their role in relation to students, Cleveland tutors often began by correcting my use of these terms:

> I'm not the teacher and I don't think of them as my students. (Tutor, Crowden and Stanage)

For some, this signalled a challenge to the power relations of the compulsory education system:

> I would never use the possessive. I'm resistant to 'my' because I'd never refer to a class as my students, because I'd think I was expected to influence them in a certain way instead of develop what was in them. When I hear it in tutors' meetings the expression jars. To me, education is the leading out of what's there. 'My' underlines inequality. (Nell)

Here Nell, like several other Cleveland tutors, is defining her practice against an over-simplified theory of education. The complex struggles within and over education, especially adult and community education, were not available to them as incentives and guides. In this, Cleveland tutors were not unusual amongst creative writing tutors, for whom the all-pervasive intuitive model of creativity has tended to construct education in terms of regulation and control that preclude developing active and transformative pedagogies.

During each visit to a course or group I asked them to describe a typical session for me. Their responses were strikingly similar. Bleaklow, Crowden, Cuillin and Stanage said they had no typical group session and described a pattern of work which utilised whole and small group work, a range of activities based on reading and responding to work and writing in class. However, during my visits they were all, with the exception of Cuillin, following the standard format. The standard format is as follows. People in turn read their work. The tutor or chair of the group comments first and then other people add their questions and comments. The only variation is whether a time or word allocation operates. It is assumed that everyone will read something each week, and that this will be new work, usually a response to a group task. Work was rarely revised and brought back to the group. Poems were often read two or three times, prose rarely read more than once. Occasionally people brought extracts from on-going work, usually a life story or less commonly a novel.

Reading work round the room in turn can become a lazy imitation of the strenuously challenging and creative activity it needs to be. Workshops are a deceptively simple method. Behind the straightforward activity of reading and responding to work, lies a complex process of imagining, discussing and negotiating change. Probing further, it emerged there had been no discussion within the groups or courses about why or how work should be discussed. Where the rationale for workshops remains tacit its potential for learning and teaching is curtailed.

An easy explanation for this state of affairs, which accounts for a lot of the negative publicity surrounding creative writing in education, is to blame it on lack of talent and focus from the individuals involved. But this will not do. The problem was pervasive, suggesting a structural explanation; and this was confirmed by talking to tutors about how they saw their role in the creative writing classroom. Students brought a long and sometimes mutually exclusive list of needs to courses, from learning craft skills to finding their voice, from motivation and discipline to advice on publication. In relation to these complex and competing needs the tutor's role is inevitably complex.

Tutors rarely talked about their role being to instruct or pass on craft and technical knowledge. Instead, they talked about a plurality of roles that included helping their students find ways into writing, manage the group dynamics and validate the students' urge to write:

My methods of tuition aren't methods at all, just my own uncertainties. I can only talk on what I've found, what moves me, how I've tried to use something in my own writing – although I never or rarely use my own writing in teaching. It's the individuality of the students' work I react best to. I have always thought of myself as a catalyst. (Tutor, Cuilllin)

Creative writing is conceptualised as exploratory, a process of discovery in which the creative writing tutor becomes a map holder, map reader, even sometimes map maker. The process of discovery is rooted in memory and consciousness rather more than craft and language. Tutors viewed this process as empowering but this was not always apparent to or appreciated by students:

It's not teaching as in teaching, it's to create a climate for people to develop in. Triggers to start people off. (...) The first thing is to get people writing. (Melanie)

To fire them with the enthusiasm and sense of worth I have had through creative writing. I want to convey that their experiences count, are of value. I want to open up people's options. (Tutor 2, Kinder)

The tutor didn't instruct you in anything. You want more guidelines, not how you should write but what publishers expect. The tutor seems to rely on your knowledge and just chairs. (Woman, Annan)

Some tutors did see their role as wider than encouraging writing and offered a full range of tutorial and group activities within the session, including one-to-one tutorials, and taking work home to read and comment on:

We hear a lot of their work, which takes the first hour. At the moment we are concentrating on three weeks of poetry. We'll be picking out things from their writing to discuss and illustrate points. By talking and doing they find out for themselves, as I did, that poetry isn't necessarily what they thought it was at school. We have a degree of structure in each lesson. I think it's important to have structure. (Tutor 2, Kinder)

CREATIVE WRITING

> We've tended to fall into a pattern reading in the first half because I feel that's what people come for. Some want quite detailed comment and some don't. I think we're gently feeling our way with that. We've done various things, we've discussed aspects like awareness of ideas, where ideas for writing come from. We've used different triggers and stimulus. Some weeks we write in the session, but we try not to keep it too long. We'll maybe start something in a session and then finish it at home. (Tutor 1, Kinder)

Tutors varied in terms of how directive they were in organising activities for and with their courses. Several reported falling into a pattern that did not necessarily arise from their aims and objectives for the course but from what they perceived as the students' expectations. It was unusual, as these tutors had done, to intervene directly into the work of the group even when, as several tutors reported, they experienced difficulty in getting the group to discuss each other's work. High Tor's tutor had also experienced this difficulty but had devised a method for dealing with it:

> They just want to get their heads down and get it read. But by trying to get them to talk about it first, that sets the context for everyone else to be able to participate in a criticism. You're not saying: 'It's not very good or anything', because you're judging it by the standard that they've just set for themselves by describing how they tackled it and how they feel about it. The first few times when I asked them to talk about their piece they'd say a few words then I'd sort of ask them a question to try and draw them out a bit more. Like, 'What do you think you've achieved?' If it was about dialogue I might ask, 'Do you think her character is as rounded as you want it to be?' or 'Have you considered the fact that you're neglecting a large part of what you could do with the story just by placing a seed earlier on for the reader to recognise?' After that's happened a few times people start to anticipate the question I might have asked, so they kind of answer it before I've asked it. It was difficult for a lot of the students and it works better if I split them into groups of three to criticise, which I've done a few times, and then I move around the groups so

they all feel that they've got some of my time and my attention.
(Tutor, High Tor)

Such interventionist strategies were unusual, both in the decision to re-organise the group into smaller working units and in taking control of its direction and purpose.

A reluctance to intervene was common amongst the tutors but it did not stem from their inability to do so. If tutors were asked to provide specific information or cover a particular topic they showed great ingenuity in doing so, as the following extract indicates. This account by Llanberis's tutor of how he responded to a request for information about children's writing illustrates the kind of quick, reactive thinking creative writing tutors must be able to do because of the very diverse ability, interests and ambitions of the people in their group:

I had a week to think of something. I thought, well, there's a lot of things in children's writing that will be the same for writing any short story, some things that are different. So I got a book out and I made some notes, and I thought about it. Then I thought some of the students have children or grandchildren, they've read stories, there's one or two who may have different opinions. There's a couple of feminists who may take issue with the type of stories that were being written. So I used the class as a resource.

I put the questions to them: what's the difference – I can't remember the question, something like what's the difference – between writing for children and writing for adults? It set up a discussion, we brainstormed and I had a checklist that I'd got from one or two books that I'd read and it worked quite well. Nobody had everything they needed on children's writing, but they were set thinking about the difference. (Tutor, Llanberis)

As a method, it has much to recommend it. It validates what students already know and encourages active, process- and knowledge-based learning which makes the students the focus of the learning. However, it can only provide the most rudimentary introduction and offers no real opportunities for the student to apply the knowledge and develop skills through repeated and detailed practice. This model of the tutor's role appears even-handed, covering inspirational and creative dimensions and technical, craft approaches, but it leans towards the inspirational by failing to provide structured and progressive opportunities for students to gain conscious, practised control of their craft. Their working practices echo and reinforce Geoffrey Adkins's finding from his interviews with creative writing tutors in 1981 where several believed 'if the approaches, circumstances and states of mind were favourable some of the technical problems faced by beginners would not even arise' (Adkins 1981: 135).

Such a position would seem ludicrous if applied to any other art form or area of knowledge. Yet where creative writing is concerned it is a widely held belief informing a great deal of practice. It is rooted in a pedagogy that understands the writing process as a welding together of late Romantic ideas about art as intuition and late-twentieth-century elisions of cultural democracy into cultural relativism. It is able to present itself convincingly, in a way that no other art form could, because its medium is language. Whereas all the other art forms demonstrate specialised uses of a specialised, and often external, medium such as paint, materials or music, writing uses the common currency of all human interaction and self-actualisation: language, memory and imagination (Ong 1982, Kress 1997, Sedgwick 1997).

But this natural art, and its expression as the several discourses of writing, is highly organised and regulated not only through aesthetic values but also through market forces, and this produces a matrix for organised creative writing activities which renders them simultaneously and contradictorily determined by self-expression and market forces. Tutors, as we saw, were at pains to avoid imposing their judgement, values and style upon their students, preferring to construct their role as facilitating existing and self-determined writing ambitions and ability. Students not only colluded with this, they often demanded it, fearful as they were of any checks to their self-expression, yet were often in much greater thrall to the rules and regulation of the market.

There were times when it felt as if tutors were doing everything in their power to dis-invest themselves of any vestige of tutoring, while students were equally reluctant to take on a student role. At the same time, outside the courses in the free-standing groups, writers expressed a desire for the guidance of tutors. Meeting these contrary views about authority and direction so frequently led me to think that something quite complex was going on. Course and group members seemed caught up in something more than the desire for what the other had.

Looked at from the perspective of cultural democracy, which privileges an organic engagement with local culture, we can see that courses mimic the form of groups as a way of validating (and creating maximum opportunities for) autonomous, self-determined and purposeful activity. However, the cultural-democratic impulse became associated with, and to some extent guaranteed by, education, it implies the need for a relationship based on the teacher and the taught. Within the groups, with the exception of Mersey and Swale, there was considerable debate about the need for guidance from people more experienced and knowledgeable than the members. In the courses, the lack of clarity about roles and boundaries produced a situation where the students and their writing were confirmed in limiting attitudes and, by not being sufficiently, continued to under-achieve.

Uncritical practices

At times, the fieldwork seemed to reveal a reductive reversal of mid-1970s cultural policy statements. Instead of policy predicated on a notion that real writers would always emerge, here it seemed that the energy was directed towards writers who seemed unable or unwilling to take responsibility for their own writing. Clearly, the processes of exclusion and subordination at work were complex and, as we shall see, what the situation revealed was the need to enable rather than assert widened participation in cultural practices.

Jim McGuigan (McGuigan 1992: 5) identifies an uncritical

populist drift in the study of popular culture within cultural studies. His project to develop a critical populism is both theoretical and applied. It engages with the work of Bourdieu (Bourdieu and Passeron 1977, Bourdieu 1990), Laclau (1977), Hall (Hall 1981, 1988, Hall and Jacques 1983), Williams (1958, 1980, 1983a, 1983b, 1989) and Hoggart (1957) to develop a grounded theory of the contradictions of everyday life, especially the gap between political ideals and social life. He brings theoretical insights to bear in new ways upon the familiar themes and positions of popular culture through case studies in youth culture and television. McGuigan concludes his study with an argument, which seeks to retain the spirit of cultural populism while strengthening its realisable political purchase through greater attention to questions of political economy, a project he continues to pursue in greater depth and complexity (McGuigan 1996, 2004).

Throughout the 1980s and early-1990s the discourse of cultural policy was not only subject to new forms of market regulation, as McGuigan has argued (McGuigan 1996), but also heavily influenced by educational values and purposes. It is the detail of the latter which concerns me next. Both processes bring in their train a set of contradictions, which make more complex the tension between alternative and oppositional cultural practices, identified by cultural critic Raymond Williams (1980: 42). Although Williams sees education as central to the processes of domination – 'The educational institutions are usually the main agencies of the transmission of an effective dominant culture' (Williams 1980: 39) – his own practice as an educator and much of his writing, reserves a critical space for certain forms of adult education. This enables us to see that the writing culture of Cleveland is clearly an alternative practice, in that it cuts across dominant understandings about writers and writing, but whether it is oppositional, is another matter. The detailed analysis of Cleveland's creative writing activities and their pedagogic practices, to which we now turn, shows a degree of conservatism, which undermined its oppositional stand.

The pedagogic practices of creative writing

The problematic nature of creative writing's pedagogic practices is illustrated by the tensions surrounding the tutor setting the group writing exercises, sometimes in class time, usually as homework. In two-thirds of the courses I visited writing themes were set weekly and then formed the entire basis of the following week's session. During my visits it became clear that this process was at the heart of the learning experience for the students. Homework took different forms. It might be one theme for everyone to write on or a choice of three or four topics or titles. Occasionally there would be an activity or discussion based around a particular aspect of craft, technique or form. Students might be asked to write in a particular style or form or given an exercise to sharpen up observation skills or use of dialogue. These were not always popular. People seemed happiest to be set simple themes and titles. This reminded me strongly of school composition but no students ever made this link. Anybody who didn't like this method of working was either not in the class or keeping quiet.

When I asked people what they valued in the class these triggers, as they tended to be called in the Cleveland writing culture, were cited more frequently than any other aspect of the course:

> Woman 1: (The tutor) gives themes, opening lines etc. We don't have to stick with it but it does give an incentive.

> Man 1: It stretches your mind more if you have guidelines. You can get stories on your own but it stretches your mind. (Woman and Man, Crowden)

Tutors stressed that themes were optional but students rarely opted out of them and there was a consensus in all the courses that 'the suggestions are the best part, they inspire you, get your mind going' (Man 2, Crowden). There was no evidence that themes were chosen to link with particular interests or needs articulated by the group. On those rare occasions when people had done their own thing, they were apologised for not doing the homework or

127

tried to make their own work fit the homework. It was as if they understood the main purpose of the course to be fulfilling the homework requirement. How to wean students from this reliance on the tutor to generate writing ideas was a perennial topic for discussion at the termly meetings organised for AEC tutors. Tutors saw their exercises as suggestions, designed to complement the students' movement towards their own writing projects, and though acutely aware that the loop was not closed until students developed independent projects they struggled to find ways to help them do so.

The courses attracted students along a broad spectrum of prior experience, levels of ambition and ability. For some students, to complete any of the exercises correctly and adequately was a considerable achievement and clearly satisfied their criteria for making progress. But for the majority of those attending, a pattern of dependency was emerging which was unconsciously encouraged by the tutor's organisation of the sessions. Students often commented that they needed the discipline and motivation of coming to the course in order to write and they put a high value on the incentive it provided. But there were students who appeared to have passed to the tutor the whole responsibility for their writing. On several occasions I observed tutors trying to encourage students to devise their own writing topics only to be met with comments such as 'I don't know what to write unless you tell me' (Woman, Bleaklow).

The guidelines were interpreted more rigidly than the tutors intended and this led to an overlap between stimulus and motivation. Only in Cuillin and Bleaklow was the question of students' independent work raised. In Cuillin there was an almost total reliance on self-originated work and in Bleaklow, which organised its work into sub-groups, this relative independence from their tutor seemed to encourage greater independence. However, as the example above shows, this was no guarantee of independence even in Bleaklow.

This highlights a set of concerns around dependence and independence. In the interviews I carried out with individual writers it became clear that many of the people attending the writing courses did have independent writing projects. People's reason for coming to courses in the first place was often that they were already writing so it would be reasonable to assume they worked on these projects during the course. However, it seemed to be difficult to make the links between an individual writing project and the work of a writing course explicit.

The advantage I had, of talking to all the students about their aims and ambitions, made it impossible to ignore the number of students who had come to the courses with improvement at the forefront of their minds. They came wanting to do better, wanting to learn, wanting to be stretched and challenged but were then drawn into an ethos which put their own projects on hold and subtly changed their expectations and practices. This was not the change people had feared, of writing to a house style, being constrained by political correctness or other restraints upon their subject matter. Rather, they adjusted to subtle peer pressure by writing to the time allowed for reading out, always sticking with the suggested themes and interpreting them in keeping with the ways that characterised the group's ethos. It was unusual for people to be aware of this process or to articulate it as clearly as this woman's account does:

> The group was pulling me in a direction I was beginning to find hard. I wasn't going with my thoughts, I was thinking: no, that's what they want me to say. It was flattering but I felt happier going back to more spontaneous writing. To me, I found writing set pieces (homework tasks) I'd written them in a way that I thought you would like to hear. I was thinking of the group and writing for you: not for me. (Woman, Etherow)

She captures the fine balance between the group developing its members as members of the group and as individuals. This tension between collective and individual imperatives is important in the debate about whether or not such initiatives are best understood as alternative or oppositional practices. It is difficult to see individual advancement as anything other than incorporation into the individualism of the dominant literary establishment. But orientation towards the group does not on its own guarantee an oppositional stance. Groups can and often do harness their energies.

Students may end up in a setting appropriate to their needs, but there is an element of chance about this as most creative writing activities are self-selecting with few guidelines to help newcomers identify and make their choices. For some, too, the concept of choice itself is dubious as practical considerations may considerably narrow their options. In an educational context, however informal, it might surely be argued that there is some obligation on tutors and organisers to ensure that the needs and aspirations students arrive with are acknowledged, negotiated and, wherever possible, met. The tutor is responsible for creating the conditions under which the group, and the individuals within it, can develop independence and responsibility for their own and each other's ambitions. Too often, community-based adult education and arts education has generated a default autonomy, in which the tutor withdraws from the tutoring role.

The passage from subordination to autonomy requires active, not passive, engagement with group dynamics and the active transference of skills and knowledge. This involves some attention to the content of creative writing (its methods, techniques, forms and genres) and to how participants understand the role and purpose of the group, including how to give, receive and act upon feedback. These issues were covered by some tutors most of the time. But at an organisational level, and within the field as a whole, there was considerable lack of clarity as to how the various creative writing activities should be organised and structured. This applied on a session-by-session basis, over the span of a course and in the organisation of several courses into a programme of study.

In chapter three we saw how differences in the way the teaching and learning of creative writing is conceptualised, particularly the debate about it being 'taught or caught', continues to influence the development and delivery of the creative writing curriculum. In the language of contemporary educational discourse, there are no standard textbooks, key stages, common curriculum or subject benchmarks for teaching creative writing. This was certainly the case when I carried out the fieldwork for this study although it is slowly starting to change. Some recent publications from the taught undergraduate sector are tending this way, outlining a core curriculum and using phrases such as coursebook or work book in their titles (Bell and Magrs 2000; Newman et al 2004). There have been attempts, within adult basic, further and higher education, to specify curriculum, often linked to developing competence and assessment frameworks whether these are for National Vocational Qualifications or the Quality Assurance Agency. These are far from fixed, and unlike other subject-disciplines do not look back to shared understandings embedded into and naturalised by long histories in the institutions. This creates fluidity and flexibility in creative writing pedagogy and curriculum that distinguishes formal and informal settings, and between undergraduate and postgraduate teaching and learning. The specific context of adult and community education adds a further openness by preferring, where possible, a student-centred, negotiated approach to teaching and learning.

This fluidity is however informally organised and regulated. It is possible to discern both local approaches and to identify certain sectoral features and characteristics. Within the different sectors, certain features are emphasised or played down, although the actual elements in play are often the same. They include building a group identity, validating the impulse to write, providing stimuli, teaching techniques and craft skills, establishing theme, form and subject matter, providing a response, audience and feedback and making public, through publication or performance, the work produced. Where the emphasis falls as this is delivered is influenced not only by which educational sector is involved but also by its underlying rationale or ruling passion in respect of encouraging expression or communication, excellence or wider participation or, indeed, refusing the implied hierarchy of these polarities.

Creative writing activities often have an ambiguous relation to structure, which is reminiscent of the forms of organisation associated with the early women's liberation movement. Like the early consciousness-raising groups, the groups are often de-centred, with no identifiable or obvious leader, and all members are encouraged to contribute and view each other's contributions as equally valuable. In the feminist movement, these practices were widely adhered to and widely critiqued. One of the earliest, and still most cogent argued that apparently open structures were less democratic and accessible than they seemed, as they made it easier for people to dominate and harder for others to challenge that domination (Freeman 1980). When observing and discussing these courses with students and their tutors I was often reminded of this pamphlet.

The situations I observed were often contradictory and chaotic, for students and tutors. The contradiction took a number of forms. First, there were apparently informal, loosely structured sessions in which the authority of the tutor, operating at a deeper structural level, was entirely unchallenged. Second, tutors established structures intended to maximise students' freedom and independence, which students resented because they wanted formal direction. Third, students were not homogeneous. On several occasions there was disagreement amongst the students themselves about the degree of comment, discussion and formal input they wanted from the tutor.

In these discussions creativity was often falsely polarised against structure. Some structures channel and stimulate creativity and others stifle it. A series of lectures on technique and form could be an uncreative and unrewarding experience – but it need not be. And just because a tutor does not stand up and lecture is no guarantee that the activity and achievement of the class will be creative.

A strongly held belief that emerged through these discussions about structure was that instruction led to uniformity. At one point, a student expressed disappointment that he hadn't learnt as much about technique as he would have liked to. Another student responded, 'Maybe that's artificial, the thing is to write' and a third student inquired, 'Wouldn't we all write in the same style?' (Men and Women, Bleaklow). As this discussion developed, drawing in other course members, it became clear that most believed the element of instruction (information about technique, form and so on) was adequately dealt with during group discussion of individual pieces of work. Although it was often the tutor who took the lead in these discussions, other group members also provided feedback and some tutors deliberately withdrew from discussion to encourage the group to take a more active part in feedback.

In some of the courses I observed this method was used effectively and skilfully. But I was also party, through direct observation or reported discussion, to some of its problems. The first of these is that many students do not trust the judgement of their peers and this working method was often described to me, as it was in Tweed, as 'the blind leading the blind' (Woman, Tweed). Sometimes, this indicates a misplaced dependency on the tutor and a formal, authoritarian style of teaching. But sometimes, of course, it is a rational response, which recognises that students do not have the skills and experience needed to evaluate work and communicate their judgement constructively.

There seemed to be something random and opportunistic at work in what tutors responded to and taught. This is partly a consequence of the student – centred imperative of adult and community education but it also suggested that any systematic approach to creative writing was anathema to students and tutors. The emphasis on stimulus and themes suggests that for many people the core activity of the creative writing course is defined by being given things to write about. The majority of writing exercises that people reported and I observed were exercises designed to generate writing rather than to teach or refine technique and craft skills. There were also exercises that were primarily about bringing social cohesion to the group. So, for example, group stories and poems were written, word association games played and several round-the-room discussions gave opportunities to share experience and views about topics ranging from names and naming to first days at school.

The kind of exercises tutors used with their groups to generate writing included: group poems, objects to stimulate writing, automatic writing or timed writing exercises, lists of titles and topics, writing from the point of view of an inanimate object, writing one poem in rhyme and one without rhyme and discussing the difference, using pictures to stimulate writing, writing about a random selection of celebrities' names or objects pulled out of a hat, the start or ending of a story to continue, exercises to generate dialogue, word association exercises and making a word hoard.

Some tutors set aside regular times to introduce various topics to the group, either in response to requests from students or, in a minority of cases, because they were following a course outline they had devised prior to, or shortly after, the first meeting of the course. Tutor-led discussions went on in just over a third of the groups, where they took up anything between half of one or two meetings to half of five or six meetings in any ten-week course.

Topics for discussion included dialogue, the forms of poetry and short stories, bringing in articles about writing to read and discuss, listing the do's and don'ts of writing, descriptive writing, English usage, introductions to metre, rhyme and rhythm and the conventions of manuscript presentation. Many of the topics were poetry-based, reflecting the extent to which poetry, although often of minority appeal, is better suited to teaching than prose. There are also more accessible poetry text books, which adopt a more formal or practical criticism approach, than their prose equivalents. This made it easier for tutors to develop sessions on forms of poetry and poetic language, and the poem itself is a more manageable unit for short, focused presentations. Poems could easily be copied and shared, just as their analysis could be demonstrated briefly to the whole group, whereas equivalent work with narrative demands greater preparation and prior knowledge from both the tutor and students. Additionally, the demystification of writing is given a boost when a form such as poetry, which is often perceived as elite and difficult, is shown to be accessible and enjoyable.

The question of technique and craft skills provides an interesting route into debates about teaching and learning creative writing. Those who argue that writing cannot be taught, because they believe it is fundamentally inspirational, will sometimes concede that it is possible to teach techniques. Many students come along to writing courses expecting to receive instruction in precisely these kinds of craft skills or writing techniques. A minority expressed cynicism about the emphasis on technique and especially if they had experienced the commercialised creative writing sector, which often emphasises technique at the expense of content and without reference to the complex and contradictory lived experience of artistic practice. Even when students had not experienced the latter they sensed that technique, whilst essential to writers, could also be limiting:

> Woman 1: Some of us have done a lot about techniques elsewhere. You can have techniques until it comes out of your ears. I linked up with (the tutor) when he started talking about looking for the soul of a poem or a piece of writing.

> Woman 2: I agree with her, you can get a bit bogged down with techniques. It's as (the tutor) says – it's something inside you that you want to get out. If you could do it all on techniques you could get a computer to do it. (Women, Cuillin)

Technique, as these students argue, must be allied to content. Writers need something to write about, or for. But there is a balance to be struck between the inspirational, imaginative and expressive side of writing and writing as a communicative act, which relies on craft skills and techniques for its realisation. Craft skills were taught, but not systematically or in any great depth as the following exchange (which is not untypical of the response received to the question: 'What do you mean when you say you've done a topic?') demonstrates:

> W1: We did the different types of poetry so we know what they mean, now we're going on to plays, we did metaphors, those kinds of things. We've learnt what all the terms are.

> M1: It would be better to call them tools rather than topics.

> M2: We get the tools and we have a go. (Woman and Men, High Tor)

There seemed to be some conflict, both between student and tutor and amongst students, about the kind and depth of instruction it was reasonable to expect within the creative writing courses. Students wanted four things from their course. These were to have their creativity and imaginations stimulated, to be introduced to specific writing techniques (point of view, characterisation, dialogue, imagery, metre, metaphor and so forth), to have various forms and genres introduced and explained to them and to have their use of English corrected. However, for the most part, they wanted this to be wholly generated by and demonstrated in their own writing. Reading and discussing other writing was often seen as a distraction from their writing.

Although these four elements are involved, however tacitly, whenever and wherever creative writing activities take place, the emphasis within the mix is determined by the specific context (a basic education class, a festival workshop given by a visiting professional writer or a weekly class). Within each setting, different individuals bring varying expectations, knowledge and ambitions so that the needs of some members of the group may be opposed to those of others. Under these circumstances, opting to stimulate or generate writing is not only a safe option from the tutor's point of view, but the only option they can be reasonably confident of achieving and being able to demonstrate they have achieved.

In this way, we can see how the absence of an institutionally regulated and codified creative writing curriculum not only makes it necessary to clarify starting points and expectations for tutor and students each time an activity is set up, but also affects how seriously the activity can be engaged with. Tutors are obliged to ascertain what expectations are in play at any one time and whether these are reasonable. For example, it may be reasonable for a student to ask how to lay out and present a manuscript, but not to use the creative writing workshop to improve general language skills such as spelling and grammar.

Within community education contexts, such as that of the AEC programme, such distinctions are harder to make and maintain. Past experiences of education, combined with the amount of time people have been out of either work or education means many came to the classes with feelings of insecurity and anxiety which often focused on their use of English. It wasn't uncommon for students to talk about not having enough words or not having enough grammar. Basic education has often adopted a model of creative writing as the medium of instruction for general writing development and within community arts and community education this writing continuum is seen as a strength.

However, for the people participating in creative writing activities within these sectors, the blurring poses difficulties if it leads to confusion about what to expect from the tutor, and what the tutor is expecting of them. It can also be an issue for tutors, who need to know what it is and is not possible to teach at any one time and to any given group of students. Lack of confidence or experience can lead tutors to organise their work around expectations such as stimulating writing and providing motivation which are uncontroversial and relatively easy to meet. The question of discipline and motivation in writing courses is a delicate one. Clearly the forces which block and hamper writing are active for many people when they first arrive at writing courses and courses can be an excellent way to overcome them. But group influences can cease to be supportive to the individual, can indeed hamper their writing development, if the group or its tutor became a substitute for their own motivation to write. Evidence of this happening comes from students who rely on their tutors for writing suggestions or writers whose entire sense of audience resided with their fellow students, producing pieces to fit exactly the word or time limit allocated for reading out.

On one occasion, interestingly when the tutor was not present, students attending Roaches talked about how their writing had been adversely affected by the group. They talked about writing for the short-term gain of the group's approval and how trite, sometimes formulaic, pieces were most likely to gain this. They identified a group style that was relatively easy to replicate and hard to break away from which they knew would get weekly praise and encouragement. Important as receiving this boost to their ego was, they also recognised that its long-term effect on their development as writers was damaging. Instead of supporting individual members, the group had commandeered the individuals to perpetuate itself.

Problematising progress

Tutors put considerable effort and imagination into generating writing. Proof of this lies in the numbers of students attracted to, and staying with, the classes and the undeniable confidence and pleasure in writing they gained there. However, once the initial learning curve had been achieved, in which students developed a sense of their entitlement to write and established, albeit in a dependent rather than independent mode, a regular habit of writing enabling them to produce their own versions of 'good enough' writing, stasis set in.

In most cases, students' work improves during their attendance at writing courses, but the progress is seen most easily across rather than within discrete pieces of work. There is a powerful argument that the role of creative writing courses and groups, especially when appealing to new writers and those traditionally excluded from participation in education and the arts, should be to establish the habit of writing in as secure and confident a way as possible. And to do so, writing must be happening in a steady, reliable flow before any attempt can be made to shape or correct it. This summary of the writing process applies to each individual piece of writing just as much as it does to the writing life as a whole. But, throughout the research visits and interviews I conducted, it was unclear when or how people would be encouraged to make the transitions necessary to develop either an independent habit of writing or the internal critical faculty that can not only generate, but also work and shape, writing towards its best possible form.

One of the reasons this transition may have been so difficult was the absence within formal group sessions of any discussion of the writing process itself. Discussions of the way people articulated their writing ambitions, perceived writing locally, regionally or nationally or compared their views with the tutor or group were rare. There was little evidence that any writing other than that produced by group members entered the life of the group in any significant way. The writers I met during these visits appeared to be reluctant readers.

This issue preoccupied some tutors more than others. Several tutors saw their role as encouraging new writers and were happy to stay with the challenges and opportunities of this boundary:

> I think it's intrinsically encouraging to know there are other people in the world writing. To be in the physical presence of people who, whatever their quality, do write and are creative. (Nell)

Others, though, expressed concern about the expectations they raised in their students and the difficulty they experienced in making explicit their own priorities and preferences within the courses and groups. Although tutors working outside as well as within Cleveland shared the concern, their response differed. Cleveland tutors tended to treat all demands from their students as equally valid. This seems to link with their different understanding of the overall purposes of creative writing courses:

> People wanted different types of things from the course. A lot of people came along wanting to write stories for women's magazines, which wasn't really my thing because I don't read them and I don't particularly like them. But I felt as a tutor I had to cater for that because that was one of the things students seemed to want. Other students want to write memoirs or things for their children. They just want to be able to express it better. There's a whole diversity of different aims and it's a very difficult job in a general course because every class is different, so the balance of those aims is different. It's very difficult. (Tutor, Llanberis)

> Are you trying to turn everyone in the class into a genius or a commercial success? And the answer is no. Not everyone has the makings of a writer and even if they do, there are many other things beside talent that may need opening up. Ambition to overcome rejection, strength for repeated rejections and a need to write that's able to say: 'Fuck you lot, I'm writing'. Not to be so poor that you can't

do this, you have to be above the level of fighting for physical survival. Ruthlessness. For a long time I've said you need as big a melting pot as possible to find your people with innate talent and enough from all the categories to give people the confidence that they as Blacks, as women, as the working class, can, could and should be heard. And then, of course, the needs for commercially successful genre writing are very different from what I'd call writing. For what I call writing you need a savage self-questioning that would disadvantage you in commercial writing. I now make it clear that if people want to write *Bella* mini mysteries then they will get nothing from me and shouldn't be there. (Gloria)

The difference here is that from her clear aim of modelling and encouraging 'being a writer' Gloria is freer to focus the content and purpose of the sessions whereas Llanberis's tutor, whose aims seems closer to 'doing writing', is caught within the several contradictions of trying to run a student-centred course drawn from a self-selected and incredibly diverse student body.

One of the challenges facing teachers and facilitators of creative writing lies in formulating the precise extent to which its knowledge base overlaps with, and is based in, its process. I do not believe these boundaries can, or should, be fixed in isolation from the particular circumstances of students and tutors in the various and distinct contexts and settings in which teaching and learning of creative writing takes place. However, it is important to recognise that within each setting there are implications and choices. Without this recognition, both tutors and students fall prey to the disempowering fallacy that writers can intuitively discover all that they need to know about creative writing simply by engaging in the activity. This assumption that writing is natural, non-academic and unintellectual strengthens the very mystification of writing that it sets out to challenge. There is also a danger that creative writing in higher education will monopolise both the knowledge production and pedagogy of creative writing, assuming that in both instances higher education practitioners are more sophisticated than those working in schools or adult education. Creative writing pedagogy shares common elements wherever it is practised, although the specific context in which teaching and learning takes place particularise and inflect its general pedagogic principles, and practitioners from all three sites borrow from each other. As creative writing consolidates itself as a subject discipline, particularly in the higher education context, it is important that it acknowledges those elements of its pedagogy developed and sustained in other sites of educational practice.

Chapter seven

Being and becoming a creative writing tutor

This chapter shifts focus from the participants in creative writing to those who lead and facilitate creative writing activities. The consolidation of a cultural policy that promoted participation, inclusion and widened participation added a new dimension to the disciplinary debate between writers and teachers about owner-ship of creative writing. Although the policy change foregrounds educational values and practices, it did not come down clearly on either side of the debate about whether writers or teachers were best placed to become creative writing tutors. It complicated matters by extending the sites of creative writing, and therefore its routes into practice, to include community action and community education in the first wave, and arts administration and social regeneration in the latter. This introduces a third term into the debate: the literature or writing development worker [LDW]. Writing, teaching writing and developing cultural activity each brings its own community of practice to the teaching of creative writing.

Each community of practice shares a tension about the boundary and nature of professional identity that mirrors, and sometimes drives, the process of legitimating creative writing as a cultural practice and subject discipline within education. In order to understand these processes, and their impact upon the day-to-day practice of teaching or facilitating creative writing, it is necessary to look in general as well as specific terms at the nature of the work and the issues it raises. My discussion of these issues draws heavily on interviews with tutors based in Cleveland but is informed by wider considerations and experience.

This chapter begins by outlining four routes into work as a

creative writing tutor and then explores four issues that are common to the practice of tutoring. These issues are the tutor's standing as a writer, locating a creative practice in an educational setting, managing feedback and criticism, and diversity of purpose and experience in the student group.

Becoming a creative writing tutor

There is an immediate and reassuring common sense about the proposition, which no one would argue with, that writers are best placed to teach writing. The Arvon foundation staffs its courses exclusively from professional writers whose role is less to teach, in the didactic sense, and more to model and encourage a professional artistic practice. For writers teaching occasional and prestigious courses and workshops in this way, there is no identity conflict. They are defined by their writing, not their teaching. However, as demand for creative writing activities increases it became impossible to satisfy it on this basis alone. Additionally, some of the increased demand was driven by an explicitly anti-elitist concept of literary culture that set out to de-centre and de-mystify expertise. Under these circumstances, professional writers were not necessarily best placed, nor always inclined to provide, tutoring and facilitation.

A further significant factor concerns the institutional location of the creative writing activity. This bears in three ways upon whether professional writers form the majority of those teaching or facilitating creative writing activity. First is the issue of how status and hierarchy operates between different sites and sectors. For example, as creative writing becomes established in higher education it has needed to guarantee its work by including high profile writers on its staff. This created demand and competition for permanent, part-time positions that enable this to happen. When post-graduate creative writing programmes were first established they put a high premium on their tutor's writing profile, often creating chairs for their directors. Pioneering undergraduate programmes in creative writing were more likely to be directed by lecturers whose primary work was in literary criticism whose published output of creative work was more modest. It was not unusual for creative writing courses in higher education to be taught by lecturers who did not primarily identify as writers. Visiting fellowships, held by a full-time writer and paid for by the regional arts boards, raised the level of professional literary standing. Today, high status posts are as likely to be attached to undergraduate as postgraduate teaching. Other sectors, with less money and less status to offer, such as further education or the voluntary sector, have relied on writers whose professional standing is less well developed.

The second factor which influences whether people providing creative writing activities identify primarily as teachers or writers is geography. Mainstream literary culture is not only pre-dominantly metropolitan but also strongly identified with London with no literary agents and very few significant publishing houses located outside London. Where this monopoly has been most successfully challenged by, for example, the poetry presses Bloodaxe and Carcanet or the independent fiction publishers Cannongate and Tindall Street Press they have de-centred London but retained a metropolitan bias, in Newcastle, Manchester, Edinburgh and Birmingham respectively. This bolsters regional identity and opportunity but still leaves significant regions without the critical cultural mass needed to challenge metropolitan bias and has career development implications for the writers who lives and work in these parts of the country.

Finally, the location of creative writing activities bears on the extent to which writers teaching creative writing can stand apart from the professional practices of education. This has most relevance to writers who work in adult and further education, which have been less successful than schools or higher education in distinguishing between their mainstream provision and that provided by writers in education. Schools have developed an organisational and funding infrastructure that give writers a clear and bounded rationale for the work they do there – despite the occasional breakdown in support or communication. Fees to writers working in schools are not calculated in relation to teacher's pay; nor are they expected to take on areas of work such as record keeping, assessment or evaluation.

In adult and further education, and in the voluntary sector, these issues are less clear-cut and have steadily become more problematic for writers. The increased scrutiny and regulation of adult and further education, especially in relation to accreditation, makes it difficult for writers to supplement their income with teaching unless they are willing to do so as education professionals. This work is often poorly paid in comparison with project work in the voluntary arts sector and it is insecure and casual in nature, due to the unpredictability of recruiting viable class numbers, and increasingly subject to bureaucratic demands in the name of quality assurance. Consequently, writers who have options to work elsewhere often do so unless they are developing their careers and prepared to do the work to gain experience, are geographically restricted in some way or belong to the beleaguered and diminishing group of people for whom teaching in adult and community settings is motivated by political as much as professional ambition.

Ten or 15 years ago, when creative writing was far rarer in higher education than it is today, adult education was a significant employer of writers as creative writing tutors. Today, these same writers are more likely to work in higher education or the voluntary arts sector, and new writers, if they decide to teach at all, will go straight into these sites.

Richard Ings's study of the background of LDWs (Ings 1992: 28–9) identified several routes into the posts, with less than one-fifth of his sample identifying as professional writers. He noted then that both writers and sponsors expressed concern about the feasibility of maintaining a writing career while working as a LDW. The issue of how writers support themselves is of perennial interest. In 1998, the 1946 *Horizon*-survey into writers' livelihoods was repeated. The majority of respondents believed that a second job was vital but nobody chose teaching creative writing, and several thought any kind of work with words and language positively damaging to a writer (Holgate and Wilson-Fletcher 1998). The survey included nationally established writers, such as

CREATIVE WRITING

Simon Armitage, Beryl Bainbridge, Adrian Mitchell and Rose Tremain.

Their view is contrary to the experience – and aspiration – of many writers further down the hierarchy for whom working with writing, in developmental or educational roles, enables them to claim identity as writers.

Being a writer has become one, rather than the defining, characteristic of creative writing tutoring. The other routes into this work, subject to serendipity as much as career planning, are cultural activism, teacher diversification and student apprentices. They are not distinct routes and individuals often blend elements from more than one source.

The activist route into teaching creative writing was very common at the end of the twentieth century. Organisations such as the FWWCP, CAM, NAWE, ACE and the myriad of feminist cultural activities had a strong evangelical impulse. They were not only motivated to extend writing activities but also had the practical knowledge to do so. This activism often came from a broader social purpose, initially related to feminist or socialist politics and later to identity based social movements such as environmentalism, sexuality, disability and race. Regional and national policy shifts that embraced participative cultural activities created a strong infrastructure within which such activism could thrive. In the mid- to late-1990s, as audit culture took hold, its negative impact on education, community development and cultural work led many people to seek greater independence in their work by opting out of formal provision and employment in favour of more entrepreneurial activities that, paradoxically, were rooted in cultural activism.

Within Cleveland's local culture of writing, three tutors (Bleaklow, Cuillin and Llanberis) had taken leading roles in establishing the groups, performances venues, publications and Writearound festival by which it was defined throughout the 1990s. Bleaklow's tutor worked full-time in adult education and this became a significant resource for local writing development work. When changes in the organisation and funding of university-based continuing education made the continuation of

146

this role impossible he resigned to develop a freelance career as a poet and writer in education, largely working with young people. In doing so, he made cultural activism more important than education. This was a courageous step at a time when a lot of people were moving the other way.

All three began tutoring as a result of encouragement from others in ways that were almost accidental extensions of their activism around writing:

> The tutorship found me rather than me finding it. I never really thought of being a teacher of any kind. It came out of a need really. I was always one of the people who got up and started something, usually on a shoestring budget, and then other people got involved at a later stage. (Tutor, Llanberis)

> Becoming a tutor was ridiculous really; I've no qualifications whatsoever to tutor. None whatsoever. I got out of school at the age of 15 and it was the happiest day of my bloody life. (...) The only people I really enjoy working with are not professionals, put it that way. They are not teachers and people like that. (Tutor, Cuillin)

A perennially popular route into teaching creative writing is to develop it as a new specialism from within education. Historically, this has been a mainstay of developing and staffing adult and higher education creative writing initiatives. In the early days of creative writing provision there were anxieties about whether these courses could be appropriately delivered within the ethos and pedagogy of the providing institution. If existing staff developed and delivered the new courses this anxiety was ameliorated. It is only recently that professional standing as a writer, demonstrated through publication, has become the prerequisite for such work.

In Cleveland, Bleaklow and Crowden and Stanage's tutors were both employed full-time, one in further education and the other in adult education, when they were asked to suggest courses for new programmes for the unemployed. The tutor, having recently become interested in it herself, suggested writing:

CREATIVE WRITING

> There was nobody really doing it. I was making mistakes and I thought
> I could do something to stop other people from doing the same.
> (Tutor, Crowden and Stanage)

This element of mutual aid connects provision with enthusiasts and activists rather than the hierarchical and scholarly approach that is coming to define creative writing in higher education.

A third route into tutoring, particularly suited to adult education, was to attend courses as a student and then progress to a tutoring role. High Tor's tutor attended the first phase of writing courses in Cleveland in the mid-1980s and went on to full-time study, which included a high proportion of creative writing. When he returned to the area, unemployed and unsure what to do next, a conversation with his original tutor led to work on the recently launched AEC community creative writing programme. Through this, and his continued development as a writer and performer, he gained further work and short residencies in community arts projects and taught on the accredited programme of AEC courses. In 1997 he was appointed to a new writing development agency for Cleveland, in 2003 became co-ordinator of the region's Creative Partnership schemes and now develops creative writing provision for part-time and full-time students at the local university. Although in some respects a model story of how the student apprentice route can work, the experience of High Tor's tutor is not typical and most student apprentices achieve more limited career development.

Student apprentices worked in different ways. Sometimes well-established tutors were too busy to take on new courses and encouraged a student to consider tutoring. Less frequently, students put themselves forward, as happened with Kinder, which was team-taught by two former students. One had thought she would enjoy the work, enquired and was taken on, which spurred on the second:

> I hadn't thought of myself as being qualified but once she did it I
> thought I could do it. I knew they needed more tutors so I put myself
> forward. (Tutor 2, Kinder)

148

This follows established adult education traditions associated with trade union studies, women's studies, return to learning and the strong mutual aid ethos of community education. The courses work, and in doing so create more demand and identify the people with potential to teach them. At this stage, the cultural democratic ethos of the AEC programme, which saw its main purpose as creating access to writing, made it advantageous to be on the same wavelength as the students. In practice, the issue was more complex than this simple 'barefoot-writing tutor' model suggests.

Only one Cleveland tutor, Beatrice, had come to tutoring from a secure position as a writer. She did not work on the community writing programme. Having combined a career break to raise her children with a full-time writing career, she had published three novels. At the time I interviewed her she was working full-time in further education, doing a small amount of creative writing teaching for full-time students, and had previously taught a 'Writing for Pleasure and Profit' course and workshops in local prisons.

In Cleveland, the writer's experience was played down and participation in creative writing activities was promoted as being within the reach of all. Beatrice was scathing about this ethos and the practices that followed from it:

> The only training you need for the job is to have been published. Writing is an apprenticeship. I don't think people who haven't been published should be teaching creative writing. You have to know what it's like; you have to have been there. Therefore you can only know the whole process people need if you have been through it. I trained as a journalist not a teacher. I got into teaching because I was a writer not vice versa. (Beatrice)

She articulated a point of view that was often put forward by those involved in running little magazines and small press publishing, who allied themselves more closely to the professional writing axis than did writing activists. Peter Mortimer, poet and founder of *Iron Press* is an articulate proponent of this view. He responded to an article in *Mslexia* that gave a reasonably positive answer to the question 'Can writing be taught?' with a provocative letter calling for 'less teaching, more truth' (Mortimer 2004). Derek Gregory, who established and edited *Tees Valley Writer* as an independent quality outlet for local writers, expressed similar concerns about the AEC community writing programme. The magazine was not widely subscribed to locally and the quality of work submitted by local writers was poor. Each issue had a competition, with a special prize for a local writer. Local writers rarely won the main prize and although the local award was always made the editorial board often declined to publish the winning entry. Derek Gregory was critical of much of the creative writing provision in Cleveland because people who were not widely enough published delivered it.

This confirms a view strongly put forward by Linda Anderson (1993) that the relationship between teaching writing and being a writer has been unbalanced by the demand for writing courses. She argued that becoming a writing tutor could distort the writer's identity. Rather than putting in the work to gain or maintain standing as a writer, people now gain status and identity by teaching writing.

Being a creative writer tutor

The happenstance with which many creative writing tutors found themselves working raises the issue of what training and support they had received. There was no specific training for creative writing tutors until the recent Arts Council initiative, currently being delivered by a consortium of the FWWCP, National Association of Literature Development Workers and NAWE. This lack of training opportunities arises for different reasons. As an innovative form of provision, creative writing only slowly codifies an entry and training scheme. Efforts to establish such a scheme, which regularly featured on NAWE's agenda, was resisted in part because of the influence of higher education, where the absence of training to teach has until recently been a well-established practice. It also dovetailed with the intuitive approach to their work held by many writers.

BEING AND BECOMING A CREATIVE WRITING TUTOR

Most creative writing tutors adapt other experiences to enable and inform their work. These include being in writing workshops themselves, seeing tutoring modelled by other tutors, general experience of teaching, including training as school teachers, intuitive practice, community arts work and their professional writing experience.

Two factors were central to the discussions with tutors about whether they wanted specific training. First, they were conscious of the training agenda, rooted in a functionalist vocationalism, which had developed during the late-1980s and early-1990s. Its emphasis on regulation and standardisation, symbolised in the creation of an accreditation culture, was received with great hostility. Not only was the relative autonomy of adult education generally felt to be under threat, but this was seen to be especially damaging to creative writing which more than most subjects depended upon the self-determination that the tutors, quite rightly, saw as threatened by these changes. Under these circumstances, it was difficult for them to see training as anything other than a further attempt to control and standardise practice.

Second, some tutors subscribed to romantic notions of writing as inspired, and saw training mechanistically, as soulless and futile. The majority of tutors formulated their role in relation to enabling or facilitating creativity and were ambivalent about training because they understood creativity as beyond planning, impossible to formulate or intervene in, needing only to be nurtured:

> I feel very mixed about training to teach creative writing. It's to do with a very romantic notion. You just feel it, do it. So much training can be stultifying. (Tutor 2, Kinder)

Although training was not viewed in a favourable light, several tutors commented on the isolation of their work and felt some form of peer-based training might counter this. This response was gendered. Women were more likely than men to view training positively, but this could reflect men's more general confidence rather than any particular demands of teaching creative writing.

CREATIVE WRITING

> Training gives you authority and confidence, you need something that makes you feel you have some authority, as this isn't an area where there are qualifications as such.
>
> (Tutor 1, Kinder)

Those tutors who thought training would have been useful wanted training that continued alongside teaching. Tutors who were already isolated as adult educators felt the isolation of working with writing even more keenly:

> Any training is useful as a way of breaking down isolation. I didn't know whether I was doing it right or wrong or whether other methods might work better. I had no one to sort of bounce ideas off, so I think that would be useful, because you would get feedback on it. (...) You experiment a bit but hearing other people experimenting and how that works, it's bound to be a benefit. (Tutor, Llanberis)

Several tutors I interviewed had trained and worked as schoolteachers. Although they felt this supported their work as creative writing tutors there was also some ambivalence:

> I'm a trained teacher, but not in creative writing. (...) It's odd, a mixed blessing. I don't think I'd have had the confidence to do it if I hadn't had that training, but that's personality, that's about lacking self-confidence and self-esteem. On the negative side I have to stop myself teaching – interfering, suggesting things – the way I would teach in school or in FE. Maybe people without teaching backgrounds approach things in a freer way. (Tutor, Crowden and Stanage)

Teacher training clearly gives confidence and some authority but the approaches that come most easily to a schoolteacher are likely to be inappropriate in adult or higher education. This would hold whatever subject was being taught, but tutors tended to discuss such pedagogical issues as if their only context were the peculiarities of creative writing as a subject discipline. Marina's comments pose an alternative set of experiences as formative:

> Who knows what prepares you to do this? What can I come up with?

BEING AND BECOMING A CREATIVE WRITING TUTOR

> I trained as a teacher years ago to teach primary. Is that a form of
> training; is that a form of preparation to work as a creative writing
> tutor? Then journalism, that teaches you to roll up your sleeves and do
> it. It's being in women's groups as much as anything, facing problems
> of being a writer myself, working very hard at it and having been in a
> writing group myself. I don't remember having thought about it
> before. I think you learn as you do it. (Marina)

She begins to say that she trained as a teacher and then stops
herself, interrogating that response by considering other possible
preparations. This enables her to set out the cluster of experiences
that brought her to the point of wanting to teach creative writing
and provided her with some of the necessary skills to do so. Her
most important observation is that teaching creative writing is a
process that sustains and engenders itself rather than a process
for which you are prepared and then go off to do. This has an
interesting bearing on the debate about publication as the
necessary pre-requisite to teach writing. Marina set great store on
confidence in one's own writing and the ability to inspire
confidence in others, neither of which necessarily correlate with
publication:

> It's being experienced as a writer. It's the ability to communicate
> something about writing to make a safe environment in which to
> constructively question and criticise. I don't think you can talk about it
> in black and white terms. (...) Writing is a very private thing and this is
> a public thing. (Marina)

These different perspectives highlight differences in how
education is defined, and consequently how the role of the
professional writer within education is perceived. On the one
hand, a collaborative method of working, with its roots in feminist,
working class and community arts, that emphasised skill sharing
and mutual aid. On the other an individual professional who
passed down advice, information and instruction without
engaging too closely in the life of the group.

High Tor's tutor shared Marina's preference for collaborative
methods:

> I think I might have said yes (to training) at the beginning but now I
> don't think so. It might have been a hindrance to have had training. I
> quite like getting thrown in and having to struggle and do it. (...) I think
> if you're honest with them instead of trying to pretend you're
> somebody who does know everything about creative writing (...) they
> are usually quite willing to go with it. (Tutor, High Tor)

His views are similar to those of Llanberis's tutor, an influential
figure in Cleveland who mentored many of the second wave CIS
tutors:

> A lot of the experience of workshops came out of just getting up and
> doing things. I think the experience of actually working with people,
> drawing things out of them, having patience, working with them, not
> expecting too much too soon, I think that rather than qualifications
> was more relevant. The fact that I'd worked with ordinary people in
> lots of different settings not just art, but welfare rights and with
> unemployed people. That experience was more relevant. (Tutor,
> Llanberis)

Tutors varied in their attitude towards the educational context
within which they worked. It was striking, though, that despite
working in adult education, the majority of tutors were unfamiliar
with its distinctive pedagogies. They had a tendency to define what
they did against a very generalised notion of education, and
sometimes, adult education, which was considerably outmoded.
They appeared unaware of debates about social purpose and
radical pedagogy and the different methods of teaching and
learning they had introduced. Marina saw working in adult
education as a means to work with writers and strongly distanced
herself from the sector as a whole:

> Their ideas are prehistoric. Boring, boring, boring. Lectures, lectures,
> lectures. (Marina)

During tutor interviews I wanted to elicit the unrehearsed answer.
This wasn't about catching tutors out; rather I hoped to lead the
discussion into areas of contradiction and difficulty. I asked them
to complete a sentence and provide a visual image or word

association for four phrases. These were: 'The group I teach'; 'My students'; 'Student writing' and 'My writing'. They completed the sentence: 'Students need …'. Often, the image undermined or contradicted their answers to previous questions. For example, in relation to 'The group' one tutor had talked about diversity and the solidarity of these people working together but the visual image was far less positive:

> A writhing mass of people, rather like worms, and me right at the bottom of it, they're overpowering me. (Tutor 2, Kinder)

Another gave a picture of 'concentration, questioning. The image is heads down' (Tutor, Crowden and Stanage) but went on to comment that this rarely happened. Responses to the phrase 'My students' hinted at tension, as with Llanberis's tutor, whose comment: 'They're all my students' suggested a struggle to include everybody. Their comments were not always negative, though. Several tutors discussed the pleasure they gained from the work students produced:

> I am amazed at what comes out of people, people that you might not think had any creative potential at all can come up with things. I find that exciting, discovering things and seeing people discovering things in themselves. (Tutor, Llanberis)

> Their range, the quality, the depth of their writing. That the writing moves me, which it does constantly, the way they are growing as writers under my eyes. (Tutor, Crowden and Stanage)

Some issues and problems

Tutors and students had very different understandings of the tutor's role in creative writing courses. Tutors' views varied, much as Geoffrey Adkins had found they did during his 1981 survey of the arts and adult education, which had identified a continuum stretching from informally chaired readings of work-in-progress through to highly organised and technical courses of study (Adkins

1981: 134–5). All tutors felt, to a greater or lesser extent, that there was a mismatch between how they and students understood their role.

Several tutors felt their students wanted more formality in the sessions. This was often linked to impatience with provisional judgements. Students expected tutors to deal in absolutes – what was right and what was wrong, good or bad – and to offer definite opinions. High Tor's tutor felt this tended to be more of a problem with new students. I asked him to think back to when he first attended a writing class. Like his students, who had initially reported they had no expectations, a little probing established that he had originally expected the rule-based formality based on his last educational experience – school:

> I thought I would get told what's right and what's wrong, the rules of doing things. The rules of doing things are all right, as long as they don't seem to be rules. (Tutor, High Tor)

The desire for rules or formula held most sway in the context of publishing, which was itself a perennial area of conflict in respect of students' expectations of tutors. Several tutors commented that their students expected them to push commercial and publishing interests more than they did. Again, High Tor's tutor recalled this need from his own experience as a student:

> That was one of the expectations that I had. I thought the tutor would act as a kind of gateway to publication. (Tutor, High Tor)

Students often wanted to learn about publishing and marketing, which were counterposed by tutors to personal development. One of Kinder's tutors saw it as part of her role to point people in the right direction if publishing was something they wanted. But, like other tutors, she was also aware that many people were unaware of other purposes for writing such as personal development or the intrinsic pleasure of the activity itself:

> I would hate anyone to think that being published was a mark of success or the ultimate aim of all writers. (Tutor 1, Kinder)

> You can't get anyone published, all you can do is give information.
> Sometimes people are disappointed if you're not published yourself.
> They think you're not a proper tutor. They are disappointed. They think
> you can help them if you're published, though you can't, and they
> feel cheated if you aren't. (Melanie)

The first comment sits oddly with the common sense understanding not only of aspirant writers but also of the general public
opinion that publishing *is* a mark of success and, however
unrealistic, will often be the aim of writers and would-be writers.
It highlights a topic none of the Cleveland tutors ever raised for
discussion, which was the quality of the writing produced by their
students. Tutors elsewhere handled this question much more
bluntly:

> I always work on the assumption that publication is the ultimate aim
> (or at least if that is what the student wants) because a poem or story
> or novel is not something you can hang on the wall and admire like a
> painting. (…) Writing is like most things in life, some are good at it and
> some aren't. But just as important is that some are good at teaching
> it and some aren't – and the bad ones, in my view, are those who
> cannot tell some of their students that they would be advised to give
> up writing and try knitting or something. (Bulman 1991)

Colin Bulman is prepared to make value judgements but still
frames them in a context of student's need. He was an early
commentator on teaching creative writing in English Studies and
made valuable contributions to the field, especially in relation to
assessment. Interestingly, though, he illustrates here a shift from
the student-centred personal development ethos of creative
writing in the 1980s to a more contemporary concern in the 1990s
with professionalising writers and writing. Two of his articles,
written a decade apart, encapsulate this. In the first, outlining a
model for assessing creative writing, his conclusion stresses that
encouragement is more important than grading (Bulman 1986:
54). The latter, titled 'Against encouragement' charts his journey
towards critical intolerance of bad writing and a conclusion that
the needs of the reader should count for more than those of the

writer (Bulman 1996: 14). The student-centredness of much creative writing teaching skews the curriculum in ways that are inconceivable in other subject disciplines. The circle of expressed and met need that it generates is disrupted by publishing, which inevitably introduces questions of selection and judgement and in their train the potential for conflict. Students avid for publication, as were many of those I observed and in other circumstances have taught, rarely consider Bulman's bottom line.

Tutors avoid it too, as I observed in Cleveland. This is not because they are bad tutors. It is because avoiding value judgements presents itself as the clearest way to manage two problems fundamental to the organisation of their work as a cultural activity taking place within educational parameters. The first is the pressure in adult education to recruit sufficient numbers to make courses viable. Self-interest determines would-be students are not turned away, and even if tutors wanted to exclude students, adult education's commitment to open access would make this difficult.

This dovetails with the second problem, which is the organisation of provision around educational values. The creative writing curriculum is not organised around absolute standards of achievement, subjective standards of taste or economic criteria of marketability, as are the literary marketplaces, but by negotiated and incremental stages of improvement. Fundamental to the misplaced expectation students had of their tutors was their inability to recognise the educational dimension of the creative writing activities they were participating in. Michelene Wandor, an established poet and playwright who is also one of the most perceptive commentators on teaching writing, offers a model of practice which neutralises this problem:

> Work to develop a critical vocabulary which outlaws all subjectivist responses: 'I like', 'I dislike', 'I prefer', all distract from the analytical process. Value judgements, if used at all, should be left to the END of the analytical process. I have found that if illuminating and exciting textual analysis takes place, value judgements effectively become unnecessary. (...) Notions such as 'positive' or 'negative' criticisms,

which accrue as correlatives to premature value judgements, thus also become irrelevant. (Wandor 2002: 13)

The conflict over publication was a tangible issue for tutors to respond to. Much more difficult for them were the contradictions that arose from being positioned between cultural and educational activity:

> Once my car broke down and I couldn't let them know I'd be late. They were still waiting to start when I got there. When I asked them why, they said: 'It's no show without Punch'. They weren't a new group, they could have started. The break, when I couldn't be there, showed this because they managed perfectly well. It's altered how I approach the group. I stand back now. I'm less interfering. (Tutor, Stanage and Crowden)

This tutor's experience indicates the degree to which independent participation must be encouraged and developed. It cannot be assumed. This in turn leads back to how tutors frame the overall purpose and activities of the creative writing course. Because most tutors are reluctant to specify aims and objectives fuzziness develops about the courses. Far from removing barriers to participation, it actually increases them as students remain unclear what exactly they are being asked to participate in and how to do so effectively.

A considerable amount of tutors' energy goes into reading and tempering the group. This is broader than reading and responding to student work or facilitating and stimulating their writing, important and time-consuming as this is. It is about teaching them how to function as a group. If the course becomes, as several of the Cleveland AEC courses did, effectively a led writers' group, then one of the tutor's roles ought to be teaching group members how to do so effectively, working towards independence for their own and other people's writing. There was little evidence of this being done. Where there was awareness of the issue, usually from those who had followed the cultural activist route into teaching creative writing, it was posed in terms of enabling students, without always recognising that there was often some conflict over what it was that students wanted to be enabled to do.

Cuillin's tutor was unusual in confronting the conflict between people who do and don't want to write for markets:

> I'm very anti the idea that writing is just another evening class. (...) You have to sacrifice that sort of person for the group. (...) I feel very strongly about other people's writing. Having come to writing very hard, I almost feel honour bound to help others on the same path. The best group I've ever been in, everyone was very certain that what they were doing was right. There was a lot of anger too and it really pushed the writing hard. Anger is a very important thing. (...) That's the minefield with creative writing, getting people to tamper with the emotions they usually suppress. (Tutor, Cuillin)

Another manifestation of the tension between directive and non-directive approaches to teaching creative writing concerned selective and specialised provision. Historically, there has been a tradition of self-selection and mixed ability in the provision of creative writing activities and it is unusual to restrict entry to courses. Some of the Cleveland tutors were beginning to see differentiated provision as a solution to what they felt to be the impossible position of trying to deal adequately with their students' diverse needs and starting points, including their sometimes unrealistic expectations, which they summarised as:

> People thinking: 'I'll go to a creative writing course and in six weeks I'll be a published writer'. (Tutor 1, Kinder)

Tutors hesitated in formulating ideas about restricting and selecting access to classes:

> A need, a very great need, for almost a masterclass, higher courses. I don't know quite what I mean by higher but almost a masterclass. Like music. You analyse what you're doing and recognise that music is intuitive but also there is so much you just have to learn, learn to hone as well. That's a masterclass. It's the depth of concentration. There's a link-up between knowing the nuts and bolts of an art form and knowing its jazz element, the spirit that only comes out of concentrated effort. (Tutor, Cuillin)

BEING AND BECOMING A CREATIVE WRITING TUTOR

Kinder 1's tutor began by saying it was impossible to teach everybody who came to the group to be a good creative writer unless there were sets. But she then interrogated herself, questioning whether it was possible to segregate people in this way before concluding it was unacceptable. However, when she checked her interview transcript she revised her view again:

> I think my reaction was an emotional one. How could we do this to people? How would I feel if I was put in a less advanced group? I now feel that having differentiated groups is the logical thing to do, but that it must be handled with sensitivity. (Tutor 1, Kinder)

Situating creative writing activities more securely within an educational framework would enable tutors to specialise rather than attempt to be all things to all students. Differentiation would also build in progress and development for students in ways that could both counter the formulaic aspirations of many students and help them achieve external success. Together, this would make the writing curriculum explicit, which in turn would highlight the power relations operating in creative writing classrooms. For the empowerment that many tutors genuinely wanted to take place through creative writing, the reality of power needed to be both acknowledged and confronted.

Several tutors thought and taught as if all power lay outside the classroom, whether in specific editors or publishing houses or in a more generalised literary establishment. They were unable to see that they too had power as a result of their structural positions as both published writers and as tutors. This power was always perceived by students to be greater than it was, but it was nevertheless an issue tutors and students needed to engage in together rather than avoid or worry about:

> People think they have to write what I will like, not for themselves. As a tutor your values and feelings do come across, but I don't want it to be so oppressive. I worry it might happen. I put my viewpoint across, but I wouldn't want to put down work I didn't like. (Tutor 2, Kinder)

> My involvement with writing is obsessive, energetic, all-consuming. I've

seen that energy communicate positively. It can have a good effect
to take yourself seriously, but sometimes it's too much, and maybe I
marginalised some students by taking it so seriously. (Marina)

Tutors do act as role models for their students and they do influence, whether consciously or not, what is acceptable within the group. To worry about this provides more evidence of how powerful the idea is of the tutor striving to be all things to all people rather than recognising both that some needs will be in conflict with others and that tutors cannot efface themselves in the classroom.

The question of how tutors present themselves – as writers, editors or teachers of writing – fed into issues of emotional risk, another source of anxiety amongst tutors. They worried that they or the students could not handle what the creative process unleashed. Several tutors felt that good, authentic writing required the writer to be clearly in touch with, and writing from, their emotions. This awareness of the emotional power of writing extends not only to what is written but to the level of commitment an art form demands from its practitioners. Cuillin's tutor, who had also worked as a semi-professional jazz musician, felt strongly about this:

> The stress on the family, the way you have to re-examine old values
> that you have led your life by. It isn't a light undertaking at all. Some
> of the people who drop out certainly hadn't realised they were going
> to have their fundamentals shook. (Tutor, Cuillin)

Although Cuillin's tutor defined good writing as writing fuelled by emotion I had observed other tutors, and their students, deflect the slightest hint of conflict. During my visit to Crowden a potentially interesting discussion about religion was halted by one of the students and the tutor did not challenge her:

> We leave all that outside the door. No religion, no politics, no
> arguments. (Woman, Crowden)

In contrast, Cuillin's tutor encouraged people to acknowledge their emotions but avoided public confrontation:

BEING AND BECOMING A CREATIVE WRITING TUTOR

> If it's getting personal I squash it straight away. There are taboo areas.
> If you tamper with people's emotions you are into a minefield. (Tutor,
> Cuillin)

He wanted individuals to confront emotions and taboos in their personal writing and only when they felt safe doing this were they encouraged to share the writing more widely. High Tor's tutor was unusual in setting out to disturb his students' preconceptions. He talked about waiting for the terror in their eyes, which he saw as a challenge to make them trust him sufficiently to learn that he would make it worth the risk.

This may seem self-dramatising, or perhaps conjure up images of clumsy encounter group sessions, but it is neither. Recalling the expectations students brought to their writing classes confirms that these tutors work with students who genuinely feel a sense of vulnerability and exposure. High Tor's tutor was adapting for his students a learning experience of his own, which had taught him the importance of risk-taking. His degree involved several elements of performance, something he had initially found daunting:

> I was terrified, absolutely terrified of movement and drama. I was on
> stage once when I was seven trying to play this guitar solo. Everyone
> sat there and I went ding ding. The most embarrassing time of my life.
> I never went on stage again until I was at college a few years ago. I
> was terrified, but you get a buzz out of it and the feeling and the
> energy that comes out of it, that's what drives you to the next one. So
> you have to overcome that fear otherwise you're going to stagnate.
> (Tutor, High Tor)

High Tor's tutor was also unusual within Cleveland because he shared his writing with the group, joining in exercises and using his own writing experiences to illustrate discussion topics. Bracketing out their own writing, which was common in Cleveland tutors, was a curious reversal of the standard approach to teaching creative writing which puts a high premium on the apprentice model which in turn relies on the status of the tutor-writer for its effectiveness.

Quite why they felt it necessary to do this was unclear. It may have been the result of their relative inexperience. More than half were also attending AEC courses as students, which perhaps left them feeling insecure about the role change from tutor to student. Unless they had considerable track records as writers (which few of them did) it would clearly have been a hostage to fortune to stake their tutoring expertise on their experience as writers. Although tutors were selfless to a fault in their desire to meet the students' needs, they were at the same time wedded to their positions of difference as the tutor. This was not elitism but indicated the anxiety that resulted from their accelerated transition from student to tutor:

> I found it frightening and off-putting how quickly I went from beginner
> to expert. (Tutor, Crowden and Stanage)

A similar acceleration was associated with cultural activism. This had the added complication that in several cases activism had severely restricted their personal opportunities for writing. Cleveland tutors may have been less willing than others to make their own writing a fundamental part of their teaching because it had been adversely affected by the demands of their roles as tutors and organisers. The conflict between developing the writing of others and your own is difficult to resolve, even for experienced and well-established writers. Some tutors talked about this openly but others expressed it in a more covert way. Elsewhere in the country tutors spoke more openly about the resentment they felt about the care lavished on encouraging new writers at the expense of sustaining writers in the early stages of their careers. Unsurprisingly, in Cleveland the only person expressing such views was Beatrice. She maintained there was no relation between teaching writing and writing but the very way she formulated this statement, as if addressing an assumed position, revealed that perhaps there was:

> I suppose I'm supposed to say it's made me more careful of what I
> write. It just reminds me how bloody difficult the whole thing is, it
> doesn't get any easier, whether you are just starting out or have had
> three novels published. (Beatrice)

BEING AND BECOMING A CREATIVE WRITING TUTOR

Writing, at the professional level that most tutors aspire to, is highly competitive. If tutors are struggling to get work accepted or have recently had work rejected then there is real conflict between helping other people and putting that time and energy into their own work.

Competition and resentment are complex issues, muffled in the discourse of widened participation, and exacerbated in the Cleveland context because of the speed with which students became tutors, however they defined that role. The enthusiasm of Kinder's Tutor 2, and the mutual benefit she saw in teaching creative writing, stands out because she expressed a view rarely articulated but surely pertinent to Cleveland tutors:

> I just get a great buzz at the moment out of talking about writing and people's experience. (...) I get ideas from people. I don't pinch them, but it's a two-way process of stimulation. (Tutor 2, Kinder)

It was not that Cleveland's tutors lacked enthusiasm. They had this in abundance and it established continuity with the evangelical cultural democracy that had brought the majority of them into the circle of creative writing activity in the first place. But the enthusiasm was as much for the whole activity of creative writing, including the drive to extend its reach, as it was for the writing itself. When talking with creative writing tutors I heard over and over again a version of this tutor's experience:

> As a writer you need time for yourself. It's advice I give the students, be selfish, be possessive of that hour of your own time and writing, and I consistently break it myself. (Tutor, Cuillin)

If we look in detail at how this situation was managed by Llanberis's tutor we can see both its individual and structural dimensions, for his position revealed some of the difficulties for practice which arise from a cultural-democratic policy. When I interviewed him he had been active in Cleveland's writing culture for almost a decade and had been at the forefront of the mid-1980s work to establish locally based democratic creative writing activities with an emphasis on publishing and performing. The sheer amount of work entailed, which was at that stage wholly voluntary, worked against the time needed to consolidate his own writing:

> It wasn't just the tutoring. I didn't really have the time to do a lot of writing. I was starting writing groups, going to Writearound meetings, staying up all night doing layouts for *Outlet*, whatever, and tutoring about four courses all over Cleveland, so there was a lot of travelling time. I did do some writing, but a lot of my creativity was going into all the rest. (Tutor, Llanberis)

Tutoring can, as several tutors attested, balance out and inspire writing. It is, in one sense, required to do so, organised as it is around tapping into and shaping creativity. But with Llanberis's tutor we see two things working against this. First, at an organisational level the basis on which Cleveland's culture of writing gained public funding often made an artificial separation between the activists and those towards whom activity was directed. Second, the impulses that had led him into the creative arts in the first place were transformed, when their expression was frustrated, into teaching and organising.

The ethos of doers and done for, a dynamic which cannot help but breed a culture of dependency, grew up alongside the earliest interventions which developed Cleveland's culture of writing:

> When we started *Outlet* it was made clear it wasn't there for us to put our own writing in, or very few pieces. As I was co-ordinating it I felt I should hold back more than anyone really, and the same with Writearound. I was hoping when I started things that there would be more outlets for me, I mean I was a writer as well, but you feel that as you're starting things that people resent it if you use it as a vehicle for your own work. (Tutor, Llanberis)

The lines were not always so clear-cut. Several members of the Writearound Committee, for example, regularly won prizes in the annual competition. Although this was judged independently and anonymously, so the prizes were fairly won, the right of the organisers to enter blurred a line that elsewhere in the culture of writing was clearly demarcated in such a way as to position activists as unable to benefit personally from the writing development work they did. As the number of LDW posts has expanded, and gained in professionalism, this has also changed. Posts held by working writers do now permit writers to continue to develop their own careers as well as creating opportunities for others. But when these activities were first funded issues of accountability had particular resonance. Historically, new literary movements coalesce around publishing ventures in which friends and supporters publish friends and supporters and this pattern spilled over into early state funding for literature so that the literary formation of the 1960s–1970s resembled a honeycomb of cliques and movements fuelled by mutual and self-promotion. Jim McGuigan's suppressed report into the grant giving activities of the Literature Department of the Arts Council of Great Britain confirmed what many suspected, namely that arts funding was a relatively closed circle in which grant-giver and recipient regularly changed places with each other (McGuigan 1977). In the late-1980s, this produced an emphasis on accountability that dovetailed with the ideology of cultural democracy and wider moves towards explicit anti-discriminatory practices in public life.

Well intended and timely as this was, it nevertheless contributed to undermining the potential for a genuinely popular movement of cultural change by absorbing and dissipating some of its energies into a struggle to demonstrate a selfless accountability. Ironically, this in turn opened the way for the professionalisation of creative writing activities, a process that added further complications to the issue of dependency, and increased the distance between critical popular direction and institutional interventions.

Llanberis's tutor made sense of all this by de-centering the individual text and his own process of writing. He developed a political analysis of creativity and cultural change that subsumed all acts of creativity into the greater whole:

> Everything I do, you know, I approach in the same way. If I'm thinking of creating a magazine or something, doing the layout, I can do it the same way that I might do if I was writing a poem. I don't see it as an aberration, I see it as all part of it. (...) I felt very strongly about wanting

better things, that was the motivation for writing, and doing that tutoring work is actually, in a small square of the world, putting those sorts of things into practice. Writers are alienated and I am sort of helping, especially people who didn't have the educational opportunities, helping them to find things in themselves and discover things like I did. I'm putting that into practice, so the reasons for writing are being translated to the developmental work and it's hopefully making a better society, a better world, or contributing to it. (Tutor, Llanberis)

The position was valiantly put, and genuinely held, but it balances on a contradiction. The value of helping others to discover writing, and discover greater self-knowledge through their writing, depends on valuing writing. Yet, as a result of helping others to discover the power and pleasure of writing, the tutor from Llanberis's own writing received steadily less and less time and attention. Doing layout is not the same as writing a poem, and it is hard to see it bringing the same rewards and satisfactions. The problem lies in a cultural formation that forced writing activists to choose between organising and developing or being organised or developed.

The distinction between what I have elsewhere referred to as 'the doers and the done-to' is not seen as sharply in writing activities which have their origins in a more overtly political tradition. Within the FWWCP and amongst feminist writing networks the principle of collective self-help prevented such distinctions arising, although achieving collective working practices does entail considerable and constant negotiation over power. This is, though, a different situation to that of the publicly funded arts or arts education worker who is charged with developing and widening participation from a base line which assumes a lack of interest or expertise amongst those they are working with and for. In these situations, as we have seen throughout the study, the tutor-writer is positioned within a contradiction. He or she is valued and employed on the basis of their achievements as a writer, but rewarded only for their ability to inspire and develop other people's writing.

BEING AND BECOMING A CREATIVE WRITING TUTOR

In discussions with Marina and Gloria about tutoring creative writing it was striking that they spoke always from the position of a writer whereas Llanberis's tutor moved between his identity as writer, writing development worker and activist. These different elements were present for the women too, but they seemed better able to inhabit several identities simultaneously:

> I've done a lot of encouraging and nurturing and felt that back. I've gained enormously in confidence and support, I've felt very supported. It is a sort of nurturing thing. We are talking here about a whole lot of things together: *Writing Women*, being in a creative writing group, teaching creative writing. I can't disentangle them from each other. (Marina)

Through discussion with several tutors it became clear that one of the issues determining the extent to which tutors were present in their groups as writers was how easy they found it to admit to and express their own vulnerabilities while retaining the authority and expertise that enable them to act as givers of confidence and holders of other people's vulnerabilities.

This had implications for the amount of time writing tutors spent with the courses and groups they tutored and whether this became the focus of their identity as writers. If their own writing became an absent presence the effect was corrosive. All writers reported reaching a plateau where the stimulus of being with other writers started working against their own writing. Those who successfully negotiated this did so because they recognised the need for change and found ways to adapt. They were in conscious control of the process rather than at its mercy:

> I think the reason teaching creative writing hasn't stopped me writing is that I am feeding as well as giving out by attending the workshops. I belong to writers' groups as well and I get stimulus from them, which balances the drain of the groups I teach. I go to writers' weekends regularly, three or four times a year. I go for the criticism and the reading of my work. (Tutor, Crowden and Stanage)

> Teaching intervenes on me because it's constant deadlines. My own

writing is changing in the sense that I'm more interested in sequences and cycles, and it feels interrupted and bitsy, but that may be because what I'm trying to work at is new. But sometimes I feel I write poetry because I can squeeze it in with other things. I've learnt how to hold the starting point when I feel there is a poem there, but I think writing a novel would be difficult. (Gloria)

These are very different strategies but have in common recognising the boundary between giving out to others and taking in for the self.

One way in which teaching can sustain writing is the inspiration generated in the taught group. Where tutors discussed the positive interaction between their teaching and writing they often drew attention to the way it sharpened their critical faculties. Only Nell talked about the group she taught directly inspiring her creative work:

I'm writing two pieces of work indirectly inspired by working here. I do use other people's experiences to relate to my own, and there's an exploitation there of what people tell you, and I do cash in on that. But there is a double truth; something interacts between the two experiences. (Nell)

Her language – exploitation, cashing in – implies that the process is problematic. It's as if one of the things that shouldn't happen in teaching writing is getting ideas you can use for yourself. Some tutors were worried about ideas that seemed to come from their students, or seeing a theme handled by a student and thinking: 'I could do that better'. There are valid issues here, but perhaps a lack of confidence in their own writing process forced many tutors to damp down these impulses in ways that ultimately damped down their impulse to write at all.

In this chapter an account of the different ways in which creative writers move into and inhabit their roles as writing tutors offers further illustration of how the cultural-democratic impulse in educational and cultural policy further complicates the already contentious issue of teaching creative writing. We have seen, too, how tutor's ambivalence about locating creative writing in

170

education helps to create a conflict of expectations between the way they and their students construct their role as tutor and the broader purpose of the creative writing activity with which they are engaged. The reluctance of tutors to take a directive, interventionist role paradoxically emphasises the dependent relationship between them and their students. This demonstrates how the rhetoric of participation and empowerment obscures the extent to which such involvement needs to be consciously and actively brought about, and it flags the importance of progress and value, in relation to creative writing, which is returned to in chapter nine. The next chapter, Myths of the common writer, offers a detailed account of who Cleveland's writers are, how they became involved in writing activities and how they live out and make sense of their engagement with writing.

Chapter eight

Myths of the common writer

Previous chapters looked in some detail at the activities of the creative writing courses and groups and related these to ideas about, and the practices of, teaching creative writing. In this and the following chapter I explore what it is that people are doing when they do creative writing. The term 'common writer' borrows from Virginia Woolf's exploration of reading and popular taste (Woolf 1925) and is not intended to be demeaning. On the contrary, setting the working lives of Cleveland writers alongside the existing literature of writers at work (Dick 1972; Wandor 1983; Chamberlain 1988; Sellers 1989) reveals structural similarities in the writing process lived and practised by writers whose professional and social circumstances differ greatly. This counters the myths that have grown up around 'common writers'. There are three myths at issue here. Firstly, that their work simply gushes out, sloppy and unworked; secondly, that they are obsessed with publication; and finally that they seek and depend upon each other's uncritical admiration. I scrutinise these myths about common writers as a way of exploring the meaning and value that writers give their creative writing activities. I look analytically at what living the writing means in terms of the social and pedagogic practices of creative writing. I consider the first two myths in this chapter and the third, uncritical admiration, in the following chapter.

'Does it matter, if they get enjoyment?' asked one respondent during a discussion about whether or not creative writing could be taught. It is an interesting question. Pleasure is often suspect in the highly moral, self and socially improving traditions of adult education and cultural policy in which these creative writing activities are located. Graham Harthill, who researched

172

frameworks for evaluating creative writing in adult education, identified a paradox at the heart of his task:

> If, as so many would seem to agree, the subject cannot in fact be taught, how and what does the student learn? (...) What does the student (or better – participant) experience in a class or workshop? And what is special or valuable in the class or workshop that makes it worthwhile to attend regularly and respond to its challenges? (Harthill 1994: 7)

Even Harthill, who argues strongly for the evaluation of creative writing activities to be rooted in their social, emotional and creative benefits, subordinates pleasure to usefulness.

Questions of value are not just abstractions but embedded and material, so it is pertinent to see how creative writing activities are lived and valued. Doing so enables us to specify the sometimes elusive writing process and to begin elaborating the relationship between an individual's writing process and the dominant social relations of literature and writing. This results in a highly differentiated practice, which in turn demonstrates the complexity of both the writing process and attempts to intervene in and foster its development. Recognition of this complexity is an important precondition for debates about value

Myth one: Letting it flow

> It's a bit like being a child really, you want it and you want it now, you want it immediate and you can't bear to sort of work through it. But I do work at it. I do most of it in bed. Actually when I'm on a night, when I've gone to bed and usually I always keep, like, paper and a pen, 'cos usually I write it in the dark as well. 'Cos when the light goes on, like, the thought I had seems to disappear with the dark. (...) I just sort of, like, scribble. If I get a thought or an idea or an image then I'll probably write the next day or whenever, the next morning maybe. I look back at it and I'll say: 'Well, what was I on about there?' and work it that way. (...) I'll write that down and I might be in the middle of doing something and I'll sit for, like, 15 minutes. I could be cooking the

tea or anything and then, like, an idea pops in and off I'll go and I'll write. I'll get, like, the basis of what I want to say, or the start of it, down and come back to it later. (...) I do that in bed as well, before I go to sleep, it's the only time I've got to myself. (Kim)

Individual interviews with writers identified an aspect of practice that may have been missed by focusing on group processes and responses. This was the amount of work people put into their writing. In groups, a rather cavalier attitude dominated. People talked about 'dashing' or 'knocking' things off and often introduced the work they read with diminutives and qualifiers – 'little', 'just' or 'rough' – as if they did not want to be seen to be taking themselves or their work too seriously. Stressing the provisional nature of their work both prepared them to receive, and invited others to give, wide-ranging feedback. Overall, much as Graham Harthill found when comparing his questionnaire returns and interviews (Harthill 1994: 23), this created an erroneous impression that participants did not work at their writing.

Writers engaged in two types of work. First the actual work of writing, re-writing, attending, and sometimes organising, writing activities. Second, and less tangibly, the work of leading what amounted to a parallel life where, alongside the demands of their everyday lives, they imaginatively inhabited the other world of their writing, conducting what for some was a lifelong dialogue with their 'writerly' self. Their quality of reflection was high, suggesting I tapped into, rather than initiated, an already established pattern of self-examination about the nature and meaning of their identity as writers. The accounts of when and where people wrote are valuable not only because they make clear that ideas, feelings and words do not simply arrive in an artless fashion but also because they begin to make complex the idea of spontaneity. Spontaneity is highly valued as a component of the writing process. It provides a rationale for those adopting non-interventionist approaches to writing in cultural policy and those advocating intervention within a framework of non-directive pedagogy. Drawing out the materialism of the writing life challenges both positions.

The strongest challenge to the myth that writers simply let it flow comes from the attention they paid to developing routine. Within the official discourse of writing, routine is presented as a given. It is dealt with in the first chapter of most books offering advice and encouragement to writers, tutors mention it in the first few sessions of their courses and it regularly crops up in interviews and talks with established writers. But routine was unevenly taken up in the writing lives of those I interviewed.

People talked about the value of writing routines but only one or two actively sought to establish them. Mona's routine was driven by necessity and thwarted by her domestic responsibilities:

> I started off with a notebook in my handbag, writing ideas down. It is still there. In practice it doesn't happen because my mind's full of all other administrative clutter. (...) When I write it's probably exactly down to three hours on a Tuesday evening, starting at 9.30 till 12.30, and that is purely driven by the fact that there is a Wednesday morning course that I still try to get to and I want to produce something for that. So every Wednesday I say 'Well, I have done something but it isn't polished and I only did it last night.' (...) I need that week to think of ideas and some weeks the idea is there by about the third day and I feel 'I ought to get that down on paper immediately' but there is usually something more urgent that I need to do. (Mona)

For Greg, routine came to the fore when regular paid acceptances led him to think seriously about writing's potential to supplement his earnings. His sense of compulsion, indicated by the repetition of the word 'should', signals the complex, unstable relationship between writing as leisure and as work:

> It's very unplanned and I tend to work in splurges. (...) I don't have any plan at all and I know I should but I don't.

> *Why do you know you should?*

> If I had stuff that was being sent off on a regular basis I would be having regular success or regular failure. I don't know but I should, I should be sending stuff off.

CREATIVE WRITING

Whose voice is that? Who is saying 'you should do this'?

My own voice, it's the very practical side of me and the very practical writer side of me that says 'Look, if you're going to make a success of this writing then you've got to be sending stuff on a regular basis'. (...) I don't think I'm as determined as perhaps I should be and I'm not as practical as I should be. (...) I treat it a lot of the time as a hobby. (Greg)

Some writers refused routine:

When I retired from teaching I sort of almost made resolutions to myself: 'I'm never going to do anything boring, I'm never going to get myself into a routine.' (Irene)

I don't have written into my timetable I am a writer so therefore ... I don't think: 'I am going to write'. But if I get an idea or perhaps I've been reading something and something has crystallised I might write that down. (Rachel)

Membership of a group or course imposed a routine for several writers. Indeed, the discipline and motivation to write which socialised writing activities provide is one of their most highly valued attributes. In practice, though, it often meant writing the night before the class met, illustrating how the obligation to the group bolstered individual resolve and enabled writing that might otherwise not have been written.

The discipline a group provided was generally felt to be a good thing but there were times when it could work against the writer. Barry described using odd snatches of time at work to make notes, which every so often he wrote up as a finished piece and sent out for publication. Once he began attending a group he found he stopped writing during its holiday break. It seemed, as several others reported, that the group's rhythm had pulled him into its orbit:

Four weeks and I never wrote a thing. I was beginning to wonder had I lost it? Had I lost the desire and had I lost the ability to write? (...)

When the course started again and I started writing again it all came
back just as if it had never left me. (Barry)

Several people expressed the view that a routine would be
beneficial but showed no real inclination towards establishing
one. This conflict between what ought to be done and what was
being done also bears on the desire sometimes expressed for
knowledge and information about writing. During the interviews
several people gave back to me wisdom about writing which they
clearly respected, but held quite separate from their practice. I
began to anticipate this aspect of the discussion whenever the
phrase 'they do say' occurred:

> They do say you should set aside, even if it's only half an hour a week,
> you should set it aside. (...) If the muse is on me I can sort of get out
> the computer or a bit of paper and scribble away happily and not
> even realise time is passing. It's all fits and starts really. (Josie)

Josie's experience of being caught up in something that demanded
to be written described her writing process much more accurately.
The ambivalence about routine signals how influential was the
intuitive approach to writing. Although many people were
sensitive to their writing rhythms and able to identify better and
worse conditions for writing they persisted in seeing routine as
mechanical rather than a valuable part of their repertoire for
writing.

Self-awareness about what encouraged their writing was most
apparent when people discussed where they wrote. This seemed
to be an aspect of the writer's life over which some control could
be exercised. Everyone reported a definite place for writing,
usually in a room or part of a room at home especially set-aside
for the purpose. Only Rachel preferred to be away from home
when writing. Most needed to be alone with reference books to
hand and access to a typewriter or, increasingly, a computer. In
some cases a study had been set aside for the use of someone else,
such as a daughter or son studying at college, or was a general-
purpose office area within the home.

Women found it hardest to escape domestic distractions.

CREATIVE WRITING

Mona describes being unable to make use of a spare bedroom kitted out as an office, illustrating that for women the issue is more complicated than physical access, important though this is:

> It's an isolated room in the house. I'm sitting up there and if my little boy cries I think 'What are they doing?' If it's quiet I'm thinking 'What are they doing?' I can't just sit in this room, nicely laid out as an office should be, and work. So what I actually do is I have a PC on a trolley in the dining room and I wheel it to where I want to be at that point in the day and I can type away on that while they're watching television or playing a game or whatever. (Mona)

Only four people, all women, lived alone and for the rest there was a great need to be able to switch off from life around them. One shared a study with his daughter, talked about needing to 'sort of be in my own little world without any other distractions at all' (Greg). Although men were most insistent about the importance of domestic peace, they more than women talked about writing opportunities created by small amounts of free time at work:

> I write on all sorts of things, on anything that's sort of blank and flat and writeable on. (…) Those bits of paper go with me everywhere. They can be pulled out for five minutes, two minutes, you can work on something. (Barry)

Many women worked in the home, where time is not so clearly demarcated into lunch breaks and slack periods. Most women working outside the home were engaged in work that was social, as teachers, nurses or clerical workers, and their work contained little opportunity for reflection or writing. Domestic space, especially in the context of motherhood, could be ambivalent. Nell had found that although motherhood made concentration difficult, it also had advantages:

> One's time is much more flexible. I mean, small children do fall asleep during the day, they do go to playgroup and in that sense a mother has more freedom than the father because he's usually in a job where he can't go off and write for an hour. (Nell)

Winifred chose her writing room for its view of the landscape, which inspired much of her writing. This freedom to keep a room for writing was a privilege that Winifred, now living alone, was very conscious of. Irene, Nell and Pearl also lived by themselves after long periods of living with others. They often talked about how much easier it was to prioritise writing and work to its ebbs and flows when there was no one else around. Irene noted a change in how much time she could spend writing when she had visitors and spoke of how difficult it was to write when living with other people:

> No matter how sympathetic they are it's much easier to say 'I have got to write this essay before we go off somewhere' than to say 'I have got to write this poem'. (Irene)

Several people talked about ideas for writing coming to them as they relaxed just before falling asleep. Some kept a notebook close by the bed and others actually got up to write but this caused friction with their partners. For many, the computer's location determined their choice of a place to write. Everyone talked about the significance of moving from pencil to pen to print while drafting work in terms of getting closer to the realisation of the idea or vision being worked on. Only two women, Tina and Mona, wrote directly onto a word processor:

> I'm quite a wordy person. (...) It's a very nice feeling to have the pen going off and off and off but it's not necessarily good for your writing. So the word processor did help me sharpen up. (Tina)

> If I write longhand the paper is just so cluttered and untidy and scribbled on I just can't organise my thoughts. (...) On a word processor you can cut in, you can say 'I'll just get this paragraph down, whether it's the beginning, middle or end, it doesn't matter. (...) It is much less binding than paper, and it's there for you to play with. (Mona)

For others, the move to print signalled closure of the generative aspect of writing and the start of a more critical, editing stance:

> Somebody I worked with said – and I took it on board – that if you're

serious about your writing you will type it up double spaced on a white sheet because that's the only way you can look at it sufficiently to see 'What is it I've got?' (Al)

When I think 'Well, yes, I can make something of this. This won't be it but it could be going to be something like this' It helps then if I type it out. (...) I can see more what it would read like, that I stood back from it a bit and then as like as not I'll just leave that lying there for a bit, a week or two. (...) It's a terribly messy business, very, very messy. (Irene)

People wrote a variety of types of work across the spectrum from non-fiction articles and sketches to historical, romantic, literary and horror novels by way of autobiography, drama, children's books, short stories, songs and poetry. There was, however, a distinct bias towards shorter pieces of writing, which may reflect the influence of reading work aloud in the groups. In most cases, what people had started to write had been a matter of chance: prompted by a tutor's suggestion, writing exercise or the preference of a writer-in-residence. Although it was rare for people to express specific interest in writing autobiography the majority identified life around them as a source of inspiration. 'Who I am and where I come from', as Tina put it. This drive to record the world they lived in was also often motivated by a desire to challenge the traditional representations of that world:

Things that I've seen, about where I live and the sort of people that I live amongst. I quite like the idea that the image people put across isn't always what they're really about. (...) That it isn't all there is to them. (Kim)

Nell used autobiographical sources and she was forceful in her views about the value of popular autobiography for readers and writers. She took great issue with the sentimentality that often characterises autobiographical work:

People write in their memoirs what they think they ought to have felt. What they actually felt was something much more complex than

what they think they ought to have felt. (...) But I think if you once dare
to face the contradictions and complexity of one's own feelings it
does nudge people into facing theirs, too. (Nell)

Such rigorous engagement with personal experience was not
always evident. Sometimes writing was rooted in personal
experience for more passive reasons. Some people believed they
could – or perhaps should – only write about events and feelings
they had experienced first-hand. Amongst writers who drew on
emotional and personal sources for writing a documentary
impulse to write was considered the most appropriate and
valuable reason for writing. Mona was the only person to express
concern about the limitation she felt this brought to her work:

The norm is thinking of a person in my past or someone in the family
and projecting that from there. I would love to get away from that.
(...) It's just putting that into practice and trying a bit harder to be
original. (Mona)

This reliance on life as a source for writing sometimes meant
writers waited to be inspired by experience rather than actively
sought out story lines or other inspirations. Cleveland's culture of
writing drew on the values and examples of the community arts
movement of the 1970s and 1980s and in particular the writers'
workshop and local publishing movement associated with the
FWWCP. A fundamental principle of that work is its rootedness in
the life experience of its writers. At its best, such life writing is an
active process combining oral and local history research methods
with rigorous exploration of individual social and psychological
formation. During its passage into Cleveland's culture of writing
this approach had lost some of its political rigour, diffused by more
general concerns with writing and widening participation.

In part this relates to how 'the local' is defined. Within FWWCP
contexts local was very local indeed, perhaps a street or ward
area. In the wider communities of Liverpool, Manchester or
London within which they existed there was a whole gamut of
writing activities, including those with a more commercial or
professional emphasis. These FWWCP groups existed within a

culture of writing in relation to which they were, in Raymond William's sense of the term, clearly oppositional (Williams 1980). In Cleveland, the absence of a well-established mainstream culture of writing created an impossible contradiction for the emerging culture of writing. It not only sought to include within 'the local' the whole county region, thereby blurring social distinctions based on class, wealth and education, but also tried to value equally all the writing aspirations that emerged.

This partly accounts for the sometimes passive relation to writing I identified in many of the people I interviewed and observed. It also illustrates a larger political contradiction of cultural democracy; which is that its concentration on getting people involved in writing did not always pay attention to the substantive writing produced.

Nell's account stands out because of the rigour with which she addressed these issues. Although she relies on inspiration too, she describes responsiveness more akin to an active readying of herself. In this she is much closer to the artistic practices and aesthetic theory of the original Romantic poets. Keatsian negative capability was a vigorous act of critical creation, not a passive waiting, just as Wordsworth and Coleridge worked to achieve meditative states of heightened consciousness. As the ideology of romantic idealism filtered down into the practice of late-twentieth century creative writing it lost much of its content and, as ideology so often does, obscured its material base, presenting culture as nature. Nell's account of how her writing takes shape avoids the vague and imprecise terms in which writing's mystical dimensions are usually described:

I'm doing something unconnected with writing, I'm dusting, and something in the external world begins to speak to me with authority and if there's any idea involved it's the idea 'I think it would be a good idea to share it'. But even that's not an idea so much as a genuine commandment, because if I leave it unexpressed the only way I can define my state would be to say that I would feel myself in a state of something analogous to a thief, someone who held something in stewardship and was not making it available. (...) This is very difficult to talk about because you feel you're always on the brink of what I call the Sunday School mentality. (...) The sort of thing where they say, you know, 'God has given me a gift.' You know, I must give it to them, whether they want it or not. There is a lovely expression of C. S. Lewis – 'She lived for others. You could tell the others by their hunted looks.' But I feel that whatever comes through me already belongs to whoever reads it, and if I were to leave it unwritten or to write it in a way that conveyed it less than accurately or brought it into focus less perfectly, then I am failing in a duty towards that person.

This is always a sort of conflict because I'm coming round to a terminology that doesn't belong to our age, like duty, like vision. But I think in a way it may be part of my task to translate these concepts of duty into a different world, a world in which they're not a narrow, moral thing. (Nell)

This strongly inspirational basis for writing was echoed by other writers although they rarely showed Nell's degree of active reflection:

It tends to be when I feel deeply about something. (...) There's always been a sense of 'I have to write that'. (...) I mean, you can't just sit down and think: 'Well, I'll write about something or other.' (Winifred)

The question of sustaining independent writing projects came up on several occasions. For some, it was a sign of confidence and maturity to be able to formulate and work on their independent writing ventures. Irene realised she could measure her progress when the poems she was most satisfied with originated with her rather than the group she attended. For the majority of writers, however, it was striking how few could identify characterising themes in their work. Indeed, several depended on the tutor or writing group to provide the stimulus to write and one or two seemed genuinely unable to develop ideas for writing without some input from their tutors.

Josie provides an interesting example of this experience. She had been involved in writing activities of one kind or another throughout her life and talked at length about trying different forms and genres. In discussing plays, something she wanted to try, it became clear that part of her problem was having nothing to write about. She talked about how things started and then fizzled out and described her main subject as 'a slice of life' but could not see the link between this and her inability to finish pieces. If a piece lacks movement, as the 'slice of life' almost always will, it is difficult material to do much with. This, combined with the absence of a strong purpose or obsession in her writing, was a problem for her, yet she did not seem aware of this. It was as if the techniques and apparatus of writing could somehow stand in for its content and motivation:

> I must admit the thought of writing something like a play, you know, appealed to me for a while and I just couldn't think of what to write a play about. (Josie)

It is as if the idea of being a writer will stand in for its reality. Yet, for all her diffidence, Josie also demonstrated tenacity as a writer and this warrants further exploration. Josie was, after all, a working mother, holding down a full-time professional job and continuing after 15 years to devote the greater part of her leisure time to writing and writing activities. If this was delusion, it was delusion on a grand scale. But the dominant impression gained from the interview, and confirmed by reading its transcript, is of deference and apology. Josie's accounts of her own writing are hedged with qualification. She talks about 'something like a play' and prefaces every reference to her work with the tag 'little'. She is trying to take writing seriously but to do so has to contend not only with external pressures in her life but also with a process which undermines her from the inside by keeping her so busy with writing activity of various kinds that she is prevented from isolating what aspects of writing she wants to get serious about.

Josie stands out not because she is typical of the common writer but because the clarity of her thwarted ambition is exceptional. To some extent her experience supports Ann Schlee's argument that creative writing activities are harmful because they muffle the necessary encounter between the writer and their writing. She argues that teaching creative writing distorts potential writer's natural talent by preventing them discovering 'what it is out of their own experience of life they most wish to write about' and before the writer has 'found the confidence to speak with his own voice' (Schlee 1982: 44).

There is limited point in pursuing the argument about whether creative writing activities are, in general terms, a good or bad thing. Much more relevant is the need to contextualise interventions seeking to widen participation in writing in terms of the broader social processes and determinations with which they are engaged. Josie's experience flags an important issue for practitioners, namely the need for writers to develop substantive content.

For the majority, creative writing activities were both perceived as, and appeared to be, a positive resource for writers and their writing. Indeed, for several of the people I interviewed, seeking out creative writing activities reinforced and developed their recognition that writing was an important aspect of their identity. The kinds of activities they became involved with ranged from correspondence courses, residential and non-residential writing courses, writers' groups and circles to the buying or borrowing of technical and discursive books about writing. No one approached these options systematically, they were inducted into various activities depending on what was available locally, what they did first and their financial and personal circumstances. What they got out of these activities was fellowship, discipline and motivation, stimulus for writing and more general social stimulus. Fellowship was always rated highly. Getting on well with the group was a vital pre-condition for its other benefits:

> I go because I experience fellowship there, which I find spiritually supportive. I don't really go to learn techniques. (…) I think if I if I went to learn anything it would be more appropriate perhaps to go to a monastery or something like that to learn meditation techniques. (Nell)

> It gives me permission to write and to talk about it. People always want to know what you write for. I never tell people I write. They think

you've got illusions of grandeur, you can see them thinking who does she think she is? (Woman, Kinder)

One of the most important benefits of the writing activities was discipline and motivation. Although creative writing activities rarely attract people who have done no writing at all, almost everybody was doing less writing than they wanted to prior to joining. The amount of confidence it takes to continue to write in a context of little recognition and encouragement is enormous. There was frequent testimony to losing motivation when it was just you and the writing:

You mess on, you think you'll do things and you don't. (Woman, Bleaklow)

It imposes a discipline. If you sit at home and think I'll write something you know no one will see it and you don't bother.

I don't think I'd write if I didn't come here. (Man and Woman, High Tor)

I need prods in the back. I am lazy. I might start, but I don't finish things. (Woman, Bleaklow)

Cleveland's culture of writing bolstered its writer's confidence by legitimating writing as an activity in general and for specific pieces of writing:

Writing is not only an all right thing to do, but it's what you're expected to do. This is so important to me in the face of so many other things crying out to be done. (Woman, Kinder)

Knowing that the work would be heard helped to get it written. In this way, the motivating aspect of creative writing activities becomes inextricably linked to the convivial aspects. However, the social side of creative writing activities was never the main focus. It was rare for participants to meet up with each other outside the groups and the groups themselves did not organise purely social events.

Myth two: in thrall to publishing

It's the first question people ask if they know you write. Are you published? Publishing isn't important to me but I think you can't call yourself a writer otherwise. (Mona)

The word 'publish' has its origins in the word 'public' which, the Shorter Oxford English Dictionary tells us, is 'Usu. opp. to PRIVATE' (Onions 1966: 1613). It is an apposite definition from which to start untangling the skein of assumptions which trail after the word as it moves, generally elusively, through the writing life of the common writer. One of the most pervasive myths about such writers, and the one that can be used so effectively to belittle them, concerns the power that the pursuit of publication holds for them.

Graham Harthill's survey of writing courses in Edinburgh found that the most popular personal goal was to get published (Harthill 1994: 9). He comments that this is a predictable enough goal but perhaps also the easiest answer to give. Arguably, it is also what many people assumed the answer to be and they gave what they believed to be the right answer. Harthill hints at the complexity of publishing for his participants, especially the 'deep possibilities for writing which are not necessarily precluded by publication' (Harthill 1994: 9). My findings confirmed his hunch, indicating how complex is the interaction between making progress, which all participants appear committed to, and achieving publication, which attracts ambivalent, often negative, feelings from the majority of participants.

Publishing is also problematic for tutors. Zoe Fairbairns offers a lucid account of, and explanation for, the difficulties it brings:

There's a feeling that getting published is like passing the driving test: you get through if you're 'good enough.' And since I'm saying this work is good, why isn't publication automatic? (...) Of course every serious writer wants to be published and paid eventually, and quite right too. And it must seem bewilderingly cruel that although I think I can identify those manuscripts which will never find a publisher, I

> cannot prescribe any formula to ensure that one will. I myself still
> expect to get rejected, and my expectations are still fulfilled.
> Rejection is shocking, humiliating and painful, and there's still no
> remedy other than to get on with the next thing. (Fairbairns 1984: 9–10)

Only a minority of Cleveland writers actively sought or achieved publication. Individuals, such as Chrissie, Doug, Nell and Irene, who prioritised publishing were reasonably successful – proving the truth of the view that persistence is crucial to publishing success. They spanned the gamut from literary to commercial outlets. Nell was regularly published in *Stand*, Chrissie in *People's Friend*, Doug in *Yachting Monthly* and all four regularly won or were placed in a variety of local and regional competitions.

The relative lack of interest in publishing suggests that writing itself and social relations short of publishing sustained by the writing culture were sufficient motivation and reward for writers. This should not be surprising. The majority of people who participate in sports and cultural activities do so able to make progress and embrace standards of excellence without any need to measure themselves against professionals within the field. In discussion with the groups and courses publishing was always given as an important indication of progress but there was a sense of this being an automatic or anticipated response which participants did not necessarily set personal store by.

Whenever comments were made during group interviews about publishing being the only reliable indicator of progress alternative viewpoints, stressing personal gains for work, study or relationships, were always voiced. Many groups, too, were at pains to distinguish themselves from the kind of group which prioritises publishing above all else:

> This isn't the sort of group that has a prize for the person who earned
> most in the preceding month and we don't clap if anyone does get
> published. (Man, Mersey)

This mythical group, the mutual admiration society, was often invoked. There were individuals who lived up to this stereotype, cheques in one hand and a subscription to *Freelance Market News* in the other, knocking off a *Reader's Digest* filler here, a greeting card rhyme there while working on the big project – a historical romance or a sitcom treatment – but they were part of the mix which characterised all but the few specialist creative writing groups and courses.

As might have been expected, publication was viewed as the main arbiter of progress more often in groups than in courses, but even there it rarely had the centrality it would in a Writers' Circle:

> To me, if something were published it wouldn't be any the better for being published. (Man, Mersey)

The importance of publication was recognised and then set aside with much more animated discussion taking place about the progress of the writing itself. This suggests that doing the writing for its own satisfaction was characteristic of courses and groups alike.

For many writers involved in creative writing activities, it is writing, not publishing, that matters. This in turn means that it is the creative writing activities themselves, rather than editorial and reader relationships within publishing networks, which provided them with a forum through which their writing is developed and validated. This is not, as the myths about publishing's importance to writers would have it, a compensatory activity for failed or aspirant writers. Rather, it suggests that publishing provides too narrow a purpose and value framework to account for the individual satisfaction, and any subsequent broader social effects, which participants gain from organised creative writing activities. In the next chapter the third myth of the common writer, the charge that they need to cluster in mutual admiration societies, is used to explore in greater detail what it is these other purposes, outcomes and values might consist of.

Chapter nine

Questions of progress and value

This chapter continues to show close-ups from the big picture of Cleveland's culture of writing and to set these accounts of practice alongside those given by cultural commentators and policy makers. Here, the concern with how participants in organised creative writing activities make sense of their activities is focused directly on questions of value and progress. The value participants identify in these activities often hinges on their progress as writers and this highlights the role of group feedback and criticism. Feedback is often a contentious issue for groups and courses, and gives rise to the third myth of the common writer: the myth of the writing group as a place of fawning mutual admiration. I want to hold that charge in mind as we explore the three aspects of progress most frequently reported by participants in creative writing activities. Firstly, they related areas of personal development, such as increased confidence, a wider social circle and general intellectual stimulus, to their involvement in creative writing activities. Secondly, they sometimes saw progress in terms of the wider educational opportunities creative writing activities introduced. Finally, as might be expected, they measured progress by changes in the writing itself.

Changing people

Writing's contribution to the development of identity is the source of one of its most fundamental values, especially if identity is formed in difficult personal circumstances. For very many people, writing was this kind of lifetime's work, stretching back into teens and childhood. As Mona demonstrates, writing had been something more than a pastime. It had played a vital part in bringing equilibrium to a chaotic life. Her teenage diary writing had been a way to cope with the many difficulties she experienced in a troubled family. Although she felt she had outgrown the purely emotional catharsis writing provided, she continued to engage with self-identity as a source and purpose for writing. She experimented with writing that drew on, but was not restricted to, her personal experience:

> Inside me there was this mass of life experiences (...) that I've come through, not unscarred, probably quite badly scarred, and it's no longer a therapy need but it's more wanting to put it to some use I suppose and to give it out rather than clutter up my inside with it.
> (Mona)

Many writers have used writing in this consciously therapeutic way and the work of Graham Harthill (1993), Gillie Bolton (1999), Fiona Sampson and Celia Hunt (1998) led to writing being recognised as a therapeutic art. In 1994 the Poetry Society established a Special Interests Group on Issue of Health, Healing and Personal Development which provided a forum for several discrete projects and activists who had previously worked in relative isolation from each other on issues to do with the arts and health care. In 1996 this group constituted itself as The Association for Literary Arts in Personal Development (LAPIDUS). This movement is rooted in the observation that many people informally use writing therapeutically and it seeks to promote this as well as to develop a more robust rationale and methodology for writing in professional therapeutic practice.

I found numerous examples of writing used for healing but I also found considerable tension about this aspect of writing in some of the courses and groups. People often made dismissive remarks about writing for therapy or writing for yourself. This emerged in a paradoxical fashion. Although the majority of participants in Cleveland's culture of writing reported that publishing was not a priority for them what they chose to write was often determined by commercial imperatives. So, for example, competent twist-in-the-tail or romance stories would be considered legitimate, serious writing while work of a more personal nature was frequently dismissed as self-indulgent. Cleveland's culture of writing contained no political rationale for writing centred on personal development. Elsewhere in Britain this strand in local cultures of writing often developed from or in dialogue with, feminist cultural activity. But Cleveland's complex relationship to feminism, as a result of the 1988 child sexual abuse cases, rendered feminism problematic as a public discourse and this severely constrained its role in organising and influencing socio-political, educational and cultural activities. Its absence from the culture of writing created space for a technical discourse centred on craft skills. As a result, form was often divorced from content and discussion of both concerned only with what was deemed marketable, even if the writers did not aspire to publication.

Tutors, just as much as students, were uneasy about emotional content and displays of vulnerability. This effectively meant there was no public acknowledgement of creative writing's role in personal development and in Cleveland this kept hidden what many other local cultures of writing promote as one of writing's major benefits:

> I want them to talk about experiences and emotions, to come to terms and deal with anger, conflict, despair – the biggies. But it's a hidden aim. Not everybody is as interested as me in self-development. (...) I worry, too, about emotional issues. People might get into deep water and go away feeling vulnerable or rejected. (Tutor 2, Kinder)

It was striking how rarely the value of writing for personal development was raised in group discussions. But, despite the absence of a public discourse of personal development, writing did change people in this way. It often took the form of small enrichments and compensations to fragile, sometimes severely damaged, self-esteem. Many people had become involved with writing activities as a result of upheaval in their personal lives, so it is reasonable to suppose that the personal value of writing expressed in one-to-one interviews was also shared by some of those I encountered in groups. But the self-realisation that people talked to me about privately was kept very close. Although highly motivating at a personal level, it was rarely expressed directly in their work and where it was, as the following extracts show, it would not necessarily be shared with others, even in the writing group:

> It lets me come out of myself without making a song and dance of it because nobody else needs see it, you know what I mean? It's like a private thing and a public thing as well. (...) It gives you a sense of being (Tina)

> When I've applied for jobs and done curriculum vitae, when it comes to hobbies and interests I dry up. But now I think: 'Well, I could say I write' and that makes me feel good. (...) It's not the reason why I am doing it but it sums up why it's important. (...) It makes me value myself more because it's an active pursuit not passive. It's something I've chosen to do. (Mona)

> If I don't keep up writing then I affect the expression of my relationship to myself, and value to myself. (Al)

Recognising and articulating progress in terms of personal development was also complicated for writers in Cleveland because the writing infrastructure made a structural separation between equal arts, which foregrounded personal development and self-expression, and its literature development functions, which were the point of contact for courses and groups. Personal development and self-expression became identified with special needs, an association that sometimes distanced them as a purpose and outcome for writers more generally. Today social inclusion has a powerful purchase and disabled people are finally beginning to claim their rightful place in society, which makes it easy to forget how recently different attitudes prevailed.

Cleveland's local culture of writing in the 1990s was no more prejudiced than other areas of the country or sector. For example, when community writing first gained popularity in the late-1970s it focused almost entirely on traditional political class politics.

CREATIVE WRITING

There were many bitter arguments within the FWWCP about this as its work extended, and especially when Olive Rogers, the second national organiser, began working with prisoners, people with special needs and people who used mental health services. At the time, some members felt not only that this was a diversion from the organisation's focus on working class writers but also that it would actively discourage working-class people's involvement. These fears were unfounded, and did not prevent this work taking place, and today the FWWCP is a profoundly inclusive organisation.

In Cleveland discussions with the students and tutor of Knarr Quarry, a closed course that was held in a day centre for disabled people, showed a clear and immediate positive articulation of personal development:

> What do I get out of coming here? It gives me a sense of purpose, it gives me something to do. With being disabled all I could do was go to town, walk about with difficulty, go home and watch television. I'd always wanted to write, but it was physically painful. The computers have dealt with that. (Man, Knarr Quarry)

For another student, a man in his early twenties, writing helped to restore the self-esteem lost following an accident in which he had sustained severe physical and neurological injuries:

> After the accident I thought I wasn't fitting in. I thought I'd never fit in. Before the accident I wouldn't give tuppence about meeting people, but I got frightened of meeting people. Learning to write again (…) I'm getting my confidence back. (Man, Knarr Quarry)

He talked about how much he had enjoyed English at school and his fear that all that side of his personality had gone for good. Several months after joining the course he was asked to edit the day centre's newsletter. Personal development of this kind, while undoubtedly therapeutic, is not therapy. Perhaps the distrust of personal development as a focus for writing stems from confusion between the two?

Changing ideas about learning

Cleveland's creative writing activities attracted a small number of people for whom it was simply one adult education course amongst the many others they had taken. For the majority, though, adult education was a new experience and for several women in particular, getting involved in creative writing activities led to more substantial involvement with education. This outcome is not precluded for men, of course, but several men were in full-time work and were always the significant minority in the classes:

> Creative writing is like a higher education without having to pass your
> lowers. (Man, Bleaklow)

Tina and Kim returned to further and higher education as a direct result of their creative writing activities. For Tina, this involved overcoming a deep-seated sense of her lack of entitlement to higher education:

> People like me just don't go to university. (...) I watched it being built
> and I'd walked through it but never for one minute had I thought it
> had any connection to me. (Tina)

Creative writing activities are well suited to encourage a return to learning of this kind. The content and nature of the sessions are so different from formal education that they create space to reconsider negative school experiences and to boost self-esteem through successful learning. The emphasis creative writing can give to personal experience and memory as a source for writing prompts the kind of reflection which, with encouragement and opportunity, can lead participants to rewrite the narratives of their lives in ways that permit new directions to emerge. However, to achieve this it is necessary to engage directly with the content and context of their experience.

Kim's experience illustrates how creative writing catalysed a return to learning. Having found her way to a writing group by chance Kim went on to join a theatre group after which she applied unsuccessfully for a degree course in drama. She

195

continued to write and became involved in voluntary youth and community work based at a combined library and community centre, which led to part-time work as a library assistant. Some years later, she was regularly performing in a poetry cabaret at venues throughout the Northeast and studying full-time for a degree in public administration. Both strands, the writing and the studying, came together after graduation when she was appointed to a full-time arts administration post in the local authority's leisure services department:

> Writing was the first thing I did that didn't involve being with the children. (...) Two or three of us were single parents, but everybody else were just normal people, you know, you weren't there as a mother, you were there as yourself and that was like totally different. It gave me a lot of confidence. And having to stand up in front of an audience and perform gave me a lot more confidence. I think I thought if I can do that I can do anything. (...) What has writing contributed to my life? It's just sort of completely changed it. (...) It made you feel that perhaps you could, you know. From saying: Well, I might be able to do this, it was: Well if I can do this, I might be able to do that as well, you know. And if I can do that, well then I can do something. (Kim)

Kim compared herself to a neighbour. Both women had attended the same mother-and-toddler group and became involved with various activities and educational opportunities provided by the local community centre. Kim's neighbour had taken a vocational route, helping out at the mother-and-toddler group, then the playgroup, and taking a child-care qualification had led to paid work with the community centre. Kim took a different route, but she felt it was almost accidental. Kim did not seek out writing, but she did choose to stay with it. Writing was thus paradoxically positioned for her as central and incidental to her process of personal growth.

Sometimes the changes, though no less far reaching at a personal level, operate in a less public forum. A severely dyslexic man talked about how realising he needed to read in order to improve as a writer had helped his motivation for dealing with reading difficulties that were causing major difficulties in his working life.

Changing writing

The most frequent response to questions about progress was to report improvement, often using that very word. It is an interesting word, compressing as it does a whole tradition of adult education which was, above all else, driven by the practice and ideology of improvement for self and others (Harrison 1961, Purvis 1989, Kelly 1992, Fieldhouse & Associates 1996). Interesting, too, that its original meaning is 'to turn to profit' (Onions 1996: 972) – something often a source of tension within creative writing. But in this context, what was significant was what improvement meant to the participants reporting it. They identified improvements in two main areas: the discipline and habit of writing and in technical and craft skill. It was unusual to hear references to content, theme or subject matter as sites of improvement.

Participants used the words 'formed', 'crafted' and 'worked' to describe the kind of changes they noticed in their writing. The guidelines against which these craft skills were developed largely came from group discussion or, in the taught courses, handouts and recommended reading. Chrissie's experience illustrates how belonging to a group enables participants to adapt and extend their writing skills.

She described her capacity to write rhyming poetry as an instinct but had used the tutor's input, gathered over several courses and from several different tutors, as the basis for experimenting. Tutors had explained the metrical organisation of poetry and introduced different poetical forms, such as the haiku, sonnet and sestina. Occasionally Chrissie wrote poems which did not rhyme but her main areas of crafting lay in organising the music and rhythm of a piece and in experimenting with different rhyme schemes. She talked about the satisfaction it gave her to re-draft poems she had written several years previously using her new and ever increasing knowledge of poetic structure:

> The instinct to write it properly is there now, whereas before it was just the instinct to write. (...) A line out of context or a line with more syllables than it should have, or the rhythm isn't right, or the rhyme isn't right, or there's something in it that's too flowery or too this or too that. I can seem to see it more now than I could when I wrote it. (Chrissie)

Chrissie was unapologetic in her defence of rhyme. She knew the argument that said rhyming poetry, especially the sentimental kind she wrote, leads to lazy writing as pursuit of the rhyme rides roughshod over meaning and predictability deadens emotional impact. But she was confident her poetry avoided these traps. She had a clear rationale for what she chose to do. Her ability to speak at length and in detail about her method shows a conscious control of her medium:

> I practice different rhyme schemes, they're not all abab. (...) I play around with a few lines in my head and write odd phrases down, and I always like to have a beginning and I always like to have an end before I start. (...) I just build on that. My poems all have the meaning there for people to see, and they're lighter. (...) You don't have to delve into it and think: 'Now what does that mean?' My meanings are always there, clear – and the rhyme helps to fix the meaning for me. (Chrissie)

One of the most powerful correctives to the mystification of writing that the inspirational paradigm creates is to make explicit how much writing depends on habit and method. Misunderstanding writing as something that is 'right first time' or the writer as someone who simply takes dictation, acts as a powerful block to writing because it is so antithetical to the incremental and provisional nature of the actual writing process. For many participants in Cleveland's culture of writing this was where they saw most progress with their writing:

> I work harder at it. I used to not write anything until ideas came to me and I'd think 'Oh, that's worth writing down and I'd write it. But now I can go and say 'I'm going to do some writing'. (Barry)

Greg described how, under the influence of his writing tutors, he had developed a method of generating stories utilising notes for planning a decision – making that saved time when he came to write. Decision-making, in the sense of choosing between options in subject matter, plot and character development, narrative style and language, is fundamental to writing. Doing this in advance gave Greg a notated skeletal structure numbered paragraph by paragraph. Summarised in this way, his method sounds stultifyingly mechanical: writing by numbers without any imaginative flow. But this method was powerful for Greg in two ways. First, it replaced the time – consuming and uncreative approach he had been using previously:

> I used to sit down with the very basic idea in front of my keyboard and write away and I could write for an hour and think: 'No, it's rubbish,' and delete it and start again. (Greg)

Second, Greg was the sort or writer who needed to work with structure. Given this, it is better he has a method which works than one which doesn't. The structure also provided him with a framework that allowed him to hold and develop ideas which advanced the story. It enabled Greg to take conscious control of judgements that for experienced or expert writers would be naturalised as unconscious processes:

> This germ might have taken quite some time coming together. I might have got it, I might have been lying in bed at night time trying to get to sleep and then this germ of an idea comes along and then I think: 'That's worth exploring, that's worth elaborating,' and over the next few days, going to work, idling time, it comes together and I start to put faces to the characters and names and so on. So I might have been sitting on it for several days before I actually sit down even and commit myself to paper. (Greg)

This method enabled Greg to start work on a major writing project. Not only had it provided the practical means to organise and develop his material, but also confirmed his sense of himself as a writer by giving him conscious control of technique and skill.

Men more often than women saw the value of a highly

structured approach to writing. One area of improvement that women talked about more than men was the use of language. Pearl was far more animated talking about her passion for words and language than when discussing particular pieces of her writing. People introducing themselves for the first time at a writing group often give a love of language as a reason for coming along. Women also paid attention to their language histories. Mona, for example, talked about the way the style demanded by her previous job in the Civil Service had seeped into and spoiled her creative work:

> Very ponderous language, ambiguous language, so you weren't putting forwards any strong opinions. You had to be very bland. (...) That really stereotyped my writing for a couple of years. (Mona)

Irene talked about how needing to find the precise word for specific feelings and incidents had made her aware that she had two distinct styles. Her explicitly political work was tightly constructed and used plain language, her more personal works had a looser structure and made more use of imagery and metaphor. Her current project, about war and gender, aimed to fuse her styles:

> The only way that one could possibly say anything at all about that has to be through poetry. I couldn't possibly do it in prose. I want to catch a feeling without delving into it deeply, because this is it and you don't have to explain it; you just feel it. I would very much like it if that could come together in one poem. (Irene)

Talking about progress

Talking one-to-one with writers made it possible to contextualise change and progress in relation to the detail of an individual writing process. Discussion of progress in the courses and groups had a different focus. There, progress most often meant internalising the habits, values and judgements of professional writers. People sometimes talked about making a serious attempt at getting work published or becoming independent from the writing group or course but this was unusual.

Answers to the question about progress were unusual in that they clustered group by group. This was especially noticeable in taught courses and it suggested their sense of what constituted progress was determined by the tutor. It formed part of a hidden curriculum, too, as it emerged that questions of good writing, bad writing, progress or stagnation had never previously been discussed in the group.

A major distinction between groups was whether indications of progress were externalised or internalised. External indicators included reactions from the rest of the group, the tutor's opinion or success in seeking publication. Internal indicators included a changed attitude towards their writing and the development of insight and judgement about how complete or effective their work was. The following quotations indicate the range:

> I've learnt to develop an inner critical ear and the group sharpens that up, confirms it. The feedback confirms where it does and doesn't work. You get approval from reading out. It gives you a good idea how a piece is coming over. (Man, Thames)

> I tend not to look to the group in terms of progress because I've yardsticks outside to measure that. I like to listen to others. It's very refreshing after the claustrophobia of getting close to your own work. It's sometimes difficult to know just how far what you've written is comprehensible to other people. Reading aloud, how far you're communicating can be answered pretty exactly by discussion in a group. (Nell)

People often talked about gaining insight into their writing as a mark of progress. Like Chrissie, several people reported moving on from the pleasure of producing anything at all to more considered writing:

> When I first came it sounded nice, but it had no substance to it. Now I'm writing things that mean something to me. (Man, Tweed)

201

CREATIVE WRITING

> You look at old work and see it's different. (Woman, Roaches)

Like Barry, several participants reported greater insight into writers' methods and habits and were often able to offer examples to support their statements:

> You go through an emotional high and then it's like a catharsis. And you wait around for it. But coming to a writers' group you learn - it's like gymnastics - you learn to do things you didn't think you could. You sit down and tackle it. (Woman, Tweed)

During visits, I was struck both by how rarely participants revised and returned work to the group and how rarely they recorded the feedback their work received. At the same time, tutors and fellow participants (as well as the writers themselves) were confident that development and change did take place, and identified feedback on work as one of the most important aspects of creative writing activities. When I was able to discuss progress directly with people I began to see how this apparent paradox was resolved.

Graham Harthill posits an organic relationship between writer and workshop in which, in line with his assertion that 'creative writing can only be learned and cannot be taught' (Harthill 1994: 5), writers improve as writers by improving as participants in the discourse about writing. This discourse is generated and sustained by the workshop, and comprises all the creative work and related critical discussion generated by its members. This is helpful in sorting out the relative importance of process and product involved in learning to improve as a writer. The product, or the piece of writing, is critical. Without it, nothing happens. But it is important only in so far as it allows access to a creative process, which cannot, in any crude sense, be read off from the product. It provides, as Harthill says, a means for writers to 'become more aware of, and involved in, the issues surrounding, and the possibilities for, their writing' (Harthill 1994: 24).

The difficulty with this, as is often the case with the arts and arts education, is that whereas process can seem too vague and insubstantial, attempts to specify it can seem correspondingly

202

crude and imprecise. During the 1990s Training Councils specified learning outcomes for vocational employment qualifications in a wide range of areas but attempts to do so for writing floundered, going no further than the consultative document (Arts and Entertainment Training Council 1993). Arthur Greenblatt and James Striby offer a model for specifying learning outcomes that distinguishes the affective from the cognitive, not just in outcomes but also in relation to the attitudes, values skills and concepts which feed into and organise the learning. They argue that learning need not be as haphazard as it frequently is. Rather than let students discover what they need to know, they advocate providing systematic opportunities to learn and apply the full range of affective and cognitive skills, which will make it easier to switch between the education and artistic discourses. They argue that some of the difficulties of arts education lie in the very different significance that the artwork has within educational and artistic discourses:

> (Art works) are critiqued, graded, sold, displayed, hidden, destroyed, given away or cherished. They reflect an individual's taste, skill, knowledge, culture, level of expertise and emotions, as well as peer and teacher input and direction. They are certainly outcomes of the learning process.

> Once removed from the learning environment, of course, art works can be judged by a different set of standards unrelated to the learning process. This judgement may be valid in the new setting, but it can confuse the learners. Even for the accomplished artists, the product may be an end of sorts during its creation, yet it is also part of the artist's ongoing development and commitment. In an educational setting, the product is likewise always a means to an ongoing end. It is a record of the individual student's learning process.' (Greenblatt and Striby 1981: 62)

In a discussion that was common to all the groups, people demonstrated the link between process and product as they talked about the delicate connections between new and old work and the mediation of change and development through group discussion.

CREATIVE WRITING

The precise form varied from person to person and group to group. For some, it was about making actual or mental notes in discussion and trying to incorporate them into current or future work:

> I remember them for next time, I bear it in mind, I make notes. I might start to write it in the same way then remind myself. You bear other people's comments in mind. (Woman, Bleaklow)

> We've learnt self-analysis really, learnt to break it down and think about it. I just know. I can't find the words for it. I do note when what I read out has had an effect. (Woman, Cuillin)

For others, it involved developing an overview which enabled them to judge work from the different periods in their writing career. Sometimes they could pinpoint actual changes in their work and sometimes they charted the growth of greater self-confidence in, and generosity towards, their own writing:

> Things I wrote when I first went looked dull and amateurish, now I look at things and have the confidence to send them out. It's rejected, but it is encouraging. (Man, Stanage)

> When I first read my work out I used to be thinking it's rubbish, but now I like some of my work. (Man, Cuillin)

It was interesting to discuss with the groups how they thought these changes had come about. Some groups, such as Cuillin, could see how their tutor's habit of saying: 'Think about this' – not – 'This is wrong', had helped them to develop their own critical insight. In this group, as in others, there was some support for a more intuitive form of knowing:

> I think instinctively you'd know. Like she (W2) said, you just know if it's right or not. (Woman 1, Cuillin)

But this statement provoked W2 to state forcefully that she had not always had the ability to know when something worked and when it didn't. Another group member supported her in this view. When asked what she thought had developed her critical faculty she answered by thinking out loud, answering the question for herself too:

> I was very timid, maybe it's confidence. Now when I've written a poem I feel I've made a contribution to life, I've done something important. I feel very pleased I've created something but I haven't always felt that way. (Woman 2, Cuillin)

The myth of mutual admiration

The phrase 'mutual admiration' is frequently heard in discussions about creative writing where it performs a symbolic rather than explanatory function. It signifies fawning uncritical approval and, by telling us what they most worry about getting wrong, alerts us to what those taking part in creative writing activities perceive to be its primary function: giving and receiving feedback on work-in-progress. References to, or accusations of, mutual admiration were always strongly, often contemptuously, expressed. Mutual admiration suggests praise which is somehow false or unwarranted, and in doing so, highlights the profound insecurity cultural activity can generate. Just what, we have to ask ourselves, would be so terrible about people being able to enjoy each other's work? Isn't it, at one level, a perfectly accurate description of what goes on in creative writing groups and courses all the time?

> I just enjoy the great difference in people's work. It's so intriguing, it's lovely to see the individuality of people. (Woman, Cuillin)

> The classes provide a vehicle for the ultimate in success, the stardom level. There is also a need fulfilled at the other end. It doesn't matter that someone comes along with something you or I or the experts feel isn't very good. It doesn't matter if they've achieved something, done a good job. (Man, Bleaklow)

The problematic nature of making both the creative work and appropriate judgements about it illustrates Pierre Bourdieu's argument about cultural capital. (Bourdieu and Passeron 1977).

205

Although Bourdieu's work is concerned with popular, or working-class, consumption of high art forms, it is possible to see the same processes of intimidation and variable competence in *knowing about* and *knowing how to respond* to cultural artefacts operating in writing workshops.

Tension surrounding feedback and criticism was a constant theme in the life of the creative writing groups and courses. It was cited as the most important aspect of the activity, and the one people most wanted to change. Feedback and criticism was the site of the main learning and teaching activities in the groups and courses. The importance to participants of feedback and criticism makes problematic the myth of adult education as primarily a social pursuit. As with Cherry Ann Knott's survey of the crafts in adult education, it was the challenge and sense of achievement that creative activity provided which drew in and retained the participants (Knott 1987: 59). Like the craft students, writers were part of a 'continual process of interchange […] realising others had the same difficulties, learning from the more experienced' (Knott 1987: 59). Feedback was highly valued as a developmental strategy for work-in-progress and to validate complete work:

> I hadn't been to a writers group for a long time when I came. The first two sessions I thought it too hard, I wasn't used to people being so hard but I wanted it because it was unlike the others, where all people ever said was: 'Lovely'. People questioned the work, said: 'This doesn't work.' (Woman, Mersey)

> It was making me think. What do you mean? Frequently a case of I don't understand it. It meant people like me had to do a lot more work. (Man 1, Mersey)

> I like it because in a busy existence it makes me do something, it sets a deadline. That produces the extra effort to force something I'm playing with into shape. (Man 2, Mersey)

People talked freely about how their writing had changed. Change included their experiments with different types of writing, greater confidence with craft skills and techniques and extending the scope of their imagination. They also frequently talked about finishing things. This demonstrated a change in how seriously they took themselves and their writing:

> I've got a file of stuff now where it used to be half-finished things turning up in odd places. I put more thought in now. When I start something I mean to finish it. I'm not just getting a good paragraph down. (Woman, High Tor)

Given that most of the writers were taking part in socialised writing activities of one kind or another it is not surprising that the majority expressed favourable views about the influence of courses and workshops on their development as writers. But not everyone who attends creative writing activities finds them productive and not everyone who writes participates in workshops and courses. Lana and Beatrice, for example, had never been to a workshop or course and Lana, unlike Beatrice, who did not teach them either, found the whole concept bizarre:

> I haven't and never would join a group. I couldn't bear the thought of the criticism and I would find it hard to connect their comments to my writing. (...) I have given talks to groups and listening to their questions and their talk I feel that what matters to me is not what matters to them. (Lana)

Several people had encountered difficulties, of varying degrees, in groups or courses. Sometimes, as happened to Doug, it was simply exasperation with other group members:

> They wrote a poem in 1955 or whenever it was and they read it every time, don't they? No matter what. Or they go to the group and they say: 'I haven't wrote anything this week. I've been very busy' and all that, week after week after week. (Doug)

For others, a group's reaction to their work brought home to them the risks that achieving their writing ambition might bring. Pearl joined a group because, having gained a degree in Local and Regional History in her fifties, she now wanted to write about her own extraordinary life. She and her eight children had been early residents of Erin Pizzey's refuge for battered women.

Her refined accent had been acquired, rather than inherited, in a working life that had ranged from Tiller girl to cleaner. Reading her autobiography to the group she realised its potential to upset her children and abandoned it. She was content to do so having by then also started to write fiction and local history features.

Others encountered greater frustration. Al described several years foraying in and out of local writers' groups, appreciating what he called the 'audience side' but getting no nearer to the apprenticeship in writing he sought. He felt strongly that his work needed to be released by the right kind of group and described his writing life as 'defined much better by the blocks and breaks and the not-writing than by anything I've ever managed to produce'. He was dissatisfied with the sense of sameness he felt about his writing and although he could articulate clearly what he felt it lacked, was unable to envisage making these changes in isolation:

> A bigger vocabulary in the sense of a vocabulary of forms or vocabulary of emotions that you deal with or a vocabulary of viewpoints. (...) I'm always buying books, especially books with significant titles like *White Paper and White Spaces* or whatever. I don't read them. I buy them. (...) There's a separate space on my shelves where I've got all these books. All these unread books about becoming a writer. So, yes, I buy them as a pledge to the future that some day I'm going to crack this problem. (Al)

Buying the books stood in for the community he believed his writing needed. It provided a way to make tangible the invisible processes of belonging to writers and writing.

Sophie found her writing was adversely influenced by the group's expectations. As a novelist it was difficult to take along work-in-progress but this was compounded because the group she joined set a weekly theme which formed the basis of readings and discussion the following week. This left very little space for independent writing projects to develop, and when she first joined the writers' group the effect was catastrophic:

QUESTIONS OF PROGRESS AND VALUE

I didn't do any writing, it stopped me from writing at first. It got me doing the bits that they wanted you to do so I stopped doing the novel. (Sophie)

Later, having persevered with the group and found a more productive relation to it, she found it influenced her work in a new way. Angry at how passive the group was, in both their writing and their critical feedback to each other, she tried to make them sit up and take notice by writing things to shock the group. As a horror writer she found this relatively easy to do but it took energy away from her own writing. Eventually she left the group completely.

Discussing the kind of problems people encounter in creative writing activities clarifies the extent to which a focus on questions of progress and improvement misses the point when attempting to pinpoint the 'ruling passion' of Cleveland's common writers (Barton and Hamilton 1998: 18). It was not that they were unable to demonstrate progress and change in their understanding and practice or writing. They could do this, across the span of a course or over several years' membership of writing groups and courses, but it became clear that development and improvement was not necessarily the point. What they valued, and what sustained their writing, was the opportunity to engage in communication and the stimulus to be creative.

It was rare for writers to bring revised work back to the groups and courses and tutors commented on the difficulty of encouraging groups to discuss work in terms of how it could be developed and improved. Such concerted refusal, by most of the people for most of the time, has to be wilful rather than accidental. It was not that they could not revise and re-write – the individual interviews with Cleveland writers offer several accounts of doing this – but rather that they did not see it as a function of the creative writing group. In the writing groups especially, informality and the freedom to set the pace of work was, by implicit comparison with the creative writing course, highly regarded:

No rules, no regulations. Honest criticism of work. (Man, Thames)

I don't feel I have to strive on and do more than I am capable of. (Woman, Goyt)

Some weeks I've done nothing and there's no feeling of being a bad lad. (Man, Goyt)

But this informality was contradicted by the high expectations they held for the quality and nature of feedback, which raised problems for them. The main issue was expressed as the conflict between the encouraging and judging functions of the group. Within courses, people tended to worry about not being knowledgeable or skilled enough to give valuable criticism in appropriate ways and in writing groups participants often felt that the friendships that had developed muffled their response to each other's work:

I'd like to be able to go to totally unbiased groups of people and get feedback. We all know what style to expect. The friendship here helps, I'm very comfortable with it, but we know what to expect. (Woman, Etherow)

We try and help each other but we don't know what we're doing ourselves. (Woman, Tweed)

We always identify the risk in reading our own work, but I think the risk is listening to other people, listening critically and helpfully, listening and trying to find something to say. I'm lately into trying to encourage groups to do this. There is a responsibility on group members to be helpful, sometimes without being given the tools to do that. I encourage them to respond to the subject matter. This image will stay with me, move me. It's a responsibility to respond. (Marina)

(The tutor) doesn't pull any punches at all, but other people they're too soft. That may be because they don't know enough about poetry. It's not always possible to have constructive criticism from fellow writers beyond whether they like or dislike it. (Man, Bleaklow)

The language which people used to describe feedback was

distinctive and it was at odds with the actual process I observed. The language was violent and aggressive. Phrases such as 'rip it to pieces', 'pull it apart', 'pull no punches', 'give it the once over' and 'brutally honest' were used frequently and unselfconsciously. It conjured up a process in which the writing and writer's feelings were literally taken apart. This language may signify a deep-seated anxiety in the writer about the worth of their work or it may allow participants to vent their frustration with discussions that do not go far enough for them. Certainly observing sessions showed that in all courses and most groups brief responses to work were the norm and people sometimes seemed unhappy about this. Managing individual time in the group is a difficult task and people's anxiety over turn-taking and dominating group time was present a lot of the time. Equally, some more forceful group members were skilled in using their impatience to control and curtail discussions that they found boring. Extended discussion about work was very rare, with people usually limiting themselves to one statement or question, and often picking up on very different aspects of the work, with the author giving single word replies. Approval and empathetic responses predominated, which tended to close work down rather than open it up.

To contextualise the discussion of feedback I now include three extended extracts which illustrate the very different ways in which creative work is discussed in groups and courses:

10.05 am

(The tutors) recapped the exercise. In pairs, the group had told each other an incident from their life and had then written each other's story as a poem.

Woman 1: I couldn't do it either. W2's story affected me emotionally when she told it me, but when I was putting it down I was concerned with feelings. I was trying to get feelings rather than contrive something.

Man 1: I think we all have the same problem – and it is not necessarily a problem. I don't know what I'm supposed to be doing when I write poetry.

Woman 3: How do you define poetry?

CREATIVE WRITING

Tutor 2: That's what I'm trying to explore with you.

W1: For me, whatever I read, the first thing that hits me is a poetical line.

M1: But what's a poetical line?

W1: I don't know. Sometimes I think: What about a beautiful line (P) like this from Dickens (quotes the opening to *Bleak House* from memory.) It's prose but it's sheer poetry.

T1: Is it the language or the imagery?

W1: It's the description, it's so descriptive. For me, that's poetry.

M1: So your only description of poetry is beautiful prose (…)

(…)

T2: To summarise then: it's to do with feelings, language, the visual.

T1: Is it anything to do with the shape on the page?

W1: It's an essence.

T1: Distilled down.

T1 raised the question of rhyme, by referring back to a poem that had been read out and which everyone but M1 had liked. This led to an exchange between M1 and T1 about poetry as a code, M1's reaction to the poem and his contention that it had not been a poem at all. T1 then asked the rest of the group for their comments.

(…)

10.15 am

T1 suggested reading out some of the work people had done. (…)

M1: Its title is Trauma.

Immediately after he had read W4 and W5 said, 'I liked that.'

W2: It was beautiful

T2: That was my experience exactly of my father dying when I was nine.

W4: It comes to me, adults are always saying children are resilient.

W5: That was exactly the same kind of thing for me.

W3: There's a picture for me of shadowy adults and a child in real grief.

W2: It's like W5's story, of the grief in the house.

T1: Have you surprised yourself?

M1: No, I've read it several times.

T2 asked for it to be re-read and made notes as he read it.

T2: I like that second part of the poem particularly. The language seemed simpler, but truer.
M1: That's the rhyme, and the iambic pentameter.
T2: I don't care, it's the emotion I feel.

A discussion then developed about interventions to help children deal with the death of their parents, in which people shared personal experience.

W6: It's important to have the choice of whether to see a dead person or not.
T2: Either way
W3: The child's feelings need respecting, not just in death. The arrival of a new sibling can be treated with great insensitivity. Children feel as vividly as adults. When I was seven I felt as big and real and full of thought as I do now.
W5: I read some of my son's writing when he was seven and it shocked me, I thought only I felt that.
W6: I think children feel more.

10.43 am
W2 read next and began by apologising to T1, saying the poem was flippant and trivialised what T1 had told her. She also talked about writing very quickly and not revising work. (Students and tutors, Kinder)

The next two extracts provide contrasting styles of feedback. In one, the market clearly structures the line of response, in the other (a smaller group that was both able and willing to devote 20 or 30 minutes to each person rather than the standard five or ten minutes) the writer is encouraged towards a deeper engagement with her work.

The meeting began by drawing people's attention to *Tees Valley Writer* and its competition:

213

CREATIVE WRITING

T: It doesn't pay well, but it is well produced.

9.45 am
M1 started to read. There was some confusion about who was who in the piece and the group questioned him about this.

T: You're trying a play? A play form?
M1: Eh?
T: How would you have got over that information?
M1: By a telephone call or something.
T: Is it a play then? The group thinks it's a play.
M1: It's a story. (Puzzled) I thought it was a story.
T: Well, you have to get over that problem then. You can't have the narrator tells us, we need to hear that invitation to the Dales. (To the group) Any ideas?

W1: Telephone
M2: A letter through the letterbox, then there would be time for thought.
T: That wouldn't work in a play.
M2: You can't include that sort of information in play directions.
W2: Is that the end of the marriage?
M1: Don't ask me, it wrote itself. Does that ever happen to you?
T: Not to me, no
M1: You're just taken over.
T: No, I know what you mean though. Now, have we anyone else?

10.00 am
W3: Mine has no title.
T: Well, let's hear it.
W3 reads her work outloud, is attentively listened to.

T: That's a nice little twist.
W4: It's pleasant to listen to, it comes over.
W3: My husband says it rambles a bit.
T: I don't think so.
W4: Yes, I liked it, I could see those violets.

QUESTIONS OF PROGRESS AND VALUE

W5: When you say she became a recluse because of being jilted, that's very true.

(Much agreement with this from rest of class.)

W3 talked about first choosing roses and then deciding to change it to violets.

T: I like the way you used the child narrator and there were lots of little touches, you're very visual. Flick, flick, flick; picture, picture, picture. We don't all have that gift. So, you're moving over more to fiction?

W4: So, it's not your own story then?

W3: Yes.

T: You were writing about yourself, weren't you?

W3: Yes.

T: Everyone becomes a short story writer in this group, however they start out, but that's too short to be saleable.

11.05 am

W1 read a love story, 'A Piece of Cake'. It was listened to very attentively and many appreciative murmurs during and at the end.

T: A nice, happy story. We don't have enough.

W4: I would have preferred to read that to myself.

W6: Oh no, I love being read to.

General discussion praising W1 for how well the story had been read.

T: It is a problem only hearing something. We do ask a lot of ourselves and each other to listen and comment. That's why I say give them in and I'll make a few comments. I think that's a *Women's Weekly* story, or People's Friend. They go in for simple, gentle stories with a change of heart.

(Students and tutor, Stanage)

*

8.00 pm

Tina prepared to read her poem. She explained that she had been reading William Lilley's *History of Middlesbrough* and writing poems based on aspects of the book. There was a discussion about different histories of Middlesbrough people had read.

Tina: The long one you heard before, 'The Jubilee Bacchae', it took all of twenty minutes to write. But this one! This must have taken two months and it's not right yet. It doesn't scan properly, the rhythm's wrong and then you get pissed off working on the one thing all the time.

Tina read 'Erimus' and stopped just before the end to comment: 'I hate that bit'. She passed it round for the others to look at.

Nell: 'A different mirth'. That's a lovely phrase, it could almost be a title in itself.
Kim: What's a mandrake?
Tina: It's a plant. There's a legend that it grows where the semen of a hung man falls. It screams as it is lifted from the ground. I was thinking that we all come from somewhere else. Most of us from Ireland, and we had to come (...) but I don't know whatever I say it's not right.
Nell: Do you think it might be that you're using general terms and words instead of concrete objects and incidents to illustrate? For example, poverty. Using the word poverty makes it more like a documentary and less like a poem.

Tina was taking notes as comments were made.

Tina: I found it difficult to write about things I really feel about. Difficult to stop them being really, what's the word, OTT.
Nell: You start to use emotive words where it might be better to describe in sensuous detail something that actually happened in history.
Tina: Yes, I see your point.
Nell: And then you wouldn't have to be so emotive about it because it would speak for itself. And you couldn't be OTT because if it's really happened, however improbably, it can't be OTT. You can cut the narrator out, put all the energy into the thing itself. You know that piece you wrote about Felling, that was very strong because you

stuck with it. You don't move outside of it and make comments on it whereas in some of your other poems, you move in and out of the text and I don't think you can.

Tina: But I always think it needs it.

Nell: You don't. It's just the things people say. It speaks for itself. You keep yourself out of it.

Kim: What did you mean about the rhythm?

Tina: Where it's not stilted, it's twee.

Kim: What do you mean twee?

Tina: Oh I'm just going to scrap it!

Kim: No! I felt it was like everything brought together. A patchwork, no, like everyone brought together. You remember all those other places, but this is where you are.

(...)

Tina: That's what I wanted in the poem. That pull from where you are to where you've been. I'll have another go. (Women, Swale)

Groups often expressed doubts about their ability to help develop each other's writing and it was not the main activity in most of the groups I observed. It is clear, as these extracts illustrate, that participants were capable of doing this work. I observed several instances of groups questioning and supporting the writer, as we saw in the exchange between Nell and Tina. This was a small group of experienced writers but the same process could be observed in larger groups with less experienced writers. Tweed provides an interesting example of how groups had this skill but were sometimes unable to recognise that they had it. The statement by one of the members that the group needed external guidance strongly divided them:

> A proper tutor. Someone consistent to take our work in and give us criticism. Someone further on to give us help and advice. (Woman, Tweed)

Some agreed with the suggestion, but others strongly resisted the idea. It would be 'like having a measuring stick' claimed one member who went on to argue that the ability to criticise your own work was an important stage of development in becoming a writer. Interestingly, just prior to this discussion, they had demonstrated their capacity to perform this role for themselves. While discussing the changes they would like to make to their own writing, a group member had said she wanted to write a novel. Again, we see the projection onto someone else of responsibility for initiating and sustaining writing:

> Somebody to inspire me to the extent that I could stop writing short stories and write a novel. I've got a synopsis and characters. (Woman, Tweed)

The group responded to this exactly the way an experienced, sensitive tutor would. They asked questions: 'What's stopping you?' 'Why don't you do that?' and suggested lack of confidence was what held her back. They asked what she meant by 'somebody to give you inspiration', prompting her to say: 'I don't know, I can write short stories, I need a push'. Another group member then asked: 'Is it knowing how much you have to write? Is it being put off by the sheer quantity of writing in the novel?' which elicited further suggestions about how to deal with this from other members of the group.

Through their questions the group provided the original speaker with the means to solve the problem she was experiencing. But for her to act on it she would have had to abandon her deeply held belief that good advice only carried weight when it came from someone with authority. That she could not recognise authority within the group illustrates one of the major problems in developing effective feedback in groups. Graham Harthill comments that full involvement in creative writing workshops requires participants 'to learn an appropriate language of comprehension and criticism' and goes on to comment that 'hopefully this language grows as part and parcel of one's experience of the course' (Harthill 1994: 18).

I found that whether participants took courses or met informally in groups this hope was not usually – and certainly not automatically – fulfilled. Neither groups nor courses took full control of the process of giving and receiving feedback and in consequence these skills and their essential contribution to creative writing activities remain underdeveloped. One of the more positive consequences of accreditation in adult and continuing education has been to identify and prioritise the need for students to learn how to give, and to receive, better feedback.

The commonest feedback scenarios that cause frustration and difficulty in writing groups and courses are obscure and dense work, anecdotal responses to writing, polite but empty responses, personal attacks upon work and its writers, controversial topics and limiting a discussion to whether and where a piece might be published. People frequently mentioned how friendship and familiarity dulled the critical edge in the groups and they hankered after anonymous feedback. Two groups, Cuillin and Tweed, were so interested in anonymous feedback that I brokered an arrangement that enabled them to try it out. It produced some interesting results, including confirmation that every group understands its own practice as the norm.

The groups took very different approaches to their task, with Cuillin correcting rather than responding to Tweed's work and Tweed responding in what Cuillin felt to be a rather dismissive fashion to their work. The absence of friendship and social relations did sanction a more direct, and possibly honest, response to the work. Some members of Cuillin were distressed by the bluntness of Tweed's comments. (Cuillin made equally robust comments about Tweed's work, especially on the issue of swearing and appropriate topics for writing – 'language and filth', as they put it – but Tweed's members took this in their stride.) At a follow up meeting to discuss and reflect upon the experience both groups had found it valuable in alerting them to the complexity of feedback, both giving and receiving it. It helped them see that while anonymous criticism had the value of directness, the potential for dialogue that a group situation provides is a vital component in ensuring that the writer can use the feedback they receive, and that it is appropriate to their experience and ambition as writers.

The value of audience

On occasions, the question: 'How can you tell if you're making progress?' provoked a defensive or surprised response. This suggested that participants rarely asked themselves this question, individually or as a group. Just as the pivotal issue of feedback was often left to chance in groups, this uncertain response to progress demonstrates how the ambivalent location of creative writing de-centres issues of evaluation and progress, locating them as the business of the tutor or the market.

Although progress was made, seen to be made, and valued by participants in the various creative writing activities in Cleveland, what was most valued by participants was the way the local culture of writing provided a place to be heard. The function of writing groups and courses in providing an audience for writers returns us to the wider meaning of the word publish, which is 'to make widely known'. It is here that we begin to find an explanation for the resistance to educational practices and values, with their emphasis on making and recording progress and improvement, which characterises not just Cleveland's culture of writing but the wider world of creative writing in education. That this culture of writing is largely made up of activities situated in educational settings adds a further complication to the already complex issue of value.

Writer's groups and courses provide a place where dialogue about writing can happen. For the majority of people who attend them, they are the only forums in which their writing will be made public:

> We get our stories read. No one would hear them otherwise. (Man, Bleaklow)

People talked a lot about how they were perceived as odd by their families because of their interest in writing. When a woman in Stanage reported 'talking about writing until their eyes glaze over' in relation to her family it prompted discussion about whether people got feedback from their families, indeed whether they showed writing to their families at all. Their comments, which

220

were often echoed in other groups, suggest families are not a good audience for new writers:

> Mine are very supportive but they are very, very critical. (Woman 2, Stanage)

> Oh no, the majority of it I wouldn't show any of them, they'd get the wrong idea. (Woman 3, Stanage)

Not being able or wanting to show writing to the family left a vacuum. Writing is often a dialogue with the self but it is also a dialogue with or about others and, as an act of communication, it is competed when someone else hears it.

There were gender differences in the reason men and women gave for choosing not to show work to partners, wives and other family members. Men were much more exercised than women about whether or not family members were competent to comment on their writing:

> Our lass, you would never get no criticism at all, constructive or otherwise out of her, so it's pointless showing it to her. (...) Me three daughters, they're not impressed or curious. I think they just think I'm weird. (...) Writing's something I do that they don't. It's the same as they don't go to the betting shop. (Doug)

> She wasn't really bothered and I don't think I wanted her to read them in case she said anything that would have put me off the story, because she's not qualified in an educational sense. I mean, she can say 'I like that story' or 'I don't like it'. So there didn't seem to me to be a lot to be gained (...) but there might be something to be lost in that she might undermine my feeling about the story. (Joe)

This is, to some extent, fair comment. Writing can be talked out before it is written out or its forward drive disrupted by feedback which, often without being intended as such, is received as negative. But these comments also reveal the way in which writing for pleasure has become entangled with commercial and educational purposes in ways that leave the writer confused about which responses are appropriate when and where. They elide general and expert readers, and berate the former for not being the latter. Both types of reader, if the writer is lucky enough to have them, are vital, and can give valuable and distinct feedback. But a reader is a reader, not an editor.

Few men or women talked about showing writing to family members simply for pleasurable exchange, validating the writer as an entertainer, recorder or commentator on events, although it was not unusual for writers to have an informal role as workplace laureate. Greg even went so far as to comment that the only feedback he needed or wanted concerned the marketability of his writing:

> The family tend to be nice and unconstructive. (...) That doesn't help you if you're considering sending it to a publisher because you're going to get a different I mean he's looking at it, full stop, as if it's marketable. I mean, he doesn't care anything about me. He doesn't care that I might be offended if he says he doesn't like it. Just the same as my family would be cagey not to be offensive. (Greg)

In contrast, women were more concerned with the effect their work might have on others. This sensitivity was sometimes ambiguous. Were a husband's feelings being spared or were women protecting themselves from the consequences of upsetting their men?

> He doesn't object to me going or anything but well, he did read a story I wrote (...) and he recognised in it some of his own family members and he was most hurt and upset. So sometimes I think it's safer not to. (Josie)

Mona showed more or less everything she wrote to her husband, finding him a sympathetic and interested reader, but she censored work she thought would distress him, such as a piece based on his mother's experiences in a nursing home:

> That would have really upset him, just because it's such a terrible situation for her. It would have upset him and I wasn't sure that I should let him read that. (Mona)

Al shared his work with his family by pinning it on the kitchen notice board. He had once tried to use poetry to communicate with his partner during a difficult time in their relationship but she had experienced this as 'an expression of my distance from her, not of my closeness'.

Although wariness about showing work to family members was widespread there were some rare instances of using writing to celebrate and strengthen relationships. Nell, whose work was often published, talked about sharing it with family and friends as something that completed the publishing process:

> I felt I'd really given them something that was part of myself, and when I came back there were some really lovely letters back from them. I think it meant a lot to people to have a book, particularly if it's based in the local area where they grew up as well. (...) There's an expression – I think Wordsworth used it of Dorothy – 'She brings forth to me my imaginations' and I think that is what I do with other people living round about here. I articulate their very deep thoughts about their own community and I think that's a sort of healing thing, releasing thing, because the book works on all sorts of different levels. (...) Even if they don't understand the deeper levels of meaning, they do recognise the parks and little houses, and that really is communication, real communication, because I share my spiritual texture with them. (...) It's real kinship, it's not a sentimental thing. (Nell)

Perhaps in this case publication had validated the writing, which then made sharing it with others legitimate. The writer is no longer seen, or sees herself, to be in the grip of an odd, slightly pathetic delusion. Tina, for example, first showed a piece of writing to her family when it had been recommended for publication after winning a local competition. Greg would show work to members of his family who expressed an interest, but was adamant it had to be finished:

> It would be like showing someone an unfinished suit of clothing. It wouldn't look right until it was finished to the last detail. (Greg)

Chrissie, who also published reasonably frequently, only showed finished work to others:

> In my eyes it's not ready to be shown until it's finished, and I think they would notice that it wasn't ready. (Chrissie)

There were only four members of the sample, all women, who had regularly shared their work with other family members over the years. Kim's children had accompanied her to various drama groups and writers' workshops. They were very positive about how different she was from other children's mothers and, as they grew older, enjoyed reading her work. Amy shared her writing with her husband and daughter who both had an interest in writing. Finally, Sophie and Josie not only shared their work with family members but also received considerable support and encouragement from them. They provided practical assistance, especially Sophie's aunt who found out about writing activities and encouraged her to attend them, but their primary role was to act as enthusiastic and sympathetic audiences for the work.

With the exception of friendships formed through creative writing activities, friends were even less likely than family to form an audience for writers' work. This was especially marked amongst the younger members of the sample who reported a strong sense of social as well as cultural isolation. Either there was nobody to show work to, as the first extract from Dean illustrates, or there were powerful psychological constraints, as Tracey's extract reveals:

> Friends don't understand what I'm talking about. (...) Family they just never listen. (...) Nobody, I just show them to myself. (Dean)

> To try and show people your work is very hard for me because I find that unless I know the person it's sort of an invasion of privacy. (...) The loneliness and bleakness. That's my personal life, that is. Really, I don't really want to show that. (Tracey)

But it was not just younger people who felt embarrassed or vulnerable when it came to sharing poems with friends. Irene's impulsive decision to read one of her poems to friends at a dinner party left her unwilling to repeat the experiment:

> We had not a bottle, plenty of wine but whether I would if I'd been stone cold sober I don't know and they were all rather nonplussed. Probably they hadn't had enough to drink. (...) People have said 'I'd like to read your poems' and I've said 'Oh. Right' and I've never done anything about it since that evening. (Irene)

Friendships formed through creative writing activities continued the generally positive experience of the writing group, although in some instances they extended the group, providing more focused and rigorous feedback than the group was able or willing to give its members. Friendships often spurred on a serious attempt at publication, with one or two friends agreeing to read each other's work and providing detailed written feedback. These friendships were often intense. Both Sophie and Mona had daily phone conversations with their writing friends:

> There'll be nothing that I've written that I wouldn't be happy to share with her because I know she values my work. But she doesn't hold back if she doesn't like it and she doesn't hesitate to compliment if she does. And I find that very supportive. I know she will say what she thinks. (Mona)

For the majority, however, friendship was limited to the social interaction the group itself provided. Participants often commented on the pleasure of being with like-minded people. This sociability is often misinterpreted as merely sociable. It fuels the myth of mutual admiration societies, promoting the idea that people put social pleasantries above genuine engagement with developing and extending their creative work. Tutors, particularly those who are sensitive to the psychological dimensions of their work, offer another perspective on sociability. They recognised the importance of paying attention to people. Gloria talked about how her own experience of therapy had helped her to realise how enormous was her own need for attention and, in turn, the value of paying attention to others. She felt strongly that one of the most important roles a creative writing group or course performed was this work of listening and paying attention. Marina, when asked to give me an image or word association for the group she taught, picked out this listening role:

> Having to be there absolutely. The talking and listening, listening, listening, listening. (Marina)

Providing people who are not often listened to with an opportunity to be heard is one of the most valuable aspects of creative writing:

> I think the groups are about validating experience: where they've been and who they have met, what they think is funny or poignant. It's like the experience of travel, a journey of a thousand miles begins with one step. It's the kind of attitude you need to cultivate to write, looking with wonder at your own life no matter what it is or was. It's not only that it is subject matter, but that it is wonderful subject matter. You can not only use but also value what you know. (Marina)

Diversity was a striking feature of the groups and courses I visited and always accompanied by tolerance towards what were often very different engagements with writing. In any one group there would be people of different ages and backgrounds, all with very diverse literary ambitions. This in itself was unusual and people appreciated crossing various social boundaries and meeting people and ideas they would not otherwise encounter:

> I enjoy the wide spread of age. People of my age don't often get a chance to meet younger people and talk to them on an equal level. (Man, High Tor)

Participants' pleasure in this expanded sociability, and the value that they put upon it, was viewed differently by the providers and organisers of many of the elements that made up Cleveland's local culture of writing. They saw the range of interests and abilities as a factor that limited the potential achievement of those writers involved. A narrower focus, it was argued, would enable individuals to progress further with their writing. But once again, progress is an imposed rather than self-determined criterion. Diversity was clearly one of the most enjoyable aspects of creative writing groups and course for the participants.

This is one small instance of how creative writing activities can encourage and validate a stand against the norms, expected behaviours and values of the social order. Writing becomes, within its own rather limited context, a subversive activity in which difference, individuality and variety are each emphasised against the assumption that we should all be the same. Some students made this connection themselves, comparing their writing activities to other, more popular, forms of leisure:

> You've got to do something else with your life besides work and watch TV. (Woman, Roaches)

> This whole thing with the arts, it's a class thing. If you're educated you have a form of expression. A lot of people have very interesting things to say but they maybe can't say it. Coming here helps people learn how to say it. (Woman, Bleaklow)

> Sometimes you do think: 'Am I wasting my time here?' But then again, what else is there? If I pack in writing I'm just like the rest of them, aren't I? Just a robot walking about. (Craig)

Peter Wollen, writing about Kathy Acker and the transition she made between avant-garde literary and visual arts, describes the mail-art networks which led to her first publications as 'based on reciprocity and a culture of the gift rather than commodity' (Wollen 1998: 9). The idea of a culture of the gift is a powerful aid to resolving the paradoxes of creative writing activities. The acts of listening and paying attention are gifts, in which the benefits and pleasures are both given and received. Reciprocity and gift, while representing and conveying many of the positive and pleasurable aspects of creative writing activities, also carry with them the sense of obligation and awkwardness which can ruffle their smooth waters and caution us against too easy or sentimental an advocacy for them. The poet Eavan Boland makes the important point that the dangers of workshops 'correspond, with symmetrical irony, to the self-deceptions of a more orthodox literary community. Both can mistake self-expression for art. Both can manufacture a critique of standards which is little more than a rhetoric of insiderism. Both can ritualise an agreed process which will, in the end, deceive them about the product' (Boland 1994: 5).

The like-mindedness of participants in a local culture of writing did not necessarily refer to shared politics, social attitudes or moral values but to their commitment to writing and the importance they gave imagination and creativity. Writers were conscious that others often saw them as deluded or pathetic for continuing to write without obvious external success. Writing is different in this respect from other cultural and leisure activities. It is as if every weekend footballer genuinely thinks he might be picked for the Premier League and is obliged never to kick a ball again once it has been pointed out he hasn't a hope in hell. But the analogy breaks down. Middle-aged men don't get to play football at Wembley but complete unknowns can quite often break into print, sometimes late in life and often from unpromising circumstances.

Writing, unlike other art forms, provides many examples of this: poet U.A. Fanthorpe (1986), novelists Mary Wesley (1984), Jeff Torrington (1992), Magnus Mills (1998) and Kate Atkinson (1995). This patterning of the literary formation is interesting in that what looks like another opportunity actually obscures how heavily weighted literary institutions are against outsiders. These people are, in Tillie Olsen's term, 'Only's'. The term itself is taken from the 1950s North American Civil Rights Movement. Ralph Abernathy described a speaking tour during which he was constantly urged to meet this and that black person: the only full Negro federal circuit judge, the only full black professor of sociology, the only black senator in the state legislature; to which he replied 'We don't want no "Only's" '. Tillie Olsen argues that 'only's' are used to rebuke, to be unrealistic role models. 'Accepting a situation of "only's" means: let inequality of circumstance continue to prevail' (Olsen 1980: 39).

Mary Stuart talks about the capacity of writing, as a social process, to offer its participants shame or self-esteem (Stuart 1998: 151). Olsen's inequality of circumstance has more often produced shame than self-esteem for aspirant writers. Local cultures of writing based on shared egalitarian values maximise the chance of self-esteem. A shared commitment to writing, and access to a wide variety of experience and approaches, provides participants with a series of applied illustrations of how the writing process works. Various people talked about how the group had supported them when doubt about their writing or writing blocks had prevented them writing.

This easing into the ebbs and flows of the writing process is one of the most valuable roles creative writing activities perform. At their best, writing courses and groups model for their members the degree to which writing is a combination of inspiration and technique and as much about discipline and habit as one-off flashes of inspired, driven writing. Some people come to creative writing activities with one important experience to write about. In most cases the experience of writing that one piece leads them to write more. As they do so, they need to learn how to create the conditions in which the writing is more likely to come and how to best take advantage of it when it does. They are learning that writing is a process, but a process that is not seamless or one-directional. Becoming a writer, for all its undeniable power, is not an upward ride to glory:

> I used to think you were either a brilliant writer or you weren't. I've learnt that's not true. Also I thought it was easy and I've learnt it's not, you have to work at things. (Woman 1, Bleaklow)

Chapter ten

Summary and conclusion

> Something that meaningful to us cannot be left just to sit there bathed in fine significance, and so we describe, analyze, compare, judge, classify; we erect theories (...); we characterise (...); we reach for scientific metaphors, spiritual ones, technological ones, political ones; and if all else fails we string dark sayings together and hope someone else will elucidate them for us. The surface bootlessness of talking about art seems matched by a depth necessity to talk about it endlessly. (Geertz 1993: 95)

The main argument

A simple question catalysed the research on which this book is based. It was this: had late-twentieth century campaigns for a more democratic and inclusive approach to writing and literature in British cultural policy and education been successful? They certainly seemed successful. The values and activities of participation had replaced those of appreciation in culture and education; cultural and educational policies now started from an inclusive rather than elite standpoint. Literature was viewed in the broadest of terms and as an activity that encompassed readers and writers, of all sorts of texts. And yet a simple 'yes' or 'no' does not quite answer the question I posed. Categorical answers are both impossible and undesirable for cultural and educational policy in general, and for the specific analysis of creative writing activities which had been my focus.

There have indeed been significant changes at the macro-level in respect of policy attitudes and values towards literature, writing and writers between the 1970s and the 2000s. Creative writing, though, is not monolithic. Its diverse history supports different traditions that have produced their own form of involvement with specific activities, purposes and motivation that take place within a wider matrix of professional and amateur participation. This produces an intricate set of relations to writing which change depending on the sector, site and tradition of creative writing involved. This in turn means that, at the micro-level of everyday life, the impact of identifiable policy changes encouraging more inclusive, anti-elitist approaches to literature also vary.

One of the reasons why answering that original question is complex and complicated is that changes in cultural and educational policy and practice were only in part brought about because of the campaigns. Like all forms of social action the resulting change was determined by forces beyond its control and was consequently sometimes the product of larger changes working through agendas less radical than those of the campaigns for social change in education and cultural policy.

I developed the concept of the local culture of writing to represent and analyse the complex ground of lived relations between writers and their writing. This holds cultural and educational policy on the one hand, and their social practice on the other, as important terms but it enables a more complex account of the interaction between them. Local cultures of writing not only mediate policy towards creative writing but also generate their own form of regulation. This is not always directed towards the same ends as that of cultural policy, whether it is driven by an older set of values and ideology, to do with elites and individual genius, or more contemporary values of diversity, inclusion and socialised activities. One of the most significant changes, in terms of policy and the public sphere, during this period was the rise of market reasoning and new managerialism (McGuigan 2004). This had a profound impact on all public institutions and radically re-structured social life and political action. I argue that, in the specific context of literature policy, the move towards this new material and ideological formation was coterminous with a belated turn towards educational values and

231

practices within the discourse of literature policy itself. The educational values of inclusivity, participation and self-development both deflected and were incorporated into the hegemonic drive of the new market reasoning in ways which, paradoxically, kept open spaces for potentially transformative radical work in writing and literature. This was in marked contrast to education, where the impact of marketisation has been far less nuanced. Educational institutions have been remade in radical, but far from progressive, ways. Non-vocational adult education in particular has to a great extent migrated out of formal provision as a result of the combined pressures of funding, institutional mission and credentialism and now survives in informal sites and practices.

The presence of educational values and practices within the discourse of literature policy made a straightforward answer to my original question impossible. The late-twentieth century cultural-democratic campaigns had largely been about art-literature and writing as expressive and communicative art forms involving display, public performance and practice – and the aesthetics of their production and reception values. What they won (in so far as they 'won' at all) involved a sleight of hand: it was education rather than art. In practice what this meant was the development of alternatives to, rather than oppositional engagements with, practices which valued scarcity in the artwork and the artists. It also generated a level of ambiguity and contradiction for practitioners and participants about the purpose and value of their activities and their relation both to education and to the wider literary formation.

In many ways the mainstream of literary and commercial writing was only marginally affected by these changes in cultural policy. This can be seen in the way the new interventions first created and then validated their own alternative cultural forums and rituals. These processes – of discipline formation, professionalisation of employment and policy implementation, as well as more immediate signs such as the founding of new journals, programmes of courses, workshops and project activities – are ambiguous, standing sometimes as a sign of positive change and at others for the incorporation and de-nerving of radical intervention.

This ambiguity is further heightened by the way in which new forms of funding the arts, especially those linked to social regeneration, has created a generation of entrepreneurial arts organisations more akin to conventional small businesses than to the collectives, charities and federations of the 1970s and 1980s. John Pick argues that this represents a nationalisation of the arts, claiming that the three-, five- and seven-year plans of Single Regeneration Budgets, lottery schemes and local authority financing produced 'the final victory of the state planners over artistic freedom' (Pick 1994: 5). I prefer to see it as an example, within the field of creative writing, of what Jurgen Habermas identifies as the penetration of lifeworld by system (Habermas 1984). Creative writing practices and activities exactly describe lifeworld: a space where understanding and meanings are made; and where the public sphere is balanced and made sense of through a protected, private space. However, the bureaucratisation of arts, cultural and educational activities on the one hand, and the commercial interests and exploitation surrounding writing activities on the other, equally well exemplify the growth of the 'monetary-bureaucratic complex' and its colonisation of the lifeworld.

The experience of writing

An important focus of this study has been the dynamic that exists between policy and practice. How does the actual lived experience of those participating in organised writing activities relate to the claims made, and expectations held, by cultural policy makers and activists? There is no simple causal relationship here. Indeed, at times it can best be described in terms of gaps or absences, for example, the lack of engagement from educational and cultural policy with more craft and commercially orientated writing organisations. Elsewhere, through writing residencies, literature development workers and festival promotions policy has acted as a means of opening pathways into and creating new sites of participation for literature, writing and social life.

My study confirmed how little those who make, implement and critique policy know about those on whose behalf they act. Engaging with those who live the writing challenges much of the common sense that exists about writers and writing, especially those who are not seeking or achieving literary or commercial publication. It demonstrates the complex engagement with writing and publication that exists in socialised writing activities, especially those widening participation in writing. In many instances this provision is founded on a rhetoric of empowerment that in practice obscures the fact of dependence. Without the active promotion of critical awareness – about the writing process, writing's substantive (and ideological) content and its broad institutional framework – the potential for individual and social transformation is unrealised. In many cases, the vacuum created by well-meant, but mis-founded, provision of writing activities organised without critical engagement is filled by commercial imperatives. This has the effect of empowering writers to participate in a profoundly anti-creative, de-personalised and conformist writing activity.

Within the broad field of creative writing, and the narrower terrain of writing in education, there is reluctance to engage with these issues. This reluctance has several sources, often of a pragmatic kind. It points to two larger issues that cut across policy and practice, providers and participants. These are avoiding engagement with questions of value and the tension between individual and social forms of participation.

The dominance of educational values and processes in organised writing activities has allowed questions of value to be bracketed out of the discourse of creative writing. Unlike the cultural-democracy campaigns of the late-twentieth century, which were in important ways argument about value, the forms of activity they produced in the twenty-first century are inscribed by a potentially damaging silence about value. This links, at a more general level, to the uncritical populism (McGuigan 1992) which permeated left-wing activism during this time but it has a special resonance for writing because of the way in which writing is so bounded by value judgements, and by individual experience and achievement. Questions of value threaten to re-introduce a competitive individualism which participatory forms of organised writing activities, especially in the context of identity politics, also often prefer to silence than to argue with and about.

Habermas addresses large societal, economic and cultural structures and shifts – modernity, the social-welfare state, capitalist society – which can seem a long way from the world of creative writing's inevitably smaller-scale organised activities. But he also points us to the 'seams between system and lifeworld' (Translator's Introduction, Habermas 1984: xxxv) and it can be argued that creative writing's organised activities form a variety of the new social movements which, he argues, is where conflicts will arise through and as part of struggles over cultural reproduction. Looking closely at local cultures of writing enables us to find some of the gaps and contradictions of partial ideological closure which McGuigan, in his project of theorising culture in the public sphere (McGuigan 1996; 2004), suggests will exist. It is important, however, to hold on to the way in which these formations contain complex and contradictory impulses and experiences in order to avoid re-mystifying, or re-romanticising, creative writing activities as inherently or inevitably socially or personally liberating. As Terry Eagleton argues, it is the political interpretation of experience, not the experience in itself, which makes it valuable:

> What could be more absurdly abstract than the notion of 'immediate experience'? Any experience is as richly concrete as it is only because it's the product of many mediations. (...) 'Growth' in itself is nothing; 'experience' in itself is nothing (...) 'Experience' in itself is blind and will teach you nothing. (Eagleton 1985: 6)

The refinement of experience-knowing has been crucial to radical adult education pedagogy. Several participants in Cleveland's culture of writing had developed their own practical understanding of this, too:

CREATIVE WRITING

Expressing yourself isn't necessarily good. You can express yourself by throwing a brick. (Woman, Bleaklow)

In order for participants in organised creative writing activities to have the possibility of a political interpretation of their experience in the group, course or project opportunities for critical reflection must accompany their experience of the process. Structures for collaborative critical reflection, and the will to use them, do not simply happen. People must, to slightly paraphrase Stephen Brookfield, be 'helped to learn what they do' (Brookfield 1996). As he goes on to say, 'experiences are constructed by us as much as they happen to us' (Brookfield 1996: 36). Issues of dependency and independence in writing, running writing groups and giving and receiving feedback on work-in-progress, were live throughout the fieldwork studies and in the theoretical and critical commentaries and debates about writing and the teaching of writing. This, the issue of dependency becomes a hinge between cultural policy and practice.

Cultures of writing have the potential to provide, as Eavan Boland puts it, an 'effective mimesis of a critical community' (Boland 1994: 61). But putting it this way assumes that the main purpose, and by extension value, of writing activities is to produce writers who conform to the criteria by which society in general acknowledges and rewards it writers. In this sense it is aligned with a reformist view of social and cultural change in which success is seen in terms of widening the number or types of people who participate in a set of activities from which they were previously excluded.

It is a political ideology which can be found across all sorts of sites and sectors, for example in twentieth-century liberal-feminist campaigns, in the 'raise and spread' impetus of the early Arts Council of Great Britain, in the late 1970s Access movement in continuing education, and which has been codified in various organisational and governmental equal opportunities and affirmative action programmes and legislation. It operates across organised writing activities, too, where it works as a kind of all purpose implicit, or default, purpose for participants and providers.

236

SUMMARY AND CONCLUSION

Clearly it can and does happen that writers with the desire and ability to function in writing's more public sphere, who might otherwise have failed to do so, have been helped to find their way through. Tillie Olsen's powerful indictment of the odds against writers who have to contend with social, economic and educational disadvantage is just as relevant now as it was 40 years ago when, as a student of the Stanford University Writing Program, she first formulated it:

> Do not forget:
> The overwhelmingness of the dominant.
> The daily saturation.
> Isolations.
> The knife of the perfectionist attitude.
> The insoluble.
> Economic imperatives.
>
> How much it takes to become a writer. Bent (far more common than we assume), circumstances, time, development of craft – but beyond that: how much conviction as to the importance of what one has to say, one's right to say it. And the will, the measureless store of belief in one's self to be able to come to, cleave to, find the form for one's own life comprehensions. Difficult for any male not born into a class that breeds such confidence. Almost impossible for a girl, a woman.
> (Olsen 1980: 256)

The way in which the process of accessing the mainstream is negotiated in the writing development project or creative writing course plays a key role in determining whether or not the outcomes will be liberating and empowering, as they are so often claimed to be, or whether people will simply slot into niches given by prevailing assumptions, across a continuum of commercial, literary and therapeutic paradigms.

Critics of the access movement in continuing education drew attention to the way in which, despite targeting specific social groups, it more often benefited individuals rather than the social group as a whole, thus risking incorporation as a 'liberal rather than liberating' practice (Fletcher 1980: 69). This criticism has a

237

particular relevance to organised creative writing activities because of the tension between writing's reliance on individual creativity and the social form of the creative writing activities through which it is supported and developed. The social form is emphasised because much writing development work either takes place in adult or community education settings or in arts projects which, as a result of the dominance of educational values and practices in the discourse of cultural policy, operate with educational paradigms. This can lead to a concern with process, reflected in the emphasis on 'the writing' – the here and now experience of producing and commenting upon work in progress – in the groups. This commitment to 'the educational value of the experience itself' has been characteristic of continuing education (Brookfield 1987: 177) and explains some of the difficulties experienced by the sector as it is repositioned in more instrumental and vocational relations of use and value.

Mary Stuart, discussing writing as a social process, talks about its capacity to offer its participants shame or self-esteem (Stuart 1998: 151). In Cleveland's local culture of writing this manifested itself in relation to guilt. It was noticeable how pervasive guilt was in participants' accounts of their writing lives. Not only did they feel guilty if they wrote, but also if they did not write, or were not writing regularly or as much as they felt they ought to be doing. All writers go through a vital stage of learning about the writing process, learning that a fallow period will usually follow a fertile period, that writing is not a machine process and cannot be regulated through the setting and meeting of targets. This is experiential knowledge but it can be triggered and reinforced by the example of others. This shared commitment to writing, and the range of experience and approaches, provides participants with a series of applied illustrations of how the writing process works. Various people talked about how the group had supported them when doubt about their writing or writing blocks had prevented them writing:

> During the barren times the group is a way of feeling you're still a writer.

> If I ever stop and ask why am I doing this, if it is a worthwhile thing, if I can see people having the same mental struggles it helps. (Man and Woman, Tweed)

> It gives me confidence to know I'll always be able to write. The more times you complete and read work out, you know you'll always be able to do that. (Man, Stanage)

This easing into the ebbs and flows of the writing process is one of the most valuable roles creative writing activities perform. At their best, writing courses and groups model for their members the degree to which writing is a combination of inspiration and technique as much about discipline and habit as one-off flashes of inspired, driven writing. Some people come to creative writing activities with one important experience to write about. In most cases the experience of writing this one piece leads them to write more. As they do so, they learn how to create the conditions in which the writing is more likely to come and how best to be able to take advantage of it when it does. They learn that writing is a process, but a process that is not seamless or one-directional. Becoming a writer, for all its undeniable power, is not an upward ride to glory:

> I used to think you were either a brilliant writer or you weren't. I've learnt that's not true. Also I thought it was easy and I've learnt it's not, you have to work at things. (Woman 1, Bleaklow)

Although the majority of people participating in socialised writing activities do value the development of skills in producing and commenting upon writing this is, paradoxically, often valued less for its influence upon them as writers than for the general contribution it makes to their growth in confidence and self-esteem:

> It's a simplification to say it, but in poetry you ought to be more honest and as your poetry improves you do get more honest, and with yourself as well as what you're actually writing. (...) Going back to the Caerleon thing, we spent a lot of time talking and we found that we

239

> couldn't tell a lie because it was spotted immediately. You couldn't be sort of trite about things because it showed immediately. (Barry)

This confidence was often linked to overcoming isolation arising from specific social causes such as illness, unemployment, redundancy or bereavement but it was also linked to challenging wider social and educational expectations as many participants had believed an interest in creative pursuits was incompatible with their life experience and role as, say, a manual worker, housewife or non-graduate until they became active in their local cultures of writing.

It was striking how consistently participants in organised creative writing activities valued the opportunity it gave them to re-appraise life experiences and identities. By definition personal and individual, this testimony was also evidence of the indivisibility of the three terms: writing, individuals and society. For example, many older people, including some in groups catering specifically for them, described the positive effects of remaining intellectually active. Unemployed men talked about the boon to them and their families of an emotional outlet and means to structure otherwise terrifying expanses of blank time. People across all permutations of gender, age, race and occupation recounted writing's power to heal personal distress and crisis.

Writing and the individual

I noted earlier the complexity of cultural policy's causal relationships with cultural practice. I do not, therefore, want to make inflated claims for writing's impact on identity and personal development. Rather, I want to insist that although these are possible outcomes, they are not inevitable. These purposes for and uses of writing will not be relevant to all writers and, even when they are, certain conditions for and approaches to the way writing activities are organised will encourage or discourage both their articulation in the groups and their legitimisation by the individuals concerned. A polarisation between the individual and the social haunts debates about socially purposeful continuing education, some areas of cultural change – especially literature – and community arts. This fixed orbit of polarity is better seen as a constant crossing and re-crossing of boundaries in and between the social and the individual. It is a way of thinking about cultural politics that draws on the work of feminist transversal politics (Cockburn 1998, O'Rourke and Hunter 2003). This transversal movement also describes the interaction between group members who offer and receive knowledge about themselves, and invite others to make similar explorations within the gift culture that characterises much organised creative writing activity. The idea of a gift culture borrows from a number of sources external to ways of thinking about creative writing and adult education. The word itself, as discussed earlier, came from Peter Wollen (1998); the appropriateness of it as a concept to explain the processes I observed in Cleveland's local culture of writing from a number of places. These include Paul Willis's notion of the grounded aesthetic (Willis 1990), Lynette Hunter's situated textualities (1999) and Ruth Finnegan's concept of music-making as an urban pathway (1989).

In *Common Culture* Paul Willis talks about the way the aesthetic effect is the product of its human receiver, not something inscribed into the text or artefact. While this is a persuasive argument and captures something of the irreducibility of human creativity and its work of producing what he calls 'expanded capacity and power' I feel his argument, that this can be enabled by, but is not dependent upon the text, is flawed (Willis 1990: 24). Its weakness is to emphasise process, as the product of creativity, at the expense of the text or artefact rather than to retain but radically de-centre the text. It suggests the aesthetic equivalent of the cultural relativism, which inspired Jim McGuigan's critique of cultural populism. The issue is not so much that texts and artefacts do not matter, as that they matter in different ways and that they are, in many instances, very different texts and artefacts to those with which we have become familiar. The work of creating a new aesthetic for these new cultural practices, practitioners and their products preoccupies Lynette Hunter in the final chapter of *Critiques of Knowing*. There she outlines a different kind of attention to the text, the standpoint critique, which she offers as a new strategy for literary analysis, reading and study developed from the kinds of communications that can – and do – take place over and through texts as they are being written:

> (It requires) a vocabulary for talking about the negotiated reality, negotiated not on plausible but on probable grounds, grounds worked on by people within a community and across communities. (...) A critique of aesthetics within standpoint would argue first for the need to value the 80 per cent of excluded art, but not through a 'critical' poetics or aesthetics that lead to a philosophical hiatus, but through a rhetorical analysis of aesthetics that offers a vocabulary for talking about the articulation of tacit knowledge by way of a textuality that understands limitations, a situated textuality. (Hunter 1999: 185–6).

One of the most striking findings of the study was the simultaneous foregrounding and backgrounding of writing. It mattered that it was writing, and not some other cultural, creative or social activity that people were engaged in yet it did not always matter to them as writing. Not that this was always clear-cut, it changed within as well as between the practices of individuals and groups. Despite my reservations about some of the detail of Paul Willis's grounded aesthetics, his underpinning argument, that creativity serves, and is sometimes to be valued for, purposes to which the core aesthetic activity is marginal, has both resonance and explanatory power for socialised writing activities.

Viewed in this way, engagement in organised writing activities (and the writing process itself) can be seen not as individuation but socialisation. As such, it is not neutral and can, as I have observed it to do, develop along lines of either conformity or resistance. Where active critical contestation goes on, organised writing activities generate a new perspective on identity and belonging. This has particular force given the political assault on identity and belonging throughout the Thatcherite years which was modified, but not substantially altered, following the New Labour victories of 1997 and 2001 which have, in some respects, made more explicit ideological appeals to family values than did the Conservative Government. Campaigns based around family values and back-to-basics not only secure a particular family form – mum, dad and the kids – but model the defeat of society by family. The potential that socialised creative writings activities provide; of a public space in which a range of identities and experiences can, but will not inevitably, be critically explored, is vital and valuable. This has the potential to benefits to two broad social groups, those who are, as single parents, single people – including lesbians and gay men – people with disabilities, members of ethnic minority groups and people on benefits, outside these new definitions of family as society and those who, married, heterosexual and economically active, resist co-option into its consensus. It benefits them individually but it can also provide them with opportunities to meet each other, opportunities that are scarce in our culture.

Writing and the social

In the discussion about art from which the quotation prefacing this chapter was taken, the anthropologist Clifford Geertz considers the various explanations – functional, aesthetic and craft based – that have arisen concerning the place and purpose of art. He questions whether art plays a significant role in social relationships, taking the Yoruba tribe of Nigeria to illustrate his argument. Nothing very much would happen to Yoruba society, he says, if Yoruba carvers ceased to carve well, or to carve at all (Geertz 1993: 99). Is he right, and if he is, could the same be said for our society and its writers? Would it matter if they ceased to write well, or to write at all? I think it would. Unlike Yoruba society and its carving, in our society writing and writers are positioned, often simultaneously, across several functional and expressive networks, which make the absence of writing difficult to imagine. It also makes it difficult to separate its creative and expressive purposes and modes from those which are instrumental and functional. This perhaps explains how tenaciously writing adapts to technological shifts (Ong 1982; Sharples 1988).

As a literate society which is rich in communication, as well as information, it is very probable that our social rules, regulations and values would 'fall apart' (Geertz 1993: 99) without writing, but this is not the only reason writing matters. Geertz suggests that, to our own as much as to Yoruba society, art both articulates and makes material experience and emotion which would otherwise 'not be said – and perhaps, after a while, might no longer even be felt' (Geertz 1993: 99).

This would be a view attested to by many participants in local cultures of writing. It is signalled by the seriousness with which they, writers for whom regular or even initial publication and acceptance as a writer is unlikely, devote their time and energy to writing. Although such conventional definitions of successful writing often seem, paradoxically, marginal to them, the writing does, and has to, matter to the writer. The self-hood, self-knowledge and self-esteem they report (and which is observable when working with writing groups in this way) is intimately bound up with the activity of writing and sharing writing. This is partly because of the greater intimacy and risk when sharing writing, especially writing rooted directly in personal experience, but also because the writing process itself is a generative activity, in which meanings are made as well as communicated:

> Writing has a power quite different from talking or thinking. Its power is similar to the other arts but dissimilar in that it uses words, our everyday communicating medium, (…) (T)he act of writing creates an object to which the writer can relate tangibly, visually and aurally. The writing is seen, it can be heard, it can be touched on the page – framed, filed with care, screwed up in a ball or burnt. And this tangibility lasts over time, to be re-experienced in different frames of mind, different stages of life.' (Bolton 1999: 213–14)

Lynette Hunter helps to locate what is going on here by drawing attention to the way the word 'aesthetics' is tied to the root word 'feelings' but insisting, through her critique of what she calls the 'gesture towards the arts', on the precise material location of this feeling and its links with social, economic and political questions of knowledge and power:

> Aesthetics and epistemology are closely intertwined, for without articulation knowledge remains tacit, and the main focus of the extension of standpoint theory into aesthetics, is to argue for an understanding of 'situated' textuality, analogous to situated knowledge. Situated textualities are where people work on words together to build common ground for the articulation and valuing of knowledge. (Hunter 1999: 2)

The exploration of this social location, what Geertz might call 'the meaning of things for the life that surrounds them' (Geertz 1993: 120), has involved trying to understand both the contradictory positioning of creative writing in its social location and the internal contradictions of creative writing as a practice. Both explorations began from a standpoint that valued the activity of socialised creative writing. Nothing I discovered led me to revise that judgement. Although I have sometimes pointed out the gaps between the rhetoric and reality of both practice and policy in relation to creative writing activities in order to argue for a practice and a rationale for practice that is both more subtle and more honest about its aesthetic and personal values. It is precisely because I am committed to, and enthusiastic about, the activity and the people who engage in it that I do so. I do not want creative writing to become just another academic subject or just another hobby, although I recognise that for some people, some of the time, this is exactly what it is.

Bibliography

Adkins, G. (1981), *The Arts and Adult Education*, Leicester: Advisory Council for Adult and Continuing Education.

Ahmad, R.M. (ed.), (1990), *Dreams into Words: The Cleveland Writers' Project*, Sunderland: The Common Trust.

Arts Council (1966), *Twenty-First Annual Report*, London: ACGB.

Arts Council (1967), *Twenty-Second Annual Report: A New Charter*, London: ACGB.

Arts Council (1968), *Twenty-Third Annual Report: Changes and Moves*, London: ACGB.

Arts Council (1970), *Twenty-Fifth Annual Report*, London: ACGB.

Arts Council (1974), *Twenty-Ninth Annual Report*, London: ACGB.

Arts Council (1975), *Thirtieth Annual Report*, London: ACGB.

Arts Council (1977), *Thirty-Second Annual Report: The Arts in Hard Times*, London: ACGB.

Arts Council (1978), *Thirty-Third Annual Report: Value for Money*, London: ACGB.

Arts Council (1980), *Thirty-Fifth Annual Report*, London: ACGB.

Arts Council (1983), *Thirty-Eighth Annual Report*, London: ACGB.

Arts Council (1984), *The Glory of the Garden: The Development of the Arts in England*, London: ACGB.

Arts Council (1985), *A Great British Success Story – An Invitation to the Nation to Invest in the Arts,* London: ACGB.

Arts Council (1987), *Forty-Second Annual Report*, London: ACGB.

Arts Council (1992), *Literature Grants 1992/93*, London: ACGB.

Arts Council (1993), *A Creative Future: The Way Forward for Arts, Craft and Media in England*, London: HMSO.

Arts Council (1998a), *Towards Cultural Diversity*, London: Arts Council of England.

Arts Council (1998b), *The Policy for Poetry of the English Arts*

Funding System, London: Arts Council of England.

Arts Council England (2002), *Arts in England: Attendance, Participation, Attitudes, Research Report No 27*, London: Arts Council of England.

Arts Council England (2003), *Ambitions for the Arts 2003 – 2006*, London: Arts Council of England.

Arts Council of England Arts and Entertainment Training Council (1993), *Writing for Publication, Writing for Production: Draft Standards*, London: Euclid.

Atkinson, K. (1995), *Behind the Scenes at the Museum*, London: Doubleday.

Atalla, J. (1993), *Interview with the Author*.

Ball, D. (1998), 'Creative writing in higher education: Its place and purpose', *Writing in Education* No 14, pp. 22–4.

Barton, D. and Hamilton, M. (1998), *Local Literacies: Reading and Writing in One Community*, London: Routledge.

Batsleer, J., Davies, T., O'Rourke, R. and Weedon, C. (1985), *Rewriting English: Cultural Politics of Gender and Class*, London: Methuen.

Bell, J. and Magrs, P. (eds), (2000), *The Creative Writing Course Book*, London: Macmillan.

Bennett, O. (1995), 'Cultural policy in the United Kingdom: Collapsing rationales and the end of a tradition', *European Journal of Cultural Policy*, Vol. 1, No 2, pp. 199–216.

Birkett, J. (1983), *Word Power: A Guide to Creative Writing*, London: A & C Black.

Bloom, U. (1938), *The ABC of Authorship*, London & Glasgow: Blackie.

Boland, E. (1994), 'In defence of workshops', *Writing in Education*, No 4, pp. 4–6.

Bolton, G. (1999), *The Therapeutic Potential of Creative Writing*, London: Jessica Kingsley.

Bornat, J. (1992), 'The communities of community publishing', *Oral History*, Vol. 20, No 2, pp. 23–31.

Boud, D. and Miller, N. (1996), *Working with Experience*, London: Routledge.

Bourdieu, P. and Passeron, J-C. (1977), *Reproduction in*

Education, Society and Culture, London: Sage.

Bourdieu, P. (1990), *In Other Words*, Cambridge: Polity Press.

Bourdieu, P. (1993), *The Field of Cultural Production*, Cambridge: Polity Press.

Braden, S. (1978), *Artists and the People*, London: Routledge.

Brande, D. (1983, first published 1934), *Becoming A Writer*, London: Macmillan.

Britton, J., Burgess, T., Martin, N., McLeod, A., and Rosen, H. (1975), *The Development of Writing Abilities (11–18)*, London: Macmillan Education.

Brookfield, S. (1984), *Adult Learners, Adult Education and The Community*, Buckingham: Open University Press.

Brookfield, S. (1987), *Developing Critical Thinkers: Challenging Adults to Explore Alternative Ways of Thinking and Acting*, Buckingham: Open University Press.

Brookfield, S. (1996), 'Helping people learn what they do', in Boud and Miller *Working with Experience*, London: Routledge.

Brown, R. (1993), *Letter to the author*.

Bulman, C. (1986), 'Creative writing in higher education: Problems of assessment', *English in Education*, Vol. 20, No 1, pp. 48–54.

Bulman, C. (1991), *Letter to author*, 11 April 1991.

Bulman, C. (1996), 'Against encouragement', *Writing in Education*, No 10, pp. 23–15.

Casterton, J. (1986), *Creative Writing: A Practical Guide*, London: Macmillan.

Central Statistical Office (1992), *Social Trends 23*, London: HMSO.

Chamberlain, M. (1988), *Writing Lives: Conversations Between Women Writers*, London: Virago.

Chase, M. (1996), 'A Different Vision? The Middlesbrough Centre', in Taylor, R. (ed.), *Beyond The Walls*, Leeds: The University of Leeds.

Cleveland Arts (1984), *Annual Report 1983–1984*, Middlesbrough: Cleveland Arts.

Cockburn, C. (1998), *The Space Between Us: Negotiating Gender and National Identities in Conflict*, London: Zed Press.

Community Development Foundation [CDF] (1992), *Arts and Communities: The Report of the National Inquiry into Arts and the Community*, London: CDF.

Croft, A. (1990), ' "A hole like that": The literary representation of Cleveland', *The Bulletin of the Cleveland and Teesside Local History Society*, No 58, pp. 31–44.

Dawson, M. (1982), 'Literature: Liasing with the public', *Annual Report 1981–1982*, Bradford: Yorkshire Arts Association, p. iii.

Dearden, S. (1998), *Letter to the author*.

Department for Culture, Media and Sport (1998), *The Comprehensive Spending Review: A New Approach to Investment in Culture*, London: DCMS.

Department for Education and Skills (2001), *National Adult Learning Survey*, London: HMSO.

Dick, K. (ed.), (1972), *Writers at Work: The 'Paris Review' Interviews*, Harmondsworth: Penguin.

Dixon, J. (1991), *A Schooling in 'English': Critical Episodes in the Struggle to Shape Literary and Cultural Studies*, Buckingham: Open University Press.

Doyle, B. (1981), *Some Uses of English: Denys Thompson and the Development of English in Secondary School*, Birmingham: CCCS, University of Birmingham.

Doyle, B. (1989), *English and Englishness*, London: Routledge.

Eagleton, T. (1985), 'The subject of literature', *The English Magazine*, No 15, pp. 4–7.

Eagleton, T. (1993), 'How do you know it's any good?', a debate with Simon Armitage as part of the twenty-fifth anniversary celebrations for the Northern Poetry Library, The Queen's Head Hotel, Morpeth, 27 November.

Elsdon, K.T., Reynolds, J. and Stewart, S. (1992), *Adult Learning in Voluntary Organisations: An Interim Progress Report*, Nottingham: University of Nottingham.

Fairbairns, Z. (1984), 'Write it again', *Arts Express*, April, pp. 9–10.

Fairfax, J. and Moat, J. (1981), *The Way to Write*, London: Elm Tree Books.

Fanthorpe, U.A. (1986), *Selected Poems*, Harmondsworth: King Penguin.

Fegan, T. (2003), *Learning and Community Arts*, Leicester: NIACE.

Fieldhouse, R. and Associates (1996), *A History of Modern British Adult Education* Leicester: NIACE.

Findalter, R. (1963), *What Are Writers Worth?* London: Society of Authors.

Findalter, R. (1966), *The Book Writers*, London: Society of Authors.

Finnegan, R. (1989), *The Hidden Musicians: Music Making in an English Town*, Cambridge: Cambridge University Press.

Fletcher, C. (1980), 'The theory of community education and its relation to adult education' in Thompson (ed.), *Adult Education for a Change*, London: Hutchinson.

Forster, W. (1983), *Arts Centres and Education*, London: ACGB.

Freeman, J. (1982, first published 1970), *The Tyranny of Structurelessness*, London: Dark Star.

Freire, P. (1974), *Education: The Practice of Freedom*, London: Sheed and Ward.

Frow, J. (1995), *Cultural Studies and Cultural Value*, Buckingham: Open University Press.

Gasse, I. (1998), *The Arts and Arts Funding in Postmodern British Culture 1945–1997*, unpublished MA dissertation, University of Huddersfield.

Geertz, C. (1993), *Local Knowledge*, London: Fontana.

Greenblatt, A. and Stiby, J. (1981), 'Outcomes for the learning artist' in Loacker and Palula (eds), *Clarifying Learning Outcomes in the Liberal Arts*, San Francisco: Jossey-Bass Inc.

Griffiths, M. and Wells, G. (1983), 'Who writes what, and why', in Kroll and Wells (eds), *Explorations in the Development of Writing*, Chichester: John Wiley and Sons Ltd.

Habermas, J. (1984), *The Theory of Communicative Action, Volume One*, London: Heinemann.

Hall, S. (1981), 'Notes on deconstructing "the popular" ', in Samuel (ed.), *People's History and Socialist Theory*, London: Routledge and Kegan Paul.

Hall, S. (1988), *The Hard Road to Renewal*, London: Verso.

Hall, S. and Jacques, M. (eds), (1983), *The Politics of Thatcherism*, London: Lawrence and Wishart.

Hansen, T.B. (1995), 'Measuring the value of culture', *European Journal of Cultural Policy*, Vol. 1, No 2, pp. 302–22.

Harper, G. (1999), *Creative Writing and Literature Development on UK Campuses*, http://www.nawe.co.uk, 26 February.

Harper, G. (2001), 'Creative writing in academe', unpublished paper given at Teaching Writing in Higher Education International Symposium, March 2001.

Harper, G. and Kerridge, R. (2004), 'Editorial', *International Journal for the Practice and Theory of Creative Writing*, Vol. 1, No 0, pp. 1–5.

Harrison, J.F.C. (1961), *Learning and Living 1790-1960: A Study in the History of the English Adult Education Movement*, London: Routledge and Kegan Paul.

Harthill, G. (1993), 'Poetry heals!', *Federation* Vol. 2, p. 5.

Harthill, G. (1994), *Creative Writing: Towards a Framework for Evaluation*, Occasional Papers Series: No 4, University of Edinburgh, Centre for Continuing Education.

Hewison, R. (1997), 'Cultural policy and the heritage business', *European Journal of Cultural Policy*, Vol. 3, No 1, pp. 1–13.

Hoggart, R. (1957), *The Uses of Literacy*, London: Chatto and Windus.

Holbrook, D. (1964a), *English for the Rejected: Training Literacy in the Lower Streams of the Secondary School*, Cambridge: Cambridge University Press.

Holbrook, D. (1964b), *The Secret Places: Essays on Imaginative Work in English Teaching and on the Culture of the Child*, London: Methuen.

Holbrook, D. (1967a), *The Exploring Word: Creative Disciplines in the Education of Teachers of English*, London: Cambridge University Press.

Holbrook, D. (1967b), *English for Maturity: English in the Secondary School*, Cambridge: Cambridge University Press.

Holgate, A. and Wilson-Fletcher, H. (1998), *The Cost of Letters: A Survey of Literary Living Standards*, Brentford: Waterstone's Booksellers Ltd.

Holland, S., Butt, M., Harper, G. and Wandor, M. (2003), *Report Series No 6, Creative Writing: A Good Practice Guide*, London: Learning and Teaching Support Network English Subject Centre.

Hooker, J. (1997), 'Developing creativity: The place of the imagination in the academy', *Writing in Education*, No 11, pp. 4–7.

Hough, S.B. (ed.), (1983), *Creative Writing*, Devon: WEA, South West District.

Hoyles, M. (ed.), (1977), *The Politics of Literacy*, London: Writers and Readers Publishing Cooperative.

Hughes, V. (1991), *Literature Belongs to Everyone*, London: ACGB.

Hunt, C. and Sampson, F. (eds), (1998), *The Self on the Page: Theory and Practice of Creative Writing in Personal Development*, London: Jessica Kingsley.

Hunter, I. (1988), *Culture and Government: The Emergence of Literary Education*, London: Macmillan.

Hunter, L. and O'Rourke, R. (1999), 'The values of creative writing', *Soundings*, No 12, pp. 144–52.

Hunter, L. (1999), *Critiques of Knowing: Situated Textualities in Science, Computing and the Arts*, London: Routledge.

Hutchison, R. (1982), *The Politics of The Arts Council*, London: Sinclair Browne.

Hutchison, R. and Feist, A. (1991), *Amateur Arts in the UK*, London: PSI.

Ings, R. (1992), *Report on the Literature Development Worker Movement in England*, London: ACGB.

Jafrate, K. (1994), 'Joined-up writing – some partial opinions from your humble researcher', Key Note Paper, *Joined-Up Writing Conference*, West Yorkshire Playhouse, Leeds, 19 November.

Kelly, O. (1984), *Community, Art and the State: Storming the Citadels*, London: Comedia.

Kelly, T. (third edition, 1992), *A History of Adult Education in Great Britain*, Liverpool: Liverpool University Press.

Knott, C.A. (1987), *I Can't Wait For Wednesday: The Crafts in Adult Education*, London: The Crafts Council.

Kress, G. (1997), *Before Writing: Rethinking the Paths to Literacy*, London: Routledge.

Laclau, E. (1977), *Politics and Ideology in Marxist Theory*, London: New Left Books/Verso.

Landry, C., Greene, L., Matarasso, F. and Bianchini, F. (1996), *The Art of Regeneration: Urban Renewal Through Cultural Activity*, London: Comedia.

McGivney, V.K. (1990), *Education's for Other People: Access to*

Education for Non-Participant Adults: A Research Report., Leicester: NIACE.

McGivney, V.K. (1996), *Staying or Leaving the Course: Non-completion and Retention of Mature Students in Further and Higher Education*, Leicester: NIACE.

McGuigan, J. (1977), *Writers and the Arts Council*, London: ACGB.

McGuigan, J. (1985), *The State and Serious Writing: Arts Council Intervention in the English Literary Field*, unpublished doctoral thesis, University of Leicester.

McGuigan, J. (1992), *Cultural Populism*, London: Routledge.

McGuigan, J. (1993), 'Discourse of cultural policy', unpublished paper given at Teaching Culture and Cultures of Teaching Conference, Brighton, March 1993.

McGuigan, J. (1996), *Culture and the Public Sphere*, London: Routledge.

McGuigan, J. (ed.), (1997), *Cultural Methodologies*, London: Sage.

McGuigan, J. (2004), *Rethinking Cultural Policy*, Milton Keynes: Open University Press.

Mass Observation (UK) Ltd. (1968), *The Potential for the Arts in Leeds*, London: Mass Observation.

Mass Observation (UK) Ltd. (1974), *The Potential for the Arts in Sheffield*, London: Mass Observation.

Mass Observation (UK) Ltd. (1974), *The Potential for the Arts in Birmingham*, London: Mass Observation.

Mass Observation (UK) Ltd. (1974), *The Potential for the Arts in Peterborough*, London: Mass Observation.

Mass Observation (UK) Ltd. (1976), *The Second Survey on the Potential for the Arts in Birmingham*, London: Mass Observation.

Mass Observation (UK) Ltd. (1990), *The Arts in London: A Survey of Attitudes of Users and Non-Users*, London: Mass Observation.

Mercer, P. (1991), *Interview with the author*.

Middlesbrough Borough Council (1998), *Middlesbrough: Official Guide*, Gloucester: The British Publishing Company.

Miller, N. (1993), *Personal Experience, Adult Learning and Social Research*, Sydney: Centre for Research in Adult Education for

Human Development, University of South Australia.

Mills, M. (1998), *The Restraint of Beasts*, London: Flamingo.

Mills, P. (1996), *Writing in Action*, London: Routledge.

Moat, J. (1985), 'The experience of Arvon', *Critical Quarterly*, Vol. 27, No 1, pp. 63–70.

Monteith, M. and Miles, R. (eds), (1992), *Teaching Creative Writing*, Buckingham: Open University Press.

Morley, D. and Worpole, K, (eds), (1992), *The Republic of Letters: Working Class Writing and Local Publishing*, London: Comedia.

Mortimer, P. (2004), 'Can writing be taught?', *Mslexia 20*.

Mulgan, G. and Worpole, K. (1986), *Saturday Night or Sunday Morning? – From Arts to Industry, New Forms of Cultural Policy*, London: Comedia.

Mulhern, F. (1979), *The Moment of Scrutiny*, London: New Left Books.

Murdock. G. and Golding, P. (eds), (1997), *The Political Economy of the Media*, Cheltenham: Elgar.

Murdock. G. and Golding, P. (1974), 'For a political economy of mass communications', in Miliband and Saville (eds), *The Socialist Register*, London: Merlin Press.

Myerscough, J. (1988), *The Economic Importance of the Arts in Britain*, London: Policy Studies Institute.

Niven, A. (ed.), (1991), *Literature: Discussion Document 29*, London: National Arts and Media Strategy Unit, Arts Council.

Northern Arts Board (1994), *Promoting the Arts in the North*, Newcastle: Northern Arts.

Olsen, T. (1980), *Silences*, London: Virago.

Ong, W. (1982), *Orality and Literacy: The Technologizing of the Word*, New York/London: Methuen.

Onions, C.T. (1966), *Shorter English Dictionary*, Oxford: Oxford University Press.

O'Rourke, R. (1982), 'Doris Lessing: Exile and exception', in Taylor (ed), *Notebooks/Memoirs/Archives*, London: Routledge and Kegan Paul.

O'Rourke, R. and Robinson, M. (1995), *Running Good Writing Groups*, Leeds: Department of Adult Continuing Education, University of Leeds.

Oxford English Dictionary Online (2000), Oxford: Oxford University Press.

Peach, L. and Burton, A. (1995), *English As A Creative Art*, London: David Fulford.

Pearson, N. (1982), *The State and the Visual Arts*, Buckingham: Open University Press.

Pick, J. (1986), *Managing the Arts? The British Experience*, London: Rhinegold Publishing.

Pick, J. (1994), 'A pick up the arts: Nationalisation of the arts', *MAiLOUT* December/January, p. 5.

Pope, R. (1995), *Textual Intervention: Critical and Creative Strategies for Literary Studies*, London: Routledge.

Puffelen, F. van (1996), 'Abuses of conventional impact studies in the arts', *European Journal of Cultural Policy,* Vol. 2, No 2, pp. 241–54.

Purvis, J. (1989), *Hard Lessons*, London: Polity Press.

RSGB (1991), *Report on a Survey on Arts and Cultural Activities in Great Britain*, London: ACGB.

RAB Website (1998), 'The big story', *Dispatches*, 2 November.

Rees-Mogg, W. (1985), *The Political Economy of Art*, London: ACGB.

Replan/Niace (1984), *Working Through Words: The Report of an Arts Education Project in Liverpool*, Leicester: NIACE.

Robins, K. (1991), 'Tradition and translation: National culture in its global context', in Corner and Harvey (eds), *Enterprise and Heritage*, London: Routledge.

Sargant, N. (1991), *Learning and Leisure: A Study of Adult Participation in Learning and its Policy Implications*, Leicester: NIACE.

Sargant, N. with Field, J., Francis, H., Schuller, T. and Tuckett, A. (1997), *The Learning Divide*, Leicester: NIACE.

Sargant, N. (1998), *Across the Learning Divide: Adults Learning in the Arts and Crafts*, Leicester: NIACE.

Sargant, N. (2000), *The Learning Divide Revisted*, Leicester: NIACE.

Saunders, J. (1983), *What Happened to a Town Without a University*, Middlesbrough: privately published.

Scammell, W. (1997), 'Letter to the Editor', *London Review of Books*, 20 February, p. 4.

Schlee, A. (1982), 'Some problems of a creative writing class', *Adult Education*, Vol. 55, No 1, pp. 43–8.

Sedgwick, F. (1997), *Read My Mind: Young Children, Poetry and Learning*, London: Routledge.

Sellers, S. (1989), *Delighting The Heart*, London: The Women's Press.

Sharples. M. (1985), *Cognition, Computers and Creative Writing*, Chichester: Horwood.

Shaw, R. (1978), 'Adult education and the arts – A case for closer integration', *Adult Education*, Vol. 50, No 5, pp. 283–8.

Shaw, R. (1987), *The Arts and the People*, London: Cape.

Shaw, R. (ed), (1993), *The Spread of Sponsorship*, Newcastle upon Tyne: Bloodaxe.

Sinclair, A. (1995), *Arts and Cultures*, London: Sinclair Stevenson.

Singleton, J. and Luckhurst, M. (1996), *The Creative Writing Handbook*, London: Macmillan.

Smith, M. (1994), *Local Education: Community, Conversation, Praxis*, Buckingham: Open University Press.

Street, B. (1995), *Social Literacies: Critical Approaches to Literacy in Development, Ethnography and Education*, London and New York: Longman.

Stuart, M. (1998), 'Writing, the self and social process', in Hunt and Sampson (eds), *The Self on the Page: Theory and Practice of Creative Writing in Personal Development*, London: Jessica Kingsley.

Teasdel, T. (1993), *A History of the Cleveland Writing Movement*, unpublished essay prepared to supplement interviews held on 1 and 15 April 1993.

The Independent, 30 December 1994.

The Times Higher Education Supplement, 7 August 1992.

Thompson, E.P.T. (1968), *The Making of The English Working Class*, London: Pelican.

Thompson, J. (2002), *Bread and Roses: Arts, Culture and Lifelong Learning,* Leicester: NIACE.

Torrington, J. (1992), *Swing Hammer Swing!*, London: Secker and Warburg.

Wandor, M. (ed.), (1983), *On Gender and Writing*, London: Pandora.

Wandor, M. (2003), 'A creative writing manifesto', in Holland, S., Butt, M., Harper, G. and Wandor, M. *Report Series No 6: Creative Writing: A Good Practice Guide*, London: Learning and Teaching Support Network English Subject Centre.

Wesley, M. (1984), *The Camomile Lawn*, London: Macmillan.

Williams, R. (1958), *Culture and Society*, London: Chatto and Windus.

Williams, R. (1976), *Keywords*, London: Fontana.

Williams, R. (1979a), 'The arts council', *Political Quarterly*, Vol. 50, No 2, pp. 157–71.

Williams, R. (1977), *Marxism and Literature*, Oxford: Oxford University Press.

Williams, R. (1979b), *Politics and Letters*, London: New Left Books.

Williams, R. (1980), *Problems in Materialism and Culture*, London: Verso.

Williams, R. (1983a), *Writing in Society*, London: Verso.

Williams, R. (1983b), *Towards 2000*, London: Chatto and Windus.

Williams, R. (1989), *The Politics of Modernism*, London: Verso.

Willis, P. (1990), *Common Culture*, Milton Keynes: Open University Press.

Wollen, P. (1998), 'Death (and life) of the author', *London Review of Books*, 5 February, pp. 8–10.

Woolf, V. (1925), *The Common Reader*, London: Hogarth Press.

Worpole, K. (1983), *Dockers and Detectives*, London: Comedia.

Worpole, K. (1991), 'The age of leisure', in Corner and Harvey (eds), *Enterprise and Heritage*, London: Routledge.

Writearound Fifth Annual Festival (1993), Chairman's Report.

Yorkshire and Humberside Arts (1991), *National Arts and Media Strategy Literature and Education Seminar*, 17 December, Unpublished Report.

Index

Titles of publications appear in *italics*

CREATIVE WRITING